The
Politics
of
New
Town
Planning

The
of New

The
Newfields,
Ohio
Story

Politics Town Planning

Frederick Steiner

 Ohio University Press, Athens, Ohio

Library of Congress Cataloging in Publication Data

Steiner, Frederick R.
The politics of New Town planning.
Bibliography: p. 252
Includes index.
1. Newfields, Ohio—City planning—History.
2. New towns—United States—Case studies. 3. City
planning—United States—Case studies. I. Title.
HT165.N44S83   307.7′6′0977172   80-12783
ISBN 0-8214-0414-8

Dedication

For My Parents

Contents

Illustrations

MAPS

FIGURES

Preface

The idea of the new town, that we can start over from scratch and do it better, is a fascinating one. It seems to be of special appeal in the United States, which was founded on utopian principles and where all communities are relatively new; yet the planning of new communities in the United States is an especially difficult task.

Take the example of Philadelphia, a community planned some 300 years ago. Dubbed the "Holy Experiment" by its Quaker founders, Philadelphia represented the most advanced physical planning of its day. Situated on the highly desirable, lush banks of the Delaware River, its original plan utilized a gridiron system, a main central square and four smaller ones, generous individual plats on large city blocks, uniform spacing and setbacks for the buildings, and an interconnecting network of country estates and townhouses.

The Quaker founders were idealists; they were opposed to armed conflict, lacked a formal hierarchy in their religious institutions, believed in the equality of all people, and practiced fairness in business and social matters. The Friends sought to build a society as closely resembling the kingdom of God as they could make it; the banks of the Delaware were to be the seat of the new Eden, and a community of love and peace governed by the spirit of God was their goal (Tolles 1948).

But both the physical plan and social organization of Philadelphia fell short of this goal. Quaker historians agree that the Holy Experiment died of materialism and secularization during the eighteenth century. Lewis Mumford notes that the plan for Philadelphia was influenced by Thomas More's desire for inner spaciousness (1961). But by the eighteenth century, as Elfreth's Alley and many similar alleys continue to remind us, the generous original blocks were subdivided by streets and alleys that reduced the living quarters to dollhouse size,

The readjusted physical arrangement was caused, according to Sam Bass Warner, Jr., by the high cost of eighteenth-century housing and the crowding of Philadelphians near their port on the Delaware River (1968). The high-density housing and subdivided large blocks destroyed the hopes of Philadelphia's planners for a "Green Town." The practice of subdividing blocks with alleys and jamming tiny houses into vacant rear yards continued strongly into the nineteenth century. Warner noted that "by the 1770's the crowding of land exceeded the sanitary capabilities of the town. The streets and alleys reeked of garbage and manure, and some private and public wells must have been dangerously polluted. The high cost of building kept houses small and in short supply. The common artisan's or shopkeeper's house was a narrow structure, about seventeen feet wide and twenty-five feet deep. A story-and-a-half high, it offered about eight hundred square feet of floor space on its ground floor and attic" (1968, pp. 15–17).

Another factor affecting the departure from the original plan was the early development of suburban areas. As Carl Bridenbaugh noted, "A unique development in Philadelphia was the appearance of suburbs. South of the town lay Society Hill, where the Shippen brothers owned a large tract of land which they began to sell off in house lots in 1739. Their advertisements made much of the accessibility of the site to a proposed new market. Another suburban development was opened up in the Northern Liberties in 1741, when Ralph Assheton disposed of his eighty-acre estate in small building lots" (1938, p. 306). Suburban development precipitated by the real estate speculation of large landowners affected both the rural and urban areas and added to the breakdown of the physical plan.

The physical plan of the idealistic Quakers succumbed to capitalist greed. Nevertheless, there were many lasting benefits of Philadelphia's plan and of the Friends' idealism. For instance, two of the green city squares and the central square remain intact and offer a welcome refuge within the busy urban environment, and the Quakers have continued to be pioneers in several areas of social reform. So it is important to look at how new communities like Philadelphia were planned. Anthony Garvan pointed out that because Philadelphia "was from 1682 a planned city, later changes in its original outline may suggest the limits and direction of successful urban modification of a planned community and, equally important, the character of those which failed" (1963, p. 185).

My aim is to report and analyze the development of the planning process of one important recent and typical case. Nearly all aspects of the planning and the development process of this new community will be touched upon, with the focus on the human and political aspects.

There are several people whom I would like to thank for their assistance in this effort. Charles Bolton, Jerome Jenkins, John Kleymeyer, Thomas Jenkins, and Harris Forusz of the University of Cincinnati, and Jon Berger, Ian McHarg, and Nick Muhlenberg of the University of Pennsylvania were invaluable in helping me gain a theoretical insight into the New Town project described here. Nick Muhlenberg was especially helpful in reviewing the manuscript and making many specific suggestions.

I should like to thank Neil Porterfield, Joanne Jackson, Greg McGinty, Robert Erwin, Hal Malt, Angela McLain, Frank Loomis, and Bill Wagner for their encouragement. My colleagues and students at Washington State University have been quite supportive in helping me apply the finishing touches on the manuscript. Professors Ken Brooks, Ken Struckmeyer, Tom Nelson, Walter Ashland, Ernie Smith, Ron Tukey, H. H. Cheng, Jerry Young, William Lassey, Eldon Franz, and Tom Bartuska must be mentioned in this regard as well.

Jennifer Hirt, Anne Toffey, and Jan Hinde did all the typing and retyping, for which I am extremely grateful. Julie Knowles, Karen Johnson, Debra Bold, and Jon Singleton assisted with the graphics. The editors and staff of the *Journal Herald* and the *Dayton Daily News* provided excellent coverage of the Newfields new community story, and I am grateful to the editors for allowing me to refer to the resulting articles. Alice Glasel Harper of the *Journal of the American Institute of Planners* was helpful as were the other publishers who permitted me to use their copyrighted material. Special thanks are in order for Patricia Elisar, Holly Panich, and Helen Gawthrop of the Ohio University Press for their support.

Finally, I wish to thank Gerwin Rohrbach, my early mentor in the planning profession; and Donald Huber, who first hired me as an undergraduate to take pictures of the Ohio cornfields that he was dreaming of transforming into a new town.

F.S.

Introduction

Every hamlet, village, town, city, and megalopolis in the world was, at one time or another, a new community. The concept of building a new community is an old one, as old as man and possibly even older if all life forms be considered to exist on some level of "community."

The first human settlements were little more than extended households of large families that lived together for mutual protection and more efficient food gathering. The first cities developed with the rise of central states as trade centers between groups of people. The first planned cities were developed by nation-states that sought to extend their political and economic control. The Egyptians had a new-town policy as early as the Ancient Empire, and later cultures followed the Egyptian lead. Throughout the Mediterranean world there are numerous cities that were planned by Greeks, Phoenicians, and Romans as military posts to protect trade routes. On the other side of the world, the Incas built new towns in conquered territories to break down established local relationships. By mixing groups that would independently resist the encroachment of the central government on traditional local and regional powers, the Incas were able to extend their rule more efficiently.

Later the Spanish, the French, the Dutch, the Portuguese, and the British built new communities in the Americas, Africa, and Asia, again to secure trade routes and extend colonial rule. Today these colonial towns include Philadelphia, New York, Santo Domingo, Cape Town, Quebec, and Sydney. The Germans, colonial latecomers, planned the extensive building of new towns in areas of Eastern Europe that they invaded during World War II (Speer 1976). The architects and planners of these proposed new towns were later involved in Germany's rebuilding efforts after the war.

The origins of the twentieth-century "new towns" are generally

1

traced to Ebenezer Howard, a nineteenth-century English court reporter who lived in London and loathed it. In his book, *Garden Cities of To-morrow*, Howard proposed building well planned smaller towns around larger central cities (1902). Howard applied his theories by building the garden cities of Letchworth and Welwyn with his chief architect Raymond Unwin. Howard's garden cities greatly influenced the development of the British new-town movement and the architecture and city-planning professions in Europe and the United States (Mumford 1961, Schaffer 1972).

To Howard, new towns were the way to escape from the congestion and social evils of urban life in Britain at the turn of the century. He saw a town as a complete social and functional structure, with sufficient jobs to make it self-supporting. He envisioned it as spaciously laid out to provide light, air, and gracious living for each resident while being surrounded by a green belt that would provide both farm produce for the community and the opportunity for recreation and relaxation. He suggested that half a dozen such towns, separate but linked by a rapid transit system, should form a city catering to the complete needs of approximately a quarter of a million people.

Howard's garden cities might be described as one pragmatic, Victorian Briton's Walden or be viewed as an important part of the British naturalist tradition. Either way, by the mid-1930s, Frank Lloyd Wright, LeCorbusier, Walter Gropius, and most of the world's other major architects were advocating Howard's proposals and presenting their own concept of future new towns (Wright 1943, 1957; LeCorbusier 1971). Shortly after immigrating to the United States from Nazi Germany, Bauhaus founder Walter Gropius commented at a conference on urbanism that "carefully planned new towns, more appropriate for showing the way to a greater economy and to better conditions for living, would provide us with the experience necessary to prepare the blueprints for the second and more complicated later step in planning, that is, the rehabilitation of large old cities."[1]

The architect Clarence Stein and the landscape architect Henry Wright, disciples of Ebenezer Howard, began planning garden city types of new communities in America with Sunnyside Gardens, New York, in 1926 and Radburn, New Jersey, in 1929. However, there were other influences that were more distinctly American that have influenced the more recent interest of new towns in the United States beginning in the early 1960s. There have been continued utopian attempts at new community planning throughout the history of the United States, such as Robert Owens's failed New Harmony, Indiana; the more successful Morman venture, Salt Lake City; and the more modern schemes like psychologist B. F. Skinner's Walden Two, architect Paolo Soleri's Arcosanti, and the various hippy communes. American landscape architects can trace their involvement in new-town planning back to the efforts of Frederick Law Olmsted and his partner Calvert Vaux who designed Riverside, Illinois, in 1869.

The greenbelt new towns of the New Deal era (Greenbelt, Maryland; Greenhills, Ohio; and Greendale, Wisconsin) were another important American influence. These towns originated largely through the effort and persistence of one man in Franklin Roosevelt's administration, Rexford Tugwell. The greenbelt new-town program was Tugwell's idea; it was an extension of his land-use programs that he envisioned as correctives to the problems of rural poverty facing millions of farm families during the Great Depression in the 1930s. Tugwell was not an urban planner, but an agricultural economist. Because of this he approached new towns differently than Howard (Myhra 1974). This is not to say that Tugwell was not influenced by Howard; indeed he was. There are just many fundamental differences between garden cities and the greenbelt new towns.

The greenbelt new towns were not the economically self-sufficient garden cities of Ebenezer Howard, but satellite suburbs that were made possible because of the universal and economical availability of the automobile. Howard's garden cities may be thought of as being escapist, reflecting his personal desire to leave London. Tugwell, on the other hand, believed that existing cities could be made more livable, but he was dismayed by their deficiencies that he felt were due to a lack of order, management, and control. In addition, with technology displacing farm workers and releasing them for industrial employment in the cities, Tugwell believed that urban growth and development had to be controlled, which meant not stopped or abandoned but guided and regulated through planning.

Another influence has been the rise of the planning profession in the United States. According to Herbert Gans, the profession of city planning (also regional, urban, and community planning) originated as a movement of affluent Eastern reformers. These reformers were upset by the arrival of European immigrants and the squalor of their existence in urban slums. There was also the threat that these immigrants, and urban industrial society generally, represented to the social, cultural, and political dominance that the reformers had enjoyed in small-town, agrarian America. These early planners did not concern themselves much with explicit goals; theirs was a movement with a missionary fervor that gave them no cause to question their own goals. Instead, they devoted themselves to developing programs calling for a change in the physical environment, for they believed that physical change would bring about social change (Gans 1968).

Gans, a sociologist and urban planner who attended the University of Chicago and the University of Pennsylvania, which were the leading institutions in those fields of his day, has been perhaps the most eloquent scholar to trace the origins of the city-planning profession and its relationship to the social sciences. He observed that as influential and powerful reform groups, businessmen, and attorneys gave city planning support, it became a profession. Its physical emphasis naturally attracted architects, landscape architects, and civil engineers who developed many planning tools. The most popular tool was the *master plan* that assumed that once land-use arrangements had been ordered comprehensively, the social and economic structure of the community would also change.

Although city planning originated as a movement to preserve the American small town, its conception of the ideal community has been influenced strongly by the suburb of the nineteenth and early twentieth centuries, which was then a residential district occupied largely by upper-middle-class people. The planner's advocacy of low density, of the single-family house, of open space, or residential areas without industry or commerce, and of small neighborhoods built around the elementary school was best realized, if imperfectly, in the suburbs that sprang up around the American city about the turn of the twentieth century.

Gans observed that planners have sharply altered their view of the suburbs since World War II (1967). This new suburbia that developed on the edge of older suburbs downgraded the prestige of these communities or took up open land that the upper middle class had used for recreation, the preservation of its privacy, and the maintenance of a pseudo-rural environment. In addition, the new suburbs drained tax monies from the cities in which the upper middle class worked or to which it returned for cultural activities. The planners, themselves members of the upper middle class in spirit, if not in income, reacted similarly. According to Gans,

> as suburban living became available to lower-middle and working-class population, and as the suburban exodus drained taxes and prestige from the city, planners turned against the suburb. Borrowing the mythical picture of suburbia that has been developed by critics and journalists, planners began to accuse the areas beyond the city limits of lacking urbanity and vitality, decried their architectural and demographc homogeneity, and sought to introduce high-density housing, industry, more population diversity, and other symbols of 'urbanity.' In the process, planners revived a goal of nineteenth century reformers, that people of all classes, ethnic groups, and races should live together in what was perceived as a balanced community. The original formulators of this idea saw maximum heterogeneity as a means to the Americanization and bourgeoisification of the new lower-class immigrants. They expected middle-class people to civilize the newcomers—but the planners of the mid-twentieth century valued heterogeneity as a means of reproducing urban vitality and, in all too few instances, of enabling poor and non-white city dwellers to leave the ghetto (1968, pp. 127–128).

Partly because of the turmoil of the 1960s that resulted in highlighting the inability of many existing institutions to cope with the problems of urban America, there has been a shift away from the traditional physical land-use base of planning, to a greater involvement with the social sciences. Nevertheless, traditional master and land-use planning has received renewed support through the revival of another nineteenth century concept: the new town. Originally conceived by Howard and others as a way of moving urban slum dwellers into the countryside and halting the growth of cities, the new town, in concept, is a fairly self-sufficient and independent community located beyond the city limits which would provide local employment opportunities for its residents, thus reducing their journey to work, the city's traffic congestion and the alleged defects of the suburbs as so-called bedroom communities. The latest development of new towns that occurred in the 1960s and early 1970s gave master planners new hope that if the master plan and related traditional schemes could not work in established cities, then they might be applied to the new town.

Two of the most publicized of the new American new towns are Reston, Virginia, and Columbia, Maryland. These pioneer efforts of the 1960s have served as models for those that followed.

Reston was begun in 1962 eighteen miles west of Washington, D.C., in Fairfax County, Virginia, near Dulles Airport by its initial developer Robert E. Simon, the onetime owner of Carnegie Hall. Early in its developmental stages Reston was heralded as an architectural marvel. But while village centers such as the Lake Anne Center were praised by critics, the new town was in trouble, because even as architectural students flocked to scenic Lake Anne Center it had become a charming white elephant forcing Simon into economic peril. Simon eventually sold the new town to the Gulf Oil Company and Gulf Reston became more of a company town than a new one. (William Magness, the director of Gulf Reston, came to the new town directly after twenty years of experience running company towns in the oil fields of Iran and Venezuela.)[2]

Columbia, perhaps the most successful of all the recent new towns, was built midway in the Washington-Baltimore corridor in Howard County, Maryland, by James W. Rouse, a mortgage-banker and shopping-mall developer. While Columbia was developed, like Reston, around the village center concept, it was built on a firmer financial base and attempted some innovative social planning (Gans 1968; Brooks 1971). Rouse attracted investments from the Connecticut General Life Insurance Company, the Teachers Insurance and Annuity Association of America, Chase Manhattan Bank, the Manufacturers Hanover Trust, and the Morgan Guaranty Trust Companies. But while social planning was attempted at Columbia, it has not been free from social problems that face unplanned communities, and it, too, has become in several ways a company town.[3]

The major problem with most new towns was that they tried to fulfill the American dream with slightly un-American governments. The developers claimed to want to build cities where people of all races and classes could live and work and develop an intangible sense of community. They did not want the first rush of affluent whites to zone out everyone who was different. To do this the developers had to maintain control over zoning. So the Gulf Reston Company in Reston and the Rouse Company in Columbia virtually became the local governments in those towns.

Both Reston and Columbia were located in counties whose executive government systems made it impossible for either to have the usual kind of municipal governments. So private governments like "home owners associations" replaced city halls. They were controlled by the developers and were designed to maintain public land and facilities deeded to them by the developers. Only when the new towns reached completion would residents gain control of the associations. Until that time developers made all the plans, sometimes asking for "citizen participation." The developers decided everything from how the land would be used to the color schemes for the front doors of townhouses.

The availability of federal funding opened the door to the generation of new towns that followed Reston and Columbia. Government-assisted financing made it possible for a greater number of potential new-town developers. The federal government's post–World War II interest in new community development began in 1966 when Section 201 of the Housing and Urban Development Act of 1965 amended The National Housing Act to create Title X. Title X provided mortgage insurance to private developers for the purchase of raw land and the development of improved building sites or new communities. But a developer could obtain similar financing terms through conventional bank loans and, therefore, did not need the assistance of the Title X program (Mields 1973).

Consequently, Title IV of the Housing and Urban Development Act of 1968 was passed. Title IV went a step further than Title X in an effort to make new community development more attractive to developers. Title IV increased the maximum obligation that could be insured in a single development, which made the program attractive to a greater number of developers. However, the federal government moved cautiously in encouraging and supporting new communities' activity under Title IV. Two years after its inception, in February 1970, the U.S. Department of Housing and Urban Development (HUD) announced its first commitment, which was to the new community of Jonathan, Minnesota then several months later to Saint Charles Communities, Maryland, and Park Forest South, Illinois.

In his 1970 State of the Union Message, President Richard Nixon stated that "the federal government must be in a position to assist in the building of new cities and the rebuilding of old ones."[4]

At the same time, HUD was working on options for expanding the new communities program. In April 1970 these options were pre-

sented to the president with the recommendation that the program encourage development of at least ten new communities. But the president, citing the inflationary state of the economy, suggested that the
program not be implemented. Congress, however, moved ahead.
Representative Thomas Ashley of Ohio along with twelve other members of the House sponsored HR 16647, and Senators Sparkman and
Muskie introduced an identical bill on the Senate side, S.3640.[5] After
a series of compromises between Congress, the administration, and
HUD, the Urban Growth and New Community Developement Act,
HUD Title VII, was finally passed by Congress in December 1970. It
immediately attracted more attention from private developers than
ever before, because it made more assistance available.

The legislation created a Community Development Corporation
authorized to make direct loans to public bodies and private developers for land acquisition, development of public infrastructures, and industrial development. To relieve some of the front-end costs of new
community development, the bill also provided for deferment of principal and interest payments on all such loans for up to fifteen years.
The bill provided grants for public services to a new town during the
initial development period with the hope of assuring that schools,
health programs, and fire and police programs would exist when the
first residents moved into the new town. The bill authorized the Community Development Corporation to undertake various demonstration projects at the direction of the president and with the approval of
Congress.

This is the history of a new town made possible by Title VII. Reston
and Columbia were made real through the efforts of individual
personalities. This book will deal heavily with the personalities who
were involved in a Title VII new town near Dayton, Ohio.

The developer of this new town was Donald L. Huber, a third-
generation home builder who made a fortune on the post–World War
II suburban ranch house. Donald Huber was also a man who was
affected by the social turmoil of the 1960s and by the criticism that
has been leveled at suburbia by social scientists, urban planners, and
others.

The initial general manager of the Dayton new town was Gerwin K.
Rohrbach, a Harvard-educated landscape architect and city planner.
Rohrbach was a man who had evolved with the planning profession,
moving from a strictly physical bias to a more social orientation after

having witnessed failure of urban renewal projects first in Pittsburgh and later in Chicago during the 1950s. He was further affected by the urban turmoil of the 1960s and the criticism levied against the many deficiencies of traditional planning programs such as urban renewal in dealing with human problems.

Because both Donald Huber and Gerwin Rohrbach were affected by the criticism of their professions, both men were in a state of transition during the early planning stages of the Dayton new town. Huber was a man trying to make the transition from small city home builder to new city developer. Rohrbach was a man trying to make the change from a physical to a systems management planner.

This story begins at the time from which Donald Huber began planning his new town (which was first called Brookwood and was later renamed Newfields) and continues to the time when it received approval from HUD. It is an important story, because this HUD Title VII new town near Dayton, Ohio, resulted in failure, as did most of the other Title VII new communities. These failures have cost millions of public and private dollars.

Among advanced civilizations the United States is unique in many ways. Unlike other cultures it is deficient in its planning for new communities. In contrast to the Greeks and Romans, the Incas and Chinese, the British, Dutch, Germans, and Japanese, the United States has no coordinated plan for the expansion of its urban areas. This is probably because land is not recognized as a scarce resource in the United States as it is in land-hungry Europe and Japan. So American cities occur accidentally as a result of the uncoordinated actions of multilayered governments and decisions made by powerful vested business interests. It should be possible to learn from the past mistakes of city and regional planning in order to develop an approach that is consistent with the democratic ideals of our nation and that is so badly needed for urban America. This look at the failure of one new community, undertaken by a private entrepreneur with government involvement, can help to illustrate some past mistakes and offer practical alternatives.

Brookwood

1 The Developer

Millionaire developer Donald Huber of Dayton, Ohio, lost money on his first construction job. "I built the back porch on a man's house one summer in my high school days," Huber commented in an interview to a newspaper reporter. "I charged him $900 and lost money all the way." It was an experience that the man, who has described himself as a "third-generation Dayton builder," referred to as "educational."[1] He was the same person who is responsible for the conception of a 5,000-acre new town in the northwest quadrant of the Dayton metropolitan area, which is often called the Miami Valley. The new town was originally conceived to have a population of between 40,000 and 50,000 persons and would cost over a billion dollars to build, including a $31 million HUD Title VII loan guarantee.[2]

Dayton, Ohio, is the city that Kurt Vonnegut, Jr., compared to Dresden, Germany, in *Slaughter-House Five*. Located on the confluence of three rivers and a large creek; the Great Miami, the Mad and the Stillwater rivers, and Wolf Creek; the Miami Valley is both a naturally attractive and fortunate area. Relatively few regions possess as many of its favorable living conditions: a temperate climate, an ideal amount of yearly rainfall for crops, a gentle terrain, an immense groundwater aquifer, and some of the finest soils in the world for agriculture and construction.

Before the white settlers arrived, the region was unsurpassed as an Indian hunting ground. On the banks of the Miami River near the town of Piqua was one of the largest native American settlements north of Mexico, with perhaps a population of 4,000. The early European settlers were comprised of the first overflow of descendants of the old New England colonists. They came with their schools, colleges, and churches, and with their capacity for industry. Quakers and others from the South who were opposed to slavery moved to Ohio.

13

They were followed by black Americans fleeing slavery on the Underground Railroad. Thrifty Pennsylvania Dutch farmers, known as the Brethren or Dunkers also established their settlements in the valley. During the 1850s German democrats, finding their hopes of freedom thwarted at home, came in large numbers first to Cincinnati, then northward into the Miami Valley.

The city of Dayton was founded by members of the Society of Cincinnatus, Revolutionary War veterans who were given land grants in what was then the Northwest Territory. From one such veteran, Jonathan Dayton, the city received its name. After its incorporation in 1830, Dayton remained a sleepy little Anglo-German farm town and trading post until the Miami-Erie Canal was opened in 1885 linking the Ohio River to Lake Erie. Dayton flourished while the nation depended on water transportation, and it was briefly the second largest city in Ohio.

Early in the twentieth century, after much work in their bicycle shop, the Wright brothers left Dayton to put man in the air, an event that was heralded by only a short paragraph on the obituary page of the local newspaper. Shortly afterwards, in 1913, the city was destroyed by a major flood. Although the 1913 flood resulted in a significant loss of lives and property, it had many long-range beneficial effects. The people of the area united; the city manager form of government and several other municipal reforms were instituted; engineer Arthur Morgan (who would later head the Tennessee Valley Authority) and the business leaders of the Miami Valley organized the Miami Conservancy District to protect the community from further floods; the Wright brothers built an airfield; and manufacturing industries sprang up throughout the area (Morgan 1951).

These industries were founded by several individuals, the foremost being Charles Kettering, whose inventions boosted Dayton's economy in several ways. His electrification of the cash register catapulted the National Cash Register Company to success. His automotive inventions, particularly the electric starter, placed him in such demand by Detroit that the automotive industry eventually had to come to Dayton in order to obtain his services. As a result, the Dayton area assumed the third largest concentration of General Motors employment in the country.[3]

The growth of Dayton's three largest employers, the Wright-Patterson Air Force Base, the National Cash Register Company, and

General Motors through the 1940s and 1950s generated a large in-migration of Appalachians and blacks. This in-migration caused an exodus of the original white population to the newly formed suburbs around Dayton. A large percentage of the housing in these suburbs was built by the Huber family.

The 1960s brought about many changes in the United States, two of which dramatically altered the character of the Dayton area. The first was the impact of federally funded programs, and the second was the inflationary nature of the economy. For several political, social, and geographic reasons, Dayton has received financial benefits generated by the new federal programs of the Kennedy and Johnson administrations. In 1967 the city was chosen to be among the first round of Model Cities. The influx of massive federal aid drastically altered the thinking of many of the Dayton political and business leaders by offering an attractive new way of financing programs and ventures.

The inflationary state of the economy affected the manufacturing base of the city. Several industries decided to move out of town because of higher wage demands by labor. Most notably, the National Cash Register Company, which had for many years depended on non-union labor, became a union shop in 1969. As a result, thousands of employees were laid off and the company moved much of its manufacturing facilities to cheaper labor market areas in southern states and Japan. These changes had a profound effect on Donald Huber, who, as a businessman, saw the possible profits in federal programs and, as a lifelong Dayton resident, was troubled by the state of the city's economy.

Donald Huber's grandfather, Jacob Huber, founded the family business in 1900 when he left his job as a rental supervisor for a Dayton attorney to build his first house. After several more houses, he built the small community of Huberville adjacent to the Wright brothers' new airfield. While the Wright brothers' small airfield evolved into the massive Wright-Patterson Air Force complex, Jacob Huber's small home-building business grew into a multimillion dollar family enterprise.

Of Jacob Huber's many sons, the one who most energetically embraced the building trades was Herbert Huber, who started in the business in 1924. In the late 1920s he built mostly north of the city. In the heart of the depression he was the only individual in Montgomery County (the county where Dayton is located) to take out a building permit. In the late 1930s he bought Far Hills Forest, formerly the estate of Frederick Patterson, son of the founder of The National Cash Register Company. The development of this area became part of Dayton's most exclusive suburban area. Herbert Huber continued building during the Second World War and subsequently shifted into the construction of veterans' housing in the post–World War and Korean War periods. Like the Levitt family, the Hubers became one of the first pioneers in total housing fabrication with the opening of their own fabrication company in 1948. In the early 1950s, Herbert Huber put his fabrication techniques to work on a wide scale south of Dayton with the start of construction of Modern Manor, the largest subdivision in the area up to that time. It was a plat that would eventually contain 2,200 homes.

Donald Huber was born on 2 September 1932, in Dayton. As a child he was not much of an athlete; instead he used to hurry home from school to read building manuals. He started building his own houses with his brother Charles in his senior year of high school. For a while, Huber considered studying architecture but decided that a background in business would better prepare him to build homes. He received his bachelor's degree in business administration from Northwestern University and studied for a year in graduate school.

Herbert Huber died in 1954 and his sons inherited the business. The two brothers finished the Modern Manor subdivision then proceeded on to their first major housing development, which would be the largest housing project to be constructed in Dayton to that time. The brothers chose a site in the northeast quadrant of the metropolitan area near the Wright-Patterson Air Force Base. That site, Huber Heights, grew to one of the largest subdivisions in the Mideast, containing well over ten thousand ranch-style houses. In the late 1950s the family business splintered.

In newspaper interviews and written biographies of the family, Donald Huber claims that the family holdings were divided between himself and Charles because the business was becoming too unwieldy. Charles Huber took over and continued to develop Huber Heights, which had been his driving interest from the beginning. Meanwhile, Donald Huber continued to develop in the southern metropolitan area and manage the family's housing fabrication business. But there are much deeper issues underlying the split.

The brothers were two basically different types of individuals.

While Donald was a shy, unassuming man with a soft smile, pleasant manner, and gentle handshake; Charles was more overbearing and had a temper and a more flamboyant life-style. Charles fit the stereotype of the millionaire subdivision developer with his private plane and swimming pool. Donald was more the refined, chamber-of-commerce type with somewhat simpler tastes, though he still maintained a fleet of Cadillacs. While most contractors and laborers preferred to work with Charles, the bankers and politicians dealt more easily with Donald. Even their philosophies of building differed: Charles favored the conventional farm-by-farm, plat-by-plat, row-by-row, house-by-house subdivision; Donald the planned residential environment. Each man was jealous of the other's success, and they were in constant competition. They were also both in the business of making money by building houses and have continued to use the same basic house design that had been developed by their father.

Charles Huber owns C. H. Enterprises, which did over $18 million dollars of business in 1973.[4] At that same time, Donald Huber operated the Springmont Company, which did $1 million in business in 1972; the Universal Corporation, a housing fabrication company, which did $2.5 million in business in 1972; and Madden, Inc., which did $3 million. Springmont, Universal, Madden, and Don Huber Rentals comprised the Donald L. Huber Development Group.

Madden was the first manifestation of Huber's growing business interest in federally funded projects. During the late 1960s, Huber developed a relationship with several leaders of the black community of Dayton in the completion of an urban renewal project, Madden Hills. Madden was the joint venture between two of those black leaders, State Representative C. J. McLin and businessman William Leigh. The company also developed training programs for black subcontractors and employed several individuals from the nearby community.

While Huber gathered experience in applying for federal programs, he revealed a naiveté in working with the black community. For one of his partners, he chose C. J. McLin, who was an individual who enjoyed an enormous popularity in parts of the black community but was not widely trusted by other large segments of either the black or white communities. The first houses constructed in Madden Hills were priced high and attracted middle-class blacks. Huber then attempted to construct federally subsidized units on the remaining lots and ran into stiff opposition from the first home owners. Although the middle-class blacks recognized the necessity for subsidized housing and were willing to accept some of the units, they resented a larger number of units located in a close proximity to where they had made a substantial investment, they resented a white developer placing subsidized units in his development in the black community instead of in his developments in the exclusive white suburbs, and they resented the compromised version of the cheap Huber ranch home. Their skepticism of Huber and McLin grew.

It was also during the 1960s that Huber grew more sensitive to the criticism of the type of suburban development for which his family had been partially responsible. He grew more critical of the type of housing that he and his brother had built in the past. Donald Huber started to look around at alternative techniques of development and soon became an advocate of planned residential development. "The quality of the environment is not as good as it could be," he said to a reporter in 1968. "We studied this abroad and hope to apply some of the ideas in the future."[5]

The "studying abroad" referred to several trips that Huber made to Europe. After his first trip in 1957 to Poland where he saw for the first time the vast differences in the way Europeans organized their cities, he commented, "In Huber Heights we were just building shelter." He made several more trips throughout the next decade to England, France, Denmark, and Belgium where he studied the development of European new towns, and he began to foster the dream of building an alternative Huber Heights, one that would be an aesthetic success that would be free from criticism.

His dream gathered more momentum after he visited the American new towns of Reston and Columbia. Then, in 1968, it was put within the realm of possibilities with the passage of the Federal Housing Act, Title IV, that cleared the way for financial insuring of community development plans. In late 1970 Donald Huber began planning his new town, and by late 1971 his plans for building one northwest of Dayton between the suburban community of Trotwood and the village of Brookville were announced.

Huber began his efforts as a thirty-eight-year-old man attempting a personal transition. He had accumulated a fortune by developing communities that he now loathed and was now looking ahead to rectify what he perceived as past mistakes. Like all men in transition, he clung awkwardly to the trappings of the past while grasping blindly at the future without a full understanding of its meaning. While he expounded the environmental benefits of planned development, Huber continued to defend stoutly the principle of the traditional single-family dwelling that he had built for twenty years. While he flashed slides of European new towns at presentations, he failed to recognize that they had been constructed in cultures more homogeneous than the pluralist American society. While he began to apply for a new source of federal financial assistance to develop a new community, he continued to practice techniques of financing and political manipulation common to those that had been used in the construction of old communities.

Finally, though he had influence on the local home-building industry and some clout in state politics, Huber was not among the banking and industrial power elite of the Dayton region. He was more what Floyd Hunter would describe as second-level individual in the lower limits of the regional power personnel (Hunter 1953). While Huber would still need the support of the banking and industrial community to be successful, he was attempting to tap a relatively new source of power in the region, the federal government.

2 The Project

Building a complete new community of over forty thousand people from open farmlands is an enormous task. There are hundreds of activities that have to be undertaken simultaneously. Once Donald Huber committed himself to building a new town, several decisions had to be made. First, a site had to be selected and the acquisition of land begun. Second, contact had to be made with HUD to establish the feasibility of the project. Then a staff and consultant team had to be assembled. Finally a process had to be developed to complete the project. All these actions had to be started before the actual planning could proceed.

The first site that Huber investigated was south of Dayton where he had been traditionally active and where he already owned several hundred acres. Some preliminary planning was begun at a site near Bellbrook, Ohio, a small hamlet in the direct path of the high-income conservative white out-migration.[1] But between Dayton and Bellbrook were the suburban communities of Oakwood, Kettering, and Centerville, the three suburbs that contained the residents with the highest income in the metropolitan area. This site was eliminated for several reasons. First, Huber's associates in the black community were unreceptive to it, because they felt it would be difficult to market to the blacks who had traditionally settled (by default and discrimination) on the west side of Dayton. Second, there was a feeling that the upper-middle-class whites of south Dayton might form strong opposition to a federally related program in their backyard, because of their concern about the blacks that it might attract. Third, there was the price of the property, which presented a major hurdle. Finally, the City of Dayton for many reasons made Huber aware of its desire that the new town be located near its city limits, a criterion that the Bellbrook site failed to meet.

Several more locations adjacent to Dayton were examined by Huber and his advisors. The general area northwest of Dayton was agreed upon as the most feasible, because it was located strategically between the predominantly black West Dayton and the more liberal middle-class community of North Dayton, and because there were several

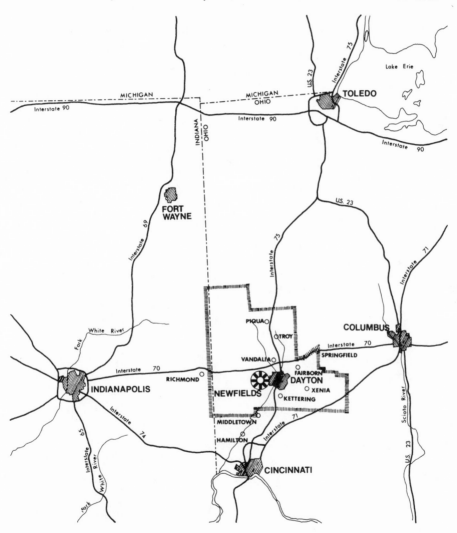

Map 1. New Town Regional Location

Scale |_____| ⇗
        40 Miles   N

LEGEND
Major Highways
Major Cities
Miami Valley Region

miles bordering the city limits that were annexable. An area close to Trotwood, Ohio, was selected as the most logical from a marketing viewpoint, that is, as an area marketable to both whites and blacks (map 1). Further investigation of surface rock and marketing data forced modifications of the site. In late 1970, preliminary engineering was started to outline specific property ownership and drainage area that fixed the location of the project. The Brookwood project's site was an approximately five-thousand-acre tract located in Madison and Perry townships of Montgomery County; between Trotwood and Brookville northwest of Dayton, Ohio; contiguous to both the northwest growth trust and the major black community of the metropolitan area[2] (map 2).

The largest concentration of population near the site was the subrural community of Trotwood, which began as Higgins Station in 1860 when it sprang up as a small railroad town. At that time there was a general store and a saloon, both owned by the town's leading citizen, Louis Pfoutz, and a tiny cluster of homes surrounded by farmland. By 1886, Higgins Station had grown large enough for Pfoutz to apply for a post office franchise. But Ohio already had a Higgins Station, so Pfoutz, an avid reader, pulled a name from the book he'd just finished, *David Copperfield*. He named it Trotwood, after Miss Betsy Trotwood, David Copperfield's aunt, friend, and protector. The town was platted in 1898 and incorporated as a village in 1901, remaining a small mideastern farm town until after World War II.

In the twenty-five years following World War II, Trotwood was a community in transition from a rural village where everyone knew everyone else to a suburban city of one-story homes inhabited by white, middle-income families. And Trotwood was beginning to suffer the growing pains similar to other areas that had undergone transition. Even before the news of the location of the new town was announced, Trotwood faced the problems of integration, low- and moderate-income housing, growth and annexation, school funding, and transportation.

Trotwood, unlike many other suburban communities, attempted to meet these problems head-on. With only 7,000 residents in 1970, Trotwood had both a full-time city manager and assistant city manager, a part-time human relations director, and a staff planner from the Miami Valley Regional Planning Commission (the official regional

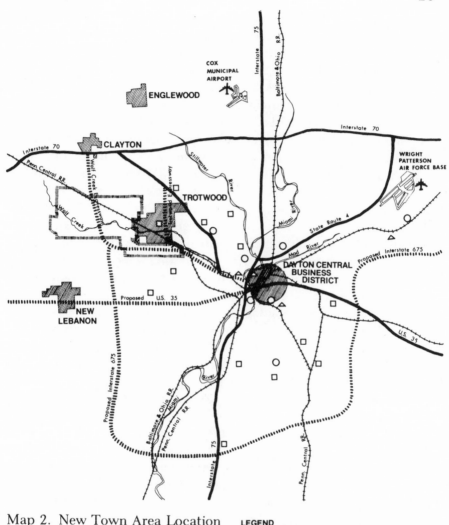

Map 2. New Town Area Location

Scale └─────────◁
      9000 Feet   N

LEGEND
▬▬▬ Existing Expressways & Main Roads
▰▰▰ Proposed Expressways
▥▥▥ New Town
□ Shopping Centers
△ Educational Institutions
○ Hospitals

planning agency for the Dayton metropolitan area), who devoted fifty percent of his time to Trotwood. The city also has had a recent tradition of devoted elected officials who have made a genuine effort to deal with problems like integration and low-cost housing with foresight.

Integration was occurring in the 1950s and 1960s at about the same

rate as in other Dayton suburbs, but Trotwood's proximity to the
black west side of Dayton and its location directly in the northwest
out-migration pattern of the city's affluent blacks made it apparent
that the situation was sure to change.

The *Wall Street Journal* described the racial distribution situation
after the 1966–67 uprisings in West Dayton's black ghetto as "one
where most of the city's black population, about half of Dayton's total
population of 250,000 is black, was crowded into the west side. Those
blacks escaping the inner city were moving west and north into suburbia, largely into Jefferson Township, with neighboring Madison
Township as the next likely escape route."[3]

The awareness of the inevitable prompted Trotwood's leadership to
deal with the reality of the situation and to take measures to insure
that the changes would occur as smoothly as possible. While most of
Dayton's suburbs have been slow in adopting the controversial housing and dispersal plan developed by the Miami Valley Regional Planning Commission in 1971, Trotwood and Madison Township were the
first suburbs to not only adopt the plan but also to take action. The
dispersal plan was one whereby new low- and moderate-income housing would be distributed throughout the five-county region on a "fair
share" basis (Bertsch and Shafer 1971, Downs 1973).

Since World War II, Trotwood has grown steadily into Madison
Township through annexation. Beginning in 1948 with its first large
expansion, the city has had a policy of annexing adjacent residential
plats. In the late 1960s, Trotwood entered into a major confrontation
with the City of Dayton. Both municipalities wanted to annex the territory around the tax-rich northern regional shopping center, the
Rouse Company's Salem Mall. Trotwood won the battle in 1969 after
it was discovered that some of the signatures on Dayton's annexation
petition had been forged. But the tactics used by both sides left each
with a great deal of mutual mistrust.[4]

In the early 1970s, two of Trotwood's most pressing problems were
its schools and transportation. School bond issues failed eight consecutive times before the news of the new town reached the voter, then
two times afterward. Consequently, the Trotwood-Madison school
system ran on split sessions. Transportation was perhaps an even more
urgent problem. The main route between Trotwood and Dayton was
Salem Avenue, which was congested with cars even in nonrush hours.
The situation was complicated by the fact that the northwest section

of Montgomery County had been neglected in regional highway planning for years. There was the proposed Wolf Creek Expressway that
would link Trotwood to the central city and the interstate beltway and
eliminate many of Trotwood's transportation problems. However, resistance from citizens, particularly in low-income areas in the
highway's path within the Dayton city limits, who opposed their
neighborhood being ripped apart for the sake of easier access by
suburbanites, had lessened the expressway's chance. In the mid-
nineteenth century a new transportation route, the railroad, had given
birth to Trotwood. There were many in the city who feared that it
would die without a new expressway or a way of adapting the old rail
line to handle the transit problems of the late twentieth century.

The problems posed by integration, low- and moderate-income
housing, growth and annexation, and school funding and transportation would be complicated by Huber's new town in both Trotwood
and Madison Township, which was linked to Trotwood socially and
economically through the school system and geography. The new
town could also stimulate the recognition of similar problems in rural
Brookville and Perry Township. Although it was Huber's contention
that his new town would eliminate these problems in the long run, he
was faced with the immediate task of getting his project off the
ground. He had to assemble almost five thousand acres of land and apply for millions of dollars in federal assistance without arousing
political controversy in the area adjacent to the project site that would
kill the new town before it was started. Because of this, he decided to
proceed with his planning secretly.

In early 1971 Huber started bolstering his political alliances and
making new contacts in Washington. He assembled a small, young
staff, most of whose members were students from the University of
Cincinnati. Among the young people whom Huber hired were his own
daughter, his future son-in-law, and a graduate student who had
worked on the staff of Senator Robert Taft's 1970 election committee.
To manage the staff of students, he hired Warren Hyser, a person with
experience primarily in local real estate development and mortgage
banking. Huber also hired a few consultants to handle specific items
that he felt would be necessary in making application to HUD for Title
VII assistance. He chose consultants who he felt would have political
influence in Washington: appraisers, attorneys, economists, engineers,
management consultants, and land planners. With a small staff and

consulting team, Huber was ready to begin his land acquisition efforts and preliminary contacts with HUD.

Huber decided to handle the land acquisition efforts in the same manner that his family had in their past large developments like Huber Heights. That is, buy enough land for the initial development stage, then purchase more land tract by tract as needed. The rolling countryside around Trotwood was inhabited predominantly by members of the Dunker Church of the Brethren who were known for their baptismal practices, opposition to legal oaths and military service, and by the simplicity of their life-style. Most of the land was owned either by elderly Dunkers who were growing too old to farm or by those who had inherited the land and had little interest in farming themselves. In the spring of 1971 Pharon Denlinger, a Dunker realtor from Trotwood, was retained to bring the land that was necessary to start the project under control. Denlinger's staff worked closely with Huber and his attorney, Robert Deddens, whose law firm had freed him to devote almost full time to the new town project. Together they identified parcels of property and investigated the various alternatives open with each.

That spring Huber also began the preparation of the necessary documents that he would be required to submit to HUD in the Title VII application process. The procedure was one in which he would have to assemble his ideas into a presentation first for a preapplication to test the project's feasibility and then for a formal application. Several of Huber's consultants would perform specific tasks for the presentation.

The key to Huber's philosophy for developing the new town was the community authority concept. This was his solution to what he perceived as several potential problems, both immediate ones with the HUD application and long-range ones with future new town residents. HUD suggested that new community applicants develop innovative proposals and strongly encouraged citizen participation. The community authority would be a quasi government having less power than established jurisdictions and more power than traditional home owners' associations (like the one at Columbia) that were beginning to present thorny problems to developers. The community authority would be made up of both representatives from the development corporation and the new-town residents. One unique feature of this was that the new-town residents' representatives would be the majority in control of the community authority from the beginning. Another was that the minority, comprised of the developer's representatives, would be phased out through the development period, which eventually would give complete control to the new-town residents. Huber decided that it would be a good strategy for the community authority and his development corporation to apply jointly for federal assistance.

To design a schedule for the joint application, planning, and development process Huber hired the management consultants McKinsey and Company. McKinsey designed a project plan for the initial stages of the development of Brookwood. They used the Program Evaluation and Review Technique (PERT) to model this process. It included a series of PERT charts illustrating the work required to complete each task and the time that each required, and it was prepared from a computer-generated critical path analysis. The primary PERT chart displayed the entire planning network in summary form that highlighted the critical path and the major dependency relationships. The focal point of the summary network was the HUD application upon which the project's success rested. McKinsey supported the summary network by detailing charts for eleven subnetworks that were consolidated on the summary chart. The subnetwork categories, which were the key areas of activity in the development process, included land acquisition, zoning, financial analysis, physical planning, the HUD application, the community authority, community services, marketing and sales, construction, utilities, and annexation.[5]

The two areas that McKinsey's network stressed as crucial to the HUD application were physical and financial planning. Huber felt that it was essential to hire consultants in these two areas who would have a favorable impact on HUD in Washington and on those who would review the project on the state level in Columbus. In the selection of consultants, Huber paid particular attention to the advice of Reuben Clark of the Washington, D.C., law firm of Wilmer, Cutler, and Pickering. Clark had been influential in writing sections of the New Communities Act and had some political connections within HUD's bureaucracy. It was Clark who suggested the firm of Llewelyn-Davies Associates as land planners. The firm's principal, Lord Llewelyn-Davies, had been involved in the planning of the New York Urban Development Corporation's new town of Amherst near Buffalo. Llewelyn-Davies began its planning efforts for Brookwood from its

New York office in June 1971 with information from Huber and his fledgling staff. At the same time Huber also provided the raw data and source material to his financial planners from the Battelle Memorial Institute of Columbus, a firm chosen because of its prestige in the state.

With his physical and financial planning efforts under way and a time schedule starting to take form, Huber began to intensify his contact with HUD that had started early in 1971. After Huber had had several meetings with officials of the Office of New Communities in Washington, they sent a representative, Spencer Lengyel, to Dayton in July to investigate the proposed new-town site and to visit other Huber projects. After the visit Huber submitted the preapplication, which included preliminary reports developed by both Llewelyn-Davies and Battelle. Then on 7 September HUD officially invited Huber to submit formal application in a letter from Samuel Jackson, HUD's assistant secretary for community planning.

A project the size and magnitude of the new community with its political and economic implications at the local, state, and national levels could not operate in a vacuum for long, and eventually the Dayton news media caught wind of Brookwood. Both the *Dayton Daily News* and the *Journal Herald* announced Huber's intentions on 5 November 1971.[6] Both newspapers covered sets of facts unknown before to the general public: first, the new town's name was Brookwood, it was being developed by Donald Huber of the Huber homebuilding family, and it would contain between ten and twelve thousand dwelling units to house about forty thousand people. Second, Brookwood would include commercial, industrial, public, and residential land uses. Third, the new town would be located northwest of Dayton between Trotwood and Brookville in Madison and Perry Townships on approximately five thousand acres. It was also disclosed that officials of the Office of New Communities at HUD admitted that "it was a project to which they were giving serious consideration." The reporters explained that HUD approval would mean that the federal government would guarantee bonds on the new town. Llewelyn-Davies of London and New York was identified as Huber's planner and the Battelle Institute of Columbus was identified as the economic consultant.

Huber had been avoiding publicity, because he feared the impact of the public reaction, especially in Trotwood. But immediately before the news leak an unusual situation presented itself to him. The mayor of Trotwood, Edward Rausch, who had worked as a manager for the National Cash Register Company, had been affected by the company's reductions in its Dayton office. Rausch was a middle manager in his early fifties who taught at a local business college and had written a book on management techniques. He had roots and family in Dayton and had no desire to relocate. As mayor he had been active in both Trotwood's annexation efforts and the city's acceptance of the Miami Valley Regional Planning Commission's housing dispersal plan. Rausch met Huber and was hired as the operations manager of the community authority.

In addition to announcing the new community, the first reports by the press and subsequent articles through November and December brought several of Brookwood's problems into the open. The first was the issue of zoning in both Madison and Perry townships. The news of large-scale urbanization in basically rural townships was bound to raise opposition at the grass roots. Huber had decided to concentrate his efforts on selling the idea of the new town to the elected officials responsible for the zoning decision instead of to the general public. Even before the new town became common knowledge, Huber had secretly flown officials to visit Columbia and Reston. But after the news reports, Huber had to deal for the first time with those responsible for the elected officials' jobs. The second problem was that of community authority legislation. By the end of 1971 the community authority was still no more than an idea with no official action having been taken on it by the state house in Columbus. The third problem was the Trotwood-Madison school system. With school bond issue after school bond issue going down to defeat and with schools running on split sessions, the news of forty thousand possible new residents further complicated an already complex situation. Then there was the growing opposition from the established jurisdictions directly affected by the new town. Some of Trotwood's anxiety had been eased when Rausch was hired as operations manager of the community authority. But as Trotwood's opposition lessened, Dayton's increased. Huber had verbally agreed with several officials to annex the new town to Dayton, but then he had turned around and hired a man who had been responsible for some of the suburban annexations that had hurt Dayton's growth substantially. The Dayton city commissioners, who were facing a dwindling tax base because key industries were moving out of town, grew distrustful of Huber. The commissioners knew that they were in a position to stop the new town, and some of them began to advocate doing just that. Lastly, Huber was facing the problem of growing concern among low- and moderate-income groups. Although Huber had stressed to HUD his working relationship with Dayton's poor, especially with poor blacks, many low-income groups, especially the powerful west-side Model Cities Agency and the Office of Economic Opportunity-sponsored Northwest Advisory Council of the Montgomery County Action Agency, felt that they had been ignored by Huber.

After a year of planning Huber was facing mounting difficulties. Besides the major questions raised by the press, there were many internal problems. The new-town operation was moved from Kettering to Trotwood, but it was understaffed. Thus it had no way of coping with either the day-to-day management of the project or the public-relations effort that the new town required after its existence became known.

The small staff at the Trotwood office included Hyser, Rausch, and a few students, as well as Huber's daughter and son-in-law. An advertising agency had been hired to build displays in the office and publish a monthly newsletter, but both were running behind schedule. Work on the HUD application dragged because of the mounting complications. Problems arose in acquiring the amount of land that would be necessary to have under control, because the newspaper articles had caused prices to soar. By the end of 1971 less than half the land needed was under any form of legal control. Then there was the problem of the name of the new project. Brookwood had been used by the press, but again and again it had to be stressed that it was only a temporary name. Consequently most people were describing the development as another Huber Heights, which was an image that Donald Huber wanted desperately to avoid. By the beginning of 1972, Huber realized that he needed help if he were to launch his dream.

3 The General Manager

With mounting opposition from local government and citizen groups; with delay in completing the HUD application; with little action taken on starting to zone the almost five thousand proposed acres; and with a project management, staff, and consultant group in a state that could be best described as the blind leading the blind, Huber desperately needed someone to plan and manage the new town. As early as October 1971 he had been in contact, through a Chicago executive search agency, with a successful, St. Louis-based planning consultant, Gerwin K. Rohrbach.

Gerwin Rohrbach was a man who mixed the toughness of a Marine drill sergeant with the zeal of an evangelist and the organizational skill of a Saul Alinsky with the mastery of a symphonic conductor. He was a man who either alienated or attracted others.

As the president of General Planning and Resource Consultants, Rohrbach had provided consulting services to private and public clients on various aspects of community planning and land development. He employed twenty-five people and made about four hundred fifty thousand dollars in annual sales. Rohrbach had been the chief officer and principal owner of the firm and had been responsible for establishing corporate philosophy and financial goals, coordinating marketing efforts, continuing necessary levels of technical competence, and maintaining relations with clients. During the period from 1960 (when he founded the firm) through 1970, he administered approximately $2.5 million in 252 consulting contracts while maintaining profits, reducing long-term debts and providing a competitive salary structure.[1]

General Planning and Resource Consultants prospered so well under Rohrbach's leadership that his little firm grew into a giant. In 1970 Rohrbach sold the firm to the Alan M. Voorhees planning

conglomerate of McLean, Virginia, and Los Angeles, California. After
the sale, Rohrbach remained as its president but grew restless and
dissatisfied with not being in complete control of the firm that he once
owned. So he quit with the apprehension that comes with having no
clear idea of where his next opportunity lay.

Gerwin Rohrbach was the son of a German immigrant who had
become a successful nurseryman. He was raised near Boston and attended Phillips Andover Academy and Harvard University. He served
in the navy during World War II for two years on a small island off
the Philippines. After the war, following years of premedical training,
he declined the family-chosen career of medicine and entered the Harvard Graduate School of Design where Walter Gropius was head of
the architecture department. When he graduated, Rohrbach became a
Fulbright scholar and traveled across postwar Germany. In Europe he
studied architecture, engineering, and town planning while observing
one of the most massive rebuilding efforts in history.

Rohrbach's character was forged in the purest form of the Protes-
tant work ethic. He was also the beneficiary of a Germanic reverence
for education. Throughout his administrative career he combined
idealism with pragmatism, and his drive was underlaid with a combination of personal ambition and a belief in the basic principles of
democracy.

The first day of February, 1972, was Rohrbach's first day as general
manager of Donald Huber's new town, which was still being called
Brookwood for the lack of any permanent name. On that day not
many people knew who Rohrbach was or what his position was, but
his arrival would have a most dramatic effect on the new town and
those involved in its development. Most of Rohrbach's first day was
spent in briefings. In the morning he met with Pharon Denlinger's real
estate men, who were desperately trying to gain control of the land
that was necessary to begin the project. In the afternoon, in the barren, confused Trotwood office, the Dayton press was briefed by
Huber, his staff, and consultants on the status of the new town.
Rohrbach sat to the side, listening and observing. The press knew only
that he was somebody who had not been introduced or whose
presence had not been explained.

"The operation," Rohrbach thought to himself that day, "is a mess.
Just exactly what does Don Huber think he is doing with all these
newsmen? He is, he said, briefing them. But, for God's sake, Huber's

people not only do not know how they are going to build what they say they are going to build, they cannot even know yet what it is going to be. And they are briefing newsmen."

"And this chart," said a consultant from Huber's prestigious planning firm with pull in Washington, "shows the depth to the water table . . ."

"If the depth to the water table is really as the chart indicates, then the new town site is the Okefenokee Swamp," Rohrbach thought; but he had driven through the site and hadn't seen any alligators. "It is just possible," he mumbled to himself, "that these guys from New York don't know what the hell they are talking about."

So Rohrbach tuned out the news briefing to ponder the Dayton new town. The project really worried Rohrbach that first day. He had decided that there was great potential in two aspects of the project; the concept and the site. These are what attracted him from St. Louis to Dayton. The site was northwest of Dayton in a location that fronted on the problems that had created the defeats of so many established urban areas: race, government overlap, rapid growth, economic instability, and incohesive communities. The site was a commitment to facing, rather than escaping, these problems. But after over a year in the heads of the creators, the system was in disarray. Then there was the concept of the community authority. It offered a solution to a problem that Rohrbach had long searched for, which was a way of promoting citizen participation with private industry in determining their joint future while not disturbing but rather utilizing present jurisdictional powers. But again no action had been taken on making the concept a reality.

At the briefing, the words "new town" were getting all the newsmen's interest.

"But, hell," Rohrbach mused, "there was nothing new about new towns. People had been building them throughout history. Most of them were company towns. Pullman built a new town for Pullman employees to live in Pullman homes buying from Pullman stores under Pullman laws. But the community authority concept, properly nurtured, should ensure that the Dayton thing would never be a company town."

So Rohrbach began planning the Dayton new town, which would no longer be referred to as Brookwood (except in official correspondence with federal officials), but as the New Town. Along the way,

Rohrbach would capture the imagination of several drifting dreamers like reporter Pat Fritz who tagged along after Rohrbach with his Hemingway beard and Indian parka, recording the events that affected the New Town's progress.

To set up the New Town "right," Rohrbach faced numerous tasks that he had to develop into a process. This could have been simplified if he had been given the McKinsey report by Huber when he arrived. Instead he was forced to develop an independent process that in the end would resemble the McKinsey report. Once he discovered the report, quite by accident, he was able to mesh it easily with his own emerging process. But before he could concentrate his efforts on process, Rohrbach had to complete several immediate, pressing tasks. He had to bring about some order through proper management within his inherited staff and consultant group, divert the mounting citizen and local government opposition, take action on zoning, complete the land acquisition, submit community authority legislation to the state legislature, and complete and submit the formal HUD application.

4 Early Planning Efforts

Raised among the trees and flowers in a nursery; educated first in biology, then in landscape architecture, Gerwin Rohrbach was a man who was innately aware of the vital interrelatedness of all living things. He realized that a system depended on a process for its birth and growth. As he began his tenure as general manager of the New Town, he was also aware that the wrong process could prove fatal to a system. He realized that he had to sow the seeds well for the process to develop and for the New Town to grow.

There were many interrelated tasks whose completion was overdue and had to be effected simultaneously. A manageable staff and team of consultants had to be organized in a positive office environment. Local and governmental opposition had to be cooled while alliances were formed with once hostile individuals. Land acquisition efforts needed to be completed while zoning efforts that would require the aid of newly formed alliances and land management policies that would smooth the transition from a rural to an urban environment were begun. Community authority legislation needed to be initiated in Columbus again with the aid of new allies. The federal application process had to be completed by both the Donald Huber Development Group, as the private developer, and the not yet created community authority, as the public developer. These tasks were completed during the same period, from February to June 1972, but I will describe in detail the activities involved in each separately, showing how all were interdependent and necessary to the New Town's planning process.

The HUD Application

Although much financial, marketing and physical research had been done when Rohrbach arrived on 1 February, the HUD application had not been completed. To complicate matters, the deadline for submission was February, because HUD required a six-month delay between the submission of the preapplication, which Huber had done in August, and that of the final application. Although the McKinsey report, which was unknown to Rohrbach at the time, had set December as a target date for submission, only fragments of a document existed two months later. When he learned about the HUD deadline soon after his arrival (again quite by accident), Rohrbach placed the completion and submission of the application first in priority on the list of tasks that had to be completed and began synthesizing the piles of information that Huber had collected.

The completion of the HUD application was essentially done in a two-and-a-half-week period in February after Rohrbach arrived. This required a herculean effort that awoke many of those connected with the New Town project to the amount of work and commitment that was necessary to the project's success. What had been essentially a nine-to-five job became an eight-to-midnight effort. This required different amounts of push-pull on the students, the secretaries, the middle managers, and the consultants.

The students were primarily cooperative students in architecture, community planning, and graphic design from the University of Cincinnati. These cooperative students were joined by Huber's daughter and son-in-law, who were also students. They had been operating out of their automobiles, driving between Huber's offices southeast of Dayton in Kettering to the New Town office in Trotwood on various tasks that Huber assigned to them by phone or at irregular weekly staff conferences. A few days after his arrival Rohrbach lined the students up for inspection on the parking lot behind the New Town office in Trotwood. He barked like a drill sergeant at the row of shaggy-haired, denim-clad youths. He gave each a broom and trash basket and told them that he wanted the area surrounding the office to be spotless. Then he gave them each specific tasks related to the HUD application with a due date for each job. "Shape up or ship out," he shouted at the students, "it's time you start learning how the real world operates." Although Rohrbach admired the younger generation's ideals and willingness to experiment, he felt that he had his work cut out for him if he was going to fit them into the process that he was developing. Colleges didn't equip individuals to function in the business world, he thought.

He used a different approach on the three secretaries who were employed at the New Town office. Because Trotwood was a small city that was vulnerable to gossip, he knew that the secretaries could play an important role in the image projected by the New Town office. So with them he stressed efficiency and established standard procedures for office routine and official correspondence like the HUD application. They typed and retyped the 200-page HUD application for two-and-a-half weeks. When the application was completed, they felt that the office had reached a new level of competency, and this was projected to the community.

There were three senior middle managers employed by the New Town when Rohrbach arrived. The first was Warren Hyser. From the start, there was conflict between Hyser and Rohrbach. Hyser had no background for a project with the scope and scale of the New Town. He enjoyed his position as confidant to Huber and head honcho on the project. The new general manager diminished Hyser's role considerably. Rohrbach blamed Hyser for much of the ineptness that he had perceived when he arrived. It had been Hyser's responsibility to spearhead the HUD application, which was not only behind schedule but, Rohrbach felt, of miserable quality. So from the beginning a situation was created where Hyser, jealous of his loss of prestige, was constantly trying to undermine Rohrbach's position covertly and overtly.

The second senior Huber New Town employee was engineer-architect Voldimere Rameika. He was a Latvian immigrant who had worked for the Huber family since the early 1950s. He had been chiefly responsible for the subdivision street grids and simple, brick ranch homes associated with the Huber family's larger developments such as Modern Manor and Huber Heights. Educated as a civil engineer before the Second World War, he was drafted by the Soviets when they invaded the Baltic nations and was put to work designing air fields. He deserted the Red army to fight with the Nazis on the Eastern Front for most of the war in a desperate attempt to free his homeland from Soviet domination. At the war's end he found himself first in Berlin cleaning the rubble off the streets; then in Dayton, Ohio, working for Donald Huber's father. Rameika had always worked out of a studio in his own home for Huber before Rohrbach arrived, but the new general manager insisted that he move into the Trotwood office to work on the many maps and documents required

in the federal application process. Rameika had mixed feelings about
Rohrbach. On one hand he resented the loss of his freedom and considered Rohrbach a tyrant. "I have worked for Stalin," Rameika
would grumble, "I have worked for Hitler, and now I have worked
for Rohrbach." On the other hand, Rameika respected Rohrbach's
ability and agreed with several of his early technical decisions. Some
of Rohrbach's findings concerning the physical planning documenta-
tion that had been done prior to February refuted some of Llewel-
lyn-Davies's findings and were closer to Rameika's, who was at the
time more familiar with the actual New Town site than was any
other individual.

Edward Rausch was the third senior Huber employee. He had
been a successful middle manager for the National Cash Register
Company and was accustomed to implementing decisions. Rausch
had felt a lack of direction from Huber when he began work. This
was replaced by a sense of optimism spurred on by the new general
manager's stress on efficiency and procedure in preparing the HUD
application. Rohrbach, away from his home and family in Trotwood, found a friend in Rausch. He entrusted him with many of the
key tasks involved in first the HUD application and then interrelated
projects in the planning effort. The one thing that worried Rohrbach
about Rausch was his position as operations manager of the community authority. Rausch had resigned as mayor of Trotwood when
he had taken the job, but now Rohrbach felt that there was a potential conflict in his being the director of a public agency while being
hired by the private developer who could be in opposition with the
same public body over certain issues. Nevertheless, the HUD application had to be applied for jointly by Huber and the community
authority to insure funding for both.

Rohrbach had to handle the consultants in a completely different
manner than he had the staff. He discovered, once he began gathering the information necessary for the HUD application, that Huber
had no contracts with his consultants, only vague letters of agreement. Because there were no binding legal contracts that specified
products, Rohrbach could not make demands for specified data that
were required for the application. He decided to proceed, acknowl-
edging in the final document possible weaknesses that there were in
what the various consultants had already produced. He would then
follow up by getting consultants under binding contracts for specific

products that could be submitted to HUD at later dates.

In this two-and-a-half-week period in February 1972 ten copies of a 1,200-page document that weighed over thirty-six pounds, including the text, plates, and various exhibits, were produced and submitted to conform to HUD guidelines that were established by the manner in which previous Title VII applications had been requested and reviewed. The application was submitted jointly by the Donald L. Huber Development Corporation, as the private developer, and the New Community Interim Non-Profit Corporation, which had been organized to act on behalf of the community authority. The application requested HUD to guarantee commitments in the total amount of $31 million comprised of $17 million for the community authority and $14 million for the private developer.[1]

The text of the application was a 400-page report that detailed the rationale of the project. It followed the statutory requirements stated in section 712 of Title VII and the administrative criteria established by HUD's Office of New Communities. Rohrbach was accustomed to writing government applications, so he followed the established criteria point by point.

Section 712 of Title VII identified eight criteria to be used by the secretary of HUD in determining whether the new community program of a private or public developer was eligible for assistance. Eligibility was conditioned on the secretary's finding that the proposed new community

1. Provided an alternative to disorderly urban growth, preserving or enhancing desirable aspects of the natural and urban environment, or so improving general and economic conditions in established communities as to help reverse migration
2. Was economically feasible in terms of its economic base or potential for economic growth
3. Contributed to the welfare of the entire area which would be substantially affected by the program and of which the land to be developed was a part
4. Was consistent with comprehensive planning [physical and social] on state, local and private levels
5. Had received all governmental review and approvals, required by state or local law, or by the secretary
6. Contributed to good living conditions in the community, and was

further characterized by well balanced and diversified land use
patterns that include public, community and commercial facilities
deemed satisfactory by the secretary
7. Provided housing within the means of persons of low and moderate
   income, and that such housing would constitute an appropriate
   portion of the community's housing supply; and
8. Made significant use of advances in design and technology for land
   utilization materials, construction methods, and provision of community facilities and services.

Administrative considerations to determine the eligibility of a project could be grouped into two categories: general and specific.
General criteria dealt with the characteristics that a new community
had to have, the types of new communities that were eligible for assistance, the sizes and locations considered desirable, and the requirement to innovate not only in physical planning but also in all other
aspects of the community's development. Specific criteria dealt with
the sponsor's capacity to manage effectively the new community process, the nature of the physical plan required, environmental impact,
the local services and facilities required, governmental and govern-
ance requirements, and the economic and financial requirements that
HUD considered to be essential.

The text of Huber's application began with an overview of the project, which was followed by the rationale of why it specifically
qualified for the program. Still using the name Brookwood, the overview in the text included first a history of the site, the developer, and
the project. The history of the project included several items that were
considered to be issues and problems: the community authority legislation, zoning in Madison and Perry townships, school facilities,
Trotwood's perennial flooding, electrical power transmission, the
pending gas shortage, local government opposition, and concern for
low-and moderate-income groups.

The overview of the site was followed by general criteria for new
communities. This included design concepts for cultural, educational,
and religious facilities; housing; transportation; utilities; industry;
commerce; open space and recreation; social and economic objectives; the impact on the surrounding area; the creation of jobs; the effect on regional urbanization; and racial and economic diversity objectives. The broad design concepts were prepared by Llewelyn-

Davies who utilized consultants, like transportation planners Barton-Aschman and Associates, with whom they had worked closely on other projects. The remaining criteria were prepared primarily by Rohrbach using his own personal experience, previous HUD Title VII new community applications, Donald Huber's personal goals, state and regional planning goals, and consultant reports as guidelines.

The general criteria included objectives that supported the rationale for the project. For instance, included in the social and economic objectives was a statement on public participation that was directed at HUD's commitment at that time to citizen and minority involvement in planning.

"Every effort will be made," the text noted, "by the Community Authority to achieve effective public participation in the development of the new community. This community involvement in the planning and management of Brookwood's development and operation will be particularly oriented towards encouraging the participation of the minority groups which have traditionally been least articulate and least able to express their aims and requirements. It is essential to the purposes of developing a self-determining new community, which will have its own system of community government, to promote public interest and participation in local affairs at all levels and in all sections of the population living and working in Brookwood."[2]

The general criteria in the application's text were followed by more specific eligibility criteria for Brookwood. The specific criteria first dealt with the size, location, and internal diversity of the project. The application projected the population of the New Town to be 42,675, which was based on housing needs projected by the Battelle Institute for the Metropolitan Dayton area, of which it calculated the New Town could capture 13,493 dwelling units in the development period from 1969 to 1992. With a site of approximately five thousand acres, this meant that there would be 2.7 dwelling units per gross acre for the overall site or a net of 5.1 units if only the residential land was considered. The location was described as ten miles northwest of Dayton's central business district on "slightly rolling open terrain, in active use for agricultural uses with a few small established residential clusters." The location was then described in relation to the diversity in population, housing, business and job opportunities, and public facilities that could be developed in the project with the existing conditions in the metropolitan Dayton region.[3]

Next, an internal development program, which related to the overall design concepts prepared by Llewelyn-Davies Associates, was proposed. The development program first included a site suitably studied based on the Llewelyn-Davies data, including topography, microclimate, soil characteristics, and existing land uses. These physical studies were based on an environmental impact statement that Huber had submitted to HUD on 17 December 1971 to adhere to the National Environmental Policy Act of 1969. A Llewelyn-Davies land-use plan was then presented for the program based on the physical studies, Battelle's population projections, and the anticipated needed facilities (water, sewer, transportation, and schools). Projected design controls, phasing, developer's innovations, and housing mixes; the necessary governmental reviews and approvals; and the various social elements were then integrated into the land-use plan.

The specific eligibility of the project was then supported further in the text. The capability of both the projected private and public developers was explained. The private developer was identified as the Brookwood Development Corporation, an entity that would be formed and headed by Donald Huber. The application outlined Huber's experience, concentrating on his family's home-building history and his more recent involvement in federal 235 and 236 housing programs. The community authority was identified as a new entity that would be organized and established under proposed Ohio legislation. Because both were new entities, financial references were offered for them through the Donald L. Huber Development Group. The application listed key Huber management personnel and stated that the Donald L. Huber Development Group had recruited Edward Rausch as acting operations manager for the community authority. It was anticipated that he would continue to be employed by the community authority once it was organized.[4] It was stressed that both developers would abide by the various federal, state, and local laws and professional standards that related to land development. Projected affirmative action programs that would show Huber's commitment to equal opportunity and civil rights laws were emphasized.

The final portions of the text were devoted to the project's economic feasibility and a general financial plan and program. The economic feasibility of the project was based on data supplied by

Battelle, which made comparisons of their own demographic projection of the region's growth potential to the development program. Using Battelle's assumptions on the growth potential of the area and its projections concerning the project's marketing feasibility, a financial plan and program was produced that detailed the costs that would be incurred by both the private and public developers. Potential financial sources, both federal and private, were compared to the costs showing how the project would be financed and equity would be built. A real estate appraisal of the site's property was used to show the predevelopment value of the land versus its potential developed value. Last, the economic model listed the terms and conditions of the federal guarantee; how much would be needed, according to the program that had been devised, for working capital, front-end costs, and long-range expenses; the security for the guarantee; and the use of the proceeds from the federally guaranteed obligations. In essence, what the economic model did was support the application's request for federally guaranteed assistance by showing the need for such a project in the area, the benefits of a new community fulfilling those needs, the cost of those benefits, the origin of the capital that would pay the cost, and the security offered on those funds.

The next section of the application was supported by appendixes, plates, and exhibits. The first appendix listed federal grants that the New Town would be applying for as part of the Title VII legislation that offered not only guaranteed loans but also first priority on federal development grants to approved new communities. These planning and construction grants could be worth additional millions of dollars to new community developers. The second appendix was a tracking schedule that compared the various regulations required by HUD to those sections of the application that fulfilled those requirements. The fifteen plates illustrated the land-use plan of the development program that had been prepared by Llewelyn-Davies. The first two plates showed the site's regional and area location (see maps 1 and 2). The next five interpreted the natural conditions such as topography, floodplain, woodland, soil types, and depth of the bedrock. The ninth plate was Llewelyn-Davies's land-use or master plan. The remaining plates illustrated supporting data such as governmental jurisdictional boundaries, planning alternatives, phasing, and the existing land ownership. There were also fifty-three exhibits in two bound volumes and separate reports that further documented and detailed what was proposed in the text.

The HUD application was essentially a physical planning document. The heart of the Llewelyn-Davies development program was a land-use plan produced from the physical studies of the site and supported by economic, marketing, and social data. It was an example of what Herbert Gans has called an adaptation of the traditional master plan approach to city planning. As Gans contended, and as Huber's Brookwood application verified, the new-town concept had revived the waning support of the land-use approach to planning that had been losing validity to social science and economic approaches. Rohrbach, the application's key organizer, although educated in the school of land-use planning, had been an innovative planning practitioner in applying social science and systems theories to real situations. Ironically, in the case of Brookwood, Rohrbach was forced by the time constraints of the application's deadline to use what had been produced before his arrival, which was primarily Llewelyn-Davies's physical planning program.

Because Rohrbach was trained as a land planner and had produced many master plans of high quality, he had been suspicious of the prior physical planning from his first day, when, during Huber's news briefing, inaccurate water table charts had been presented. After investigating the site himself and interviewing those who were most familiar with the property, he was certain that most of the biophysical data were inaccurate. This awareness prompted him to consider the possibility that other information that had been produced for the application by other consultants was also faulty. Rohrbach had decided to submit the application anyway and then work with HUD to correct the discrepancies.

The first indication from the HUD officials that they shared Rohrbach's observations about the physical data came in March when they rejected the environmental impact statement. This was a key document, and its rejection meant that HUD approval would be delayed for several months.

A second indication came in the review process several months after the application's submission. At that time, HUD questioned several deficiencies in its content. Specifically the land acquisition program, the low- and moderate-income housing plan, the security offered by Huber, and the real estate appraisal were criticized by the officials.

Market studies provided by Battelle were also not acceptable to HUD.

The confirmation by HUD that Rohrbach's suspicions were correct about the physical, economic, and marketing data presented him with several difficult problems. There was the matter of the ability to trust the competence of the consultants. Even if the project had been poorly managed by those who had preceded him, the consultants were experienced enough that they should have investigated the data that had been provided for them more thoroughly and should have made investigations of the site to verify their own reports. This raised the question of how Rohrbach was to deal with his employer's top management, which he felt had to share the blame for the poor output of the consultants.

Rohrbach was amazed at the lack of control that Huber had over his consultants because Huber had failed to negotiate specific contracts that would bind them to needed products and price controls. Many of the consultants had been suggested because of their influence with HUD, and Rohrbach had to question the motives of those suggesting the firms and of Huber, who allowed himself to be swayed because of their alleged influence. All of this raised the question of how a productive, working relationship could be established with HUD.

For the competence of the New Town to be established with HUD, it had to be proven in its performance during the process required by the review of the application. The first step after the submission in that process was the A-95 review. This was the procedure required by law, in which the application was reviewed by state and local governments. For Huber's request for assistance to be approved by the federal government, it was necessary first for the project to be recommended by all the affected state and local entities. The review process began when the preapplication was submitted, and it was intensified when HUD released the final application to the reviewing agencies.

The purpose of the A-95 review was to coordinate, evaluate, and review federally assisted projects and to coordinate planning efforts of intergovernmental jurisdictions on all levels. Its goal also was to receive comment from regional and local governments about federal projects in their area and to coordinate their efforts with those of federal agencies.

The unofficial review at the state level for the New Town was first established in May 1971 upon request by Donald Huber to the Ohio

Department of Development, which, at the time, was the official state clearinghouse review agency. Huber's move for early involvement was prompted by his recognition that the project would require approval on myriad governmental levels. It became apparent immediately to the state officials that they were not equipped to deal with a project the size of Huber's. Because of the absence of criteria for review and the lack of clear state policies to deal with the project, the state officials decided to restrict their preliminary review to satisfy the federal requirement for review of federally funded projects by interested state agencies and to use the Brookwood project in determining policies for reviewing other future new community projects.[5]

Because Huber's project was the first of its type in Ohio and because of Huber's personal relationships with officials from state representatives to the governor, he was in an extremely advantageous position. The Office of Development used Title VII guidelines for its review, giving specific emphasis to those guidelines that would be beneficial to the project's success, such as the state enabling legislation for the community authority. Emphasis was also given, on paper, to zoning and subdivision regulations; the relationship with local governments, public utilities, and services; the economic feasibility and impact on local governments; and the control of fringe development and the interests of a low-income population. But, on the whole, the Department of Development tried to avoid controversy and appease Huber. In fact, it decided not to involve other state agencies because it was perceived that the disclosure of certain facts might jeopardize the project's success.[6]

In August 1971 the Department of Development intensified its review after receiving a copy of the preapplication from Huber. During the course of the preapplication review the state clearinghouse function shifted from the Department of Development to the Department of Finance, but this did not affect the state's approach to the project. The state's official stance was that it recognized the preliminary nature of the preapplication and focused its attention on only the determination of potential areas of concern and conflict. Most of the information that the state used in making these determinations was provided by Huber during a series of meetings in late 1971. Immediately before Rohrbach began as general manager, the Department of Finance gave the project preliminary clearance based on its review of the preapplication, stating that "no major serious concerns were anticipated" in its further review process.[7]

The final application was received by the state in March 1972. Soon afterwards Huber and Rohrbach met with state officials who presented them with twenty-seven questions about the New Town. The major questions concerned overlapping governmental jurisdictions; community authority legislation (which, in the meantime, had been submitted to the Ohio House of Representatives presenting new issues at the state level); school funding, disparities between the anticipated population absorption rate and the housing absorption rate; control of fringe development; the incorrect physical data included in the application and the environmental impact statement; transportation planning; and charges that had been leveled against the project by the Northwest Advisory Council of Montgomery County concerning low- and moderate-income persons' involvement in the project's planning.[8]

Rohrbach responded to these questions in a letter to Andris Priede, deputy director of the Development Planning Division on 17 May 1972. By that time the issue of overlapping jurisdictions had become very heated and an outside consultant had been retained to mediate the differences. (This issue, which was also a major concern of the local A-95 review, will be discussed later.) The several questions raised concerning the community authority legislation were also being decided concurrently with the state A-95 review process. The legislation had direct bearing on the options available for school financing. In the letter, it was stressed that the passage of community authority legislation would greatly benefit financing the construction and operating expense of schools in the New Town. Because of the many questions raised by HUD and the state and local authorities about the economic projections in the application, Rohrbach decided that it would be best to have a set of projections alternative to those of the Battelle Institute. He chose Real Estate Research Corporation of Chicago, whose market projections were lower than Battelle's in the early years. This meant, for one thing, that the amount of pupils would be less at the outset and result in less of a drain on an already overburdened system. The disparities between population and housing absorption rates were also clarified by the new Real Estate Research Corporation figures.

In his letter to the state, Rohrbach did not respond to the questions about control of fringe development, because both he and Huber realized that any control would be advantageous to the marketing potential of the New Town. Both the physical data and transportation planning had been completely rewritten for a second environmental impact statement, which was submitted in April. The low- and moderate-income citizen opposition was also to be resolved at the time Rohrbach wrote the letter. Both the new physical planning and citizen involvement efforts will be investigated later in depth. The state A-95 review process was expected to be completed by early summer when the vital questions concerning the community authority and the environmental impact statement would be answered.

The local A-95 review was administered by the Miami Valley Regional Planning Commission (MVRPC), which established a special New Town Review Committee that was comprised of representatives from affected jurisdictions. The committee was advised by MVRCP staff and solicited input from various local officials such as those responsible for police and fire protection, power transmission, and health and educational facilities. The committee's membership included two representatives each from Montgomery County, Dayton and Trotwood, and one representative each from Madison Township and MVRPC. Other representatives participating in the committee's deliberation were those from the Montgomery County Community Action Committee, who represented the interests of minorities and low-income groups, and the First National Bank of Dayton, which represented the area's power establishment.[9]

The review process began in the preapplication stage and continued through the state and federal reviews of the final application. Using a sixteen-page checklist of items, the special New Town Review Committee released its report in May. The material on the checklist included public utilities and facilities (sewage, solid waste disposal, gas, electricity, and communications); transportation facilities (streets, highways, parking, mass transit, and pedestrian and bicycle ways); housing, education; open space and environmental quality; community facilities; historical and cultural preservation; public safety; governmental structure; community organizations, social services, and citizen participation; equal opportunity; the economic and social impact on the urban area; and the relationship of the New Town to unacquired property near the site. Each item and subitem was compared against the text of the application to decide if the committee felt that the application's response was satisfactory, incomplete, not necessary or possible at the time of review, in the process of being resolved, in conflict with the established regional plan, concerned local governments, or was in need of being resolved before final HUD approval. Based on its checklist the committee approved Huber's application with a long list of "conditions and recommendations."[10]

Included in the conditions were some stipulations that greatly benefited Huber's efforts. The committee recommended that Huber be asked to include in his proposal an agreement to provide land for a college campus. Huber and Rohrbach felt that a college could be beneficial to the New Town's image and to its marketing potential. The committee also lent its support to community authority legislation in its report.

Most of the other conditions, however, were not so helpful. The committee's members were local officials who were sensitive to the pressures of the local press and their constituents, and they were unable to give Huber the blue-ribbon treatment that he received at the state level. Recommendations were made for more public housing than the initial plans had provided for and for various rent supplements to be provided for low- and moderate-income families. In the Dayton area "low- and moderate-income" meant black, and both Huber and Rohrbach were fearful that the image of the New Town would be black because of the press coverage of the review committee's report. This also complicated the growing resistance by home owners in the Trotwood-Madison Township area to whom "federal project" was also synonymous with black. Some of the committee's other suggestions included that commitments be made for the New Town to become a member of the regional transit authority, to adopt affirmative action programs in the hiring of staff for the public and private developers, to work with MVRCP in future planning and development, and to work with local governments to resolve jurisdictional issues.[11]

The jurisdictional issues became more complex when, in the review process, Mayor James H. McGee of Dayton wrote a six-page letter relating the city's position to Dale Bertsch, the director of MVRCP. In his letter McGee made several demands on behalf of the City of Dayton many of which, like low-income housing quotas and affirmative action programs, were incorporated into the committee's report. Most of the conditions could be relatively easy to follow, but there was one major harnessing condition.

"The City of Dayton's recommendation," the Mayor's letter stated, "for favorable review is contingent upon commitments of the developer for annexation of the significant portion of the New Town to the City. If the developer is unable to make good his commitment, the City's support will be withdrawn in terms of the A-95 Review and in terms of transportation, utilities and other services to the New Town."[12]

Dayton's insistence on annexation had reignited the feud between the city and Trotwood, which forced Huber and Rohrbach to bring in a mediator to resolve the differences. The mediator's efforts resulted in an "agreement in principle" concerning annexation in which Huber made certain commitments. The McGee letter then was an attempt to ensure that those commitments would be kept.

The McGee letter was a personal blow to Huber because he had considered the mayor to be an ally. A black man, McGee had been the attorney for Madden. After his election, he found himself opposing Huber in a confrontation with residents of Madden Hills who claimed that Huber had lowered his building standards after receiving the federal financing for the project. McGee lost some confidence in Huber after the confrontation. He lost more when several Dayton city councilmen began publicly expressing their mistrust of Huber because they felt that he had no intention of fulfilling verbal commitments that he made for annexing the New Town as early as the spring of 1971. Dayton's only alternative was to make stipulations concerning the New Town when it had the opportunity before funds were approved by HUD.

With the release of the New Town Review Committee's report, the executive committee of MVRPC passed a resolution approving the New Town subject to the conditions attached by the report and the McGee letter, thus ending the local A-95 review process.

The local approval marked the culmination of much progress on the HUD application. Although the many strings that had been attached to the project by local and state officials still needed to be addressed, the application had grown from several loose, unrelated documents in February to a completed report. With many ongoing additions and corrections provided by Rohrbach and new consultants, it was gaining credibility with local, state, and federal officials by June 1972.

The Community Authority

By the time both the local and state A-95 review processes were well under way, community authority legislation had been introduced and was being advocated by both review agencies. To understand the full implications of the legislation, it is first important to know the motives of its originators and then to trace its history from the drafting stages through the state house to when the community authority became legal.

Donald Huber approached the New Town first and foremost as a businessman. He felt that the success of a new community depended largely on its ability to market itself. In his investigation of other new-town developments, he had found that one of their major marketing problems was the adverse publicity generated by early residents. Unlike traditional housing developments, which are sold in a few months or years, new towns are marketed over a long period of time, in some cases twenty or thirty years. These sales efforts continue after some residents have settled. In many cases, these residents experience a sense of powerlessness resulting from frustration or disillusionment, because most of the new community's key decision-making power still rest with the developer. Some new-town developers, like James Rouse of Columbia, have tried to combat the adverse publicity generated by the residents' frustration by forming home-owner's associations. But these associations offer little real power to the residents and, in some cases, have been used to coerce opinion and manipulate citizens.

To alleviate these problems while making the application more attractive to HUD, which was at the time an advocate of citizen participation, Huber conceived the community authority that would provide for a special district to organize, plan, finance, and implement the New Town's public improvements and human services. In this way, Huber could rid himself of the responsibility of providing these services by making a joint application for federal-guaranteed assistance to have the community authority finance the public areas of the New Town. The community authority would thus provide an attractive amenity package for Huber while alleviating the burden of direct confrontation with residents about services.

Huber had briefly considered incorporating the New Town into a separate jurisdiction. But, according to a new state law, no new village, town, or city could be incorporated within three miles of an existing incorporated entity. Because Brookwood was within three miles of three such jurisdictions, this alternative was ruled out and the idea of community authority was pursued.

Gerwin Rohrbach approached the New Town as more of an idealist. He felt that the success of any community depended largely on the ability of its residents to control their own destiny. In his experience as a planner, he had found one of the major problems with many American communities, especially the new ones, was the lack of real power that citizens had in decisions that affected their communities. Different planners and other community organizers had approached this problem with various strategies that resulted in various degrees of success.

When Huber first approached Rohrbach in October 1971, it was the community authority concept that impressed him most about the project. Here was a way to provide a body on a different level of financial and political control for residents of a community from the outset than had ever been available in any new town or any other subdivision or tract development. In the complex, multilayered jurisdictional bureaucracy of urban America, the community authority offered a way of providing the ordinary citizen with the power to dictate his own future in an environment that was too often controlled by private business interests and faceless, unresponsive governmental systems. It was this potential that ultimately convinced Rohrbach to take the job with Huber.

But when Rohrbach arrived at the New Town on 1 February he found the state of the community authority to be in worse shape than even the HUD application. The legislation necessary to make the concept a reality had not only not been submitted to the Ohio General Assembly, but no workable draft had been produced nor had any worthwhile lobbying been started. Rohrbach realized that it was the first task to be completed after the HUD application. But, in that request for federal assistance, it was necessary to make a joint application for both the private and public developers to assure financing. So a nonprofit corporation, The New Community Interim Non-Profit Corporation, was formed under Ohio law by Huber to act on behalf of the community authority until it could become a reality.

The drafting of the Community Authority Bill and the lobbying efforts in Columbus began in earnest soon after the HUD application was submitted. In many ways the drafting and lobbying became the

same activity. Rohrbach realized from past experience that a bill
with the community authority's implications was certain to gather
opposition from many groups who were fearful of losing their own
power. So the bill was drafted by Huber's three law firms, Squire,
Sanders, and Dempsey of Cleveland, who drafted the financing sections of the bill; Wilmer, Cutler, and Pickering, Reuben Clark's
Washington firm, which participated in the drafting from the stand-
point of qualifying the community authority for Title VII purposes;
and Gould, Bailey, and Farquhar, Huber's Dayton attorneys who
developed the bulk of the bill and coordinated all of the various suggested changes that would come from the other law firms, the Ohio
Legislative Service Commission (the legislative drafting arm of the
Ohio House), and various lobby groups. After the initial drafting,
the bill's sponsor, State Representative Frederick Young, who had
been a childhood friend of Donald Huber, introduced it to the Housing Subcommittee of the assembly in February.

The Community Authority Bill, House Bill 1063, received an extensive review by legislators (Young claimed that the bill received
more scrutiny than ninety percent of the proposed legislation in
Ohio) and lobbyists. Many of these were potential enemies of the bill
who in the end actually wrote sections of the legislation. The drafting and lobbying efforts were spearheaded by Representative Young;
Robert Deddens of Gould, Bailey, and Farquhar; and Robert
Husted, a public relations man from Huber's advertising agency,
Kircher, Helton, and Collett. As it was introduced to the assembly
from the Housing Subcommittee, House Bill 1063 was designed primarily to authorize a publicly controlled developmental entity that
would provide a sensible alternative to typical home-owner's associations in other new communities. Although written specifically for
the Dayton New Town, the legislation had to be applicable to other
possible new community situations. The proposed bill had three
primary stated purposes:

1. To provide a means whereby the residents of a new community could
   participate in the planning process through the entire development
   period and, especially, through trustees selected to represent their interests, participate in the all-important *initial* decisions made effect-
   ing public facilities;
2. To provide a flexible means whereby communit   d amenities could be financed to the end where that th   lves

would pay for these facilities and amenities over their useful life (which, typically, would be substantially longer than the development period itself); and

3. To enable new communities to make maximum use of the new federal financing available under Title VII and to pass the substantial savings arising out of such financing on to the resident of the same communities.[13]

To convert potential enemies to allies, Rohrbach advocated an approach that made each special-interest group feel that it had a vital part of the content of the bill. In this way each group became protective of its own work and instead of opposing the legislation, supported it. In late February, many lobby groups were contacted, given copies of the proposed bill, and requested to suggest how the bill might be improved. In early March, Deddens and Husted, representing the developer, contacted these groups by phone and requested appointments to discuss the bill in detail. For use at these appointments the New Town staff produced an audiovisual presentation that explained the concept of the bill, how a community authority would function, how it would be financed, and the various benefits of both the Brookwood Community Authority and the New Town itself. Armed with draft copies of the bill and the audiovisual presentation, Deddens and Husted contacted a wide range of lobby groups that had potential interest in the legislation, including the state school board association, the various governmental associations, state banking and other financial leagues, professional councils of all types, church conferences, and the housing coalition.[14]

One of the most powerful lobbies that had to be negotiated with was the Ohio Municipal League. When Deddens and Husted made their initial contact with its general counsel, John Gotherman, it became quickly apparent that passage of the Community Authority Bill depended, in part, on support from this powerful city lobby. There were meetings between the New Town representatives and Gotherman that were designed to mediate the delicate balance between the "municipal powers" of cities and the proposed community authority powers. As a result of the discussions, the community authority was, in essence, given broad powers to develop the community facilities and to provide social services that were not normally provided by municipalities. At the same time it was stripped of the municipal powers to provide police, fire protection, and water and sewers, except where these services could not be obtained from municipalities.[15]

Another issue discussed with the Ohio Municipal League was the power of taxation. It was decided that the community authority would be able to collect a community development charge. The charge would be based on income and would not be a tax because it would not be levied by a unit of government for general government support, nor would it be established by government action. Like the usual assessments for the support of home-owners' associations, it would be created by a private covenant running with the land placed in deeds, which, when recorded, would bind all subsequent purchasers to pay the charge. It was the same method used to finance Columbia's home-owners' association. It differed from an income tax in that it simply placed a fee on property owned or used within a new community.

Perhaps two of the most dramatic and certainly unexpected sources of support for the bill eventually came from the City of Dayton and a group representing the same low- and moderate-income groups from the Northwest Montgomery County Community Action Agency. The support was unexpected because both groups had been publicly opposed to the project. Nevertheless, remarks in favor of the legislation were introduced to the state legislature from both Dayton officials and a citizen's New Town committee, which was an ad hoc group comprised of the low- and moderate-income citizens.

Anthony Char, speaking for the city, said, "We believe the legislation is a positive step in giving central cities the opportunity to evaluate the input and determine the effect such development would have on the cities. Mrs. Francis Brown of the citizen's committee said, "We feel this law will assure the success of the new communities throughout Ohio that will provide an opportunity for anyone to live in them and have a part in planning their communities."[16]

This support, along with that of the state and local A-95 review agencies, bolstered the bill's position in the legislature. The City of Dayton supported the bill primarily because of the agreements reached in drafting the legislation with the Ohio Municipal League, which secured many of the central city's powers, and because of agreements reached concerning annexation arrived at through the efforts of Rohrbach and an outside mediator. The support of the low- and moderate-income groups was gained primarily through Rohrbach's persuasive powers. He was able to convince the citizen's organizer Harlan Johnson of the far-reaching positive implications of the bill. Rohrbach and Huber also promised citizen representation on the Interim Non-Profit Corporation.

Also involved in the lobbying effort was the Interim Non-Profit Corporation. Its operations manager, Edward Rausch, was a Huber employee, and he let the main thrust be provided by Huber, Rohrbach, Young, Deddens, and Husted. According to the HUD application the Interim Corporation would "have the power to develop and review physical, economic, social and related plans for the development of the proposed new community of Brookwood, and to negotiate for guaranteed assistance, grants, loans and other forms of assistance from the office of New Community Development Department of Housing and Urban Development as well as other federal, regional, state, local and private sources."[17]

The corporation's purpose was also to "facilitate the orderly transfer of public responsibility of planning and development to the Community Authority" or to act as an alternative much like a homeowner's association in case the Community Authority Bill was not approved. Three public trustees (veterinarian Thomas Dillman, former Brookville postmaster Jerald Leiber, and insurance salesman Cecil Swank) and three trustees representing the developer (Huber, Rohrbach, and Madden vice-president William Leigh) were selected by Huber and then appointed by the Montgomery County commissioners to direct the corporation.

As proposed in the final version of House Bill 1063, a community authority governing body, which, in the case of Huber's New Town, would replace the Interim Corporation Trustees, would be comprised of a nine-person board to be appointed by the appropriate county commission, or a municipal government if the new community was within a municipal jurisdiction. During the planning and development period, four of the members would be trustees to protect the rights of future residents, one member would represent local government, and four members would represent the private developer. These appointed officials would then be gradually phased out and replaced by elected trustees throughout the development period,[18] so that never during or after the planning and development period would the private developer have the majority representation on the board.

Under the umbrella of public facilities and social services, the board would be responsible for coordinating and developing park land, community centers, pathway and bikeway systems, recreation facilities, transportation systems, health systems, and community identification and maintenance programs. It would also be empowered to coordinate cultural, environmental, social, religious, governmental, and other human services. Funds to operate community development and activities would be provided by bonds issued by an authority and, in the case of Title VII new communities, guaranteed by the federal government. These bonds would then be retired through resident assessments, community improvement charges, and users fees.

Once the bill was passed, a community authority could be established by petition to the appropriate county commission with the approval of the most populous city in the county and of any city that was contiguous to a new-town area. The veto provisions were specifically added on Rohrbach's urging both to protect the rights of local jurisdictions in all cases where the law might apply and to appease the cities of Dayton and Trotwood in the case of the project for which the bill was written. For a tract to be a "new town area" as defined by the Community Authority Bill, it had to encompass at least 1,000 acres and had to be zoned for comprehensive development. Public notice and hearings were required for the adoption of any resolution established by a community authority.[19]

On 31 May 1972, after several months of drafting and lobbying, and after being approved by all the appropriate legislative committees, the Community Authority Bill breezed through the Ohio House by a vote of seventy-eight to ten. Two weeks later the bill received unanimous approval by the senate and was passed on to Ohio governor Gilligan to sign.

Huber expected Gilligan to sign the bill quickly, because he was a heavy contributor to the governor's campaign fund. But pressure was put on Gilligan not to sign the bill by the Economic and Community Development Department. Arnold White, deputy director for legal services of the department wrote a strong memorandum to the governor urging him not to sign the bill. White had been on vacation in Europe when the legislature acted on the bill. Upon his return, he found a memorandum from Rusty Matthews, pointing out what he thought were deficiencies in the bill. Matthews and then White were concerned that the mechanics for electing board members to the community authority board of trustees were not "democratic"; they feared that the bill did not provide enough protection for investors, specifically homebuyers; they thought that there was not enough state involvement in the planning; and they were concerned that the bill "may have implied that you do not have to consider racial integration."[20]

With loyalties split between his staff and a campaign contributor, Gilligan pocket vetoed the bill, thus allowing the community authority to become law without his signature.

Land Acquisition and Zoning

One of the prerequisites of petitioning for the establishment of a community authority, according to House Bill 1063, was that a new-town area had to be zoned for comprehensive development. By state law it was necessary for an individual to own land or to have it under legal control before zoning could be requested. So before the community authority could be formed, there had to be the necessary land for zoning. But because no comprehensive new-town zoning laws existed in Montgomery County, it was necessary first for new zoning laws to be created so that once there was enough land under control, zoning could be requested.

As in the other early planning efforts, there was no schedule being adhered to for land acquisition when Rohrbach arrived. There was only a nebulous deadline for final HUD project approval that Huber had derived from the McKinsey report. According to the McKinsey schedule, which in no way was being followed except for the approval date, land for the first phase of the project was to have been secured by October 1971, a land-control statement for HUD was to have been prepared by November, and acquisition of the four to five thousand acres needed for the project was to have been completed by December.[21] But as of February 1972, less than half the land for the first phase had been secured; the statement for HUD had been only partially prepared, because control of the land had been only partially completed; HUD had commented that the land acquisition report that had been submitted in the application needed considerable elaboration; and only about seventeen hundred acres were under some form of legal control.

The major reason why Huber had delayed his land-acquisition program was his past experience in real estate development. In his family's previous subdivision developments, one tract of land at a time had been purchased. Although land prices rose because of adjacent development, the amount was less than the interest on the mortgage and other holding costs that would have resulted if the land had been purchased at the beginning of the development. Subdivision zoning in the 1950s and 1960s was also relatively easy to obtain from local jurisdictions, which were equipped to process tract development with traditional procedures.

The New Town presented a completely different type of development. The stories in the local newspapers had an impact on the acquisition efforts. The coverage of the project's scope and size and its economic potential caused land prices to soar. It soon became apparent to Huber, realtor Pharon Denlinger, and the others involved in acquisition that most of the land in the tract would have to be controlled from the initial stages of development (as the McKinsey report had suggested). The community authority law also made it necessary for there to be a complete tract for comprehensive zoning.

A new approach to acquisition began to take shape soon after the HUD application had been submitted and the community authority legislation introduced, when there was added pressure on zoning caused by opposition from some local officials. In the early spring an intense communications effort was begun by the New Town staff that attempted first to convince landowners to sell their property at competitive prices both because the project would be beneficial to the area and the economic potential alleged in the newspapers was long range and risky. The program was also designed to pave the way for zoning. The communication effort consisted of an audio-visual presentation similar to the one that was used to present the case for the Community Authority Bill, the delayed display panels for the Trotwood office, and the informative newsletter (which had been published irregularly up to that time) mailed to every resident in Trotwood, and Madison and Perry townships. The presentations were advertised locally with handbills and were given at the schools, churches, fraternal lodges and grange hall by Rausch and Denlinger (who were familiar with the local residents) and by Huber, Rohrbach, and Deddens.

Most of the old Dunker farmers were skeptical of urbanization. They had seen its evils, and, with their attachment to the land and their strong religious convictions, this made it difficult to convince them to sell. They were also skeptical of Huber whose name to them was synonymous with the worst use of the land in the Dayton area. Rohrbach offered an alternative image to that of the smooth, citified Huber. The farmers watched the gruff little German make his way around the community, learned of his love for the land, and grew to trust him. This trust, coupled with the public-relations effort, convinced many of the old farmers to sell. There was also a substantial amount of land controlled by real estate speculators and the children of farmers who had died. These individuals were more willing to sell and needed little convincing. By late spring, most of the needed land had been brought under some form of legal control, including practically all the land needed for the first phase, and the land ownership statement for HUD was nearing completion.

The zoning of the New Town area was controlled by two bodies. Zoning in the Madison Township section was under the control of the Madison Township Zoning Board, an appointed body of the township trustees. The zoning in the Perry Township area was under the jurisdiction of the Montgomery County Rural Zoning Commission, whose members were appointed by the county commissioners. The Rural Zoning Commission had jurisdiction over all areas in the county that had not elected to exercise zoning control. Madison Township had so elected; Perry Township had not. Although a Planned Unit Development (PUD) Ordinance existed in Montgomery County, there were no ordinances that covered comprehensive new community development of the size that Huber was proposing. This meant that an amendment establishing a category for new communities had to be introduced and approved by each jurisdiction before zoning for the New Town could be requested.

Huber had flown the township trustees, county commissioners, and the zoning officials to Columbia and Reston to visit other projects like the one that he was proposing. He had also initiated the needed zoning amendment in both the township and county, but his amendment ran into stiff opposition from the local officials. It was the first overt official opposition that the New Town had encountered. The headline of the local paper read "New Town Plan Put Off" in February as Rohrbach was hurriedly getting adjusted to a new job and trying to produce the HUD application. It soon became apparent that trips to other new towns alone would not persuade the officials who were responsible for zoning and who had to answer either directly or indirectly to local voters to approve zoning. There would have to be little opposition and even some support from their constituents before they would do so.

So when Rohrbach arrived he was faced with hostile zoning administrators. He would have to rewrite Huber's proposed amendment, have it reviewed and approved, and then submit the specific zoning request simultaneously to both township and county commissions. To complicate matters, land control had not yet been completed, and the mapping and comprehensive physical planning would be found faulty in the HUD application process. Both the control and the physical planning were vital to the success of the final request.

Rohrbach decided that the best approach was to sell the concept of the new town through the communications program and quell potential opposition with knowledge. At the same time that they would be trying to buy the necessary land, the New Town staff would attempt to convince residents of smaller tracts that would remain as "out-parcels" adjacent to or, in some cases, surrounded by the New Town, that it would be beneficial to their property. This was done night after night in the schools, churches, and other meeting places chosen for the audiovisual presentations. Questions were fielded and answered, potential opposition was eased by alliances between the municipalities that were begun at the meetings and then were followed up with one-on-one meetings at the New Town office. While the communication program was in process, Rohrbach was meeting with the local officials, discussing the proposed zoning amendment. He was always careful to listen to their ideas and tried to incorporate them into the proposal, making the officials feel as though they were a part of the project. That was the same technique that had been used with the lobby groups in the case of the Community Authority Bill and it was equally effective. Rohrbach was constantly endeavoring to build trust with the individual officials and dispel the idea that the New Town was just another Huber subdivision. He tried to get them to see it as a project that would be utilizing the most advanced land-planning methods known.

Rohrbach, who as a consultant had been employed as a community advocate, was skillful at compromising potential opposition by answering questions before they were asked, using the ideas of others, always stressing competence, being prepared, and being as open as possible. Before long the communication program and the meetings with officials began to produce results.

On 2 March the county planning commission, the first zoning amendment review board, recommended to both the county commissioners and the township trustees that the new community provision be adopted. The amendment was then reviewed and recommended by both the Montgomery County Rural Zoning Commission and the Madison Township Zoning Board. Final approval came in May when first the Madison Township trustees and then the Montgomery County commissioners adopted the amendment, making it possible for Huber to request zoning.

The new community zoning amendment took several months to be approved and was hampered along the way by the persistent reports of Dayton's and Trotwood's opposition to the project. Negotiation was necessary to gain the support of these municipalities. During the review process, however, there was very little opposition in the open hearings by local residents to the project. In fact, there were several local residents, including a former county commissioner who had sold his land to Huber, who came to the hearings in support of the zoning concept. The communication program had succeeded in arresting a potential ground swell of opposition.

There were several special provisions in the amendment to which new community developers would have to adhere. Before applying for the new community zoning classification, a developer would have to have a 4,000-acre planning area and own at least 2,000 acres of which 1,000 were contiguous. New community zoning called for a general plan that showed all the planning area that was to be eventually developed, and it required a specific plan that showed the section that was to be developed immediately. At least 40 percent of the land had to be used for residential purposes, between 2 and 15 percent for offices and businesses, 5 percent for industry, and 20 percent as open space. Overall, an average of four dwelling units per acre was permitted. All utilities, with the exception of high-tension lines, had to be underground. A 300-foot buffer strip had to be provided around property owners of out-parcels who chose not to become a part of a new community development. This provision did not allow a change in land use in the area in the buffer strip. Thus, if a farmer opposed a change in neighborhood land use from agricultural to residential, the developer would have to leave a 300-foot-wide buffer zone around the farm.[22]

Although on the surface the new zoning greatly restricted a new community developer, it really provided Huber much flexibility. The requirements for residential density were in many ways much more lax than in traditional subdivision zoning. The density requirements would allow Huber to produce more housing units at less cost than any of his competitors. This position was enhanced by the fact that because he had more than enough land under control by the time the zoning amendment was approved, he was the only new-town developer in the area. The major problem now facing the New Town staff in zoning was the production of the necessary graphics.

When Rohrbach arrived there was no graphics department but only a few architecture and design students who spent most of their time in automobiles or in cornfields shooting photographs. Rohrbach hired a competent draftsman who was responsible for map production and the supervision of the students. Once the base maps with the physical data and a land-use plan were redone with accurate information, they could be used for zoning. The completed plan would have to go through the same process as the amendment had, which was from the county planners to the township and rural zoning commissions and then on to the township trustees and county commissioners for final approval.

Jurisdictional Relationships

The opposition that the New Town encountered in zoning was mild when compared to the opposition mustered by the cities of Dayton and Trotwood. Early in Donald Huber's informal discussions with local officials he had promised several city commissioners to annex the New Town to Dayton. The rumors of this promise angered Trotwood officials who had a close geographic and social relationship with the area of Madison Township in which the New Town was located. Many Trotwood officials were also afraid of the out-migration of blacks that they felt annexation would cause. When Huber appointed Rausch as operations manager for the community authority, the Dayton officials felt betrayed. As Trotwood's mayor, Rausch had been chiefly responsible for outmaneuvering Dayton in the annexation battle that had caused a great deal of bitterness on both sides. During the preapplication, however, most of this bitterness remained bottled up, and both sides viewed Donald Huber as just another wealthy home builder who was about to start another subdivision development outside their realm of control.

When the official approval process began, the officials began to realize what the scope of the project was and what power they had over its success or failure. Each began to unleash the pent-up frustration that it felt toward the other on the New Town. Both started to exercise their power during the A-95 review process, the community authority legislation, and finally zoning. These were proceedings on which they had either a direct impact or an indirect influence through the news media and public opinion. Either way the cities presented a force that Rohrbach had to reckon with.

The first Dayton city commissioner to come out publicly against the New Town was Thomas Andrews, who had demanded from the first private meetings with Huber that the New Town be annexed to Dayton. Andrews was followed by Charles Curran, who, in an April local A-95 review session, blasted the project, calling it a "nirvana" and predicting that it would evolve into a separate entity that would be competitive and possibly fatal to the city.[23] Soon both commissioners were vowing not to support the project unless the New Town were annexed to Dayton. Their logic was clear. Dayton, the old city, had faced depopulation during the 1960s like most American central cities. The middle class had fled to the suburbs, leaving the central city black and poor. In the early 1970s in Dayton, several key industries were moving out or shutting down, causing the tax base to dwindle even more. The two commissioners saw the New Town as a threat and were determined not to let it hurt the city.

The publicity about annexation frightened the residents of Trotwood and Madison Township. They were the middle class who had fled the city in the 1960s. Annexation to the central city meant that blacks would be moving out and with them all the associated stereotypes such as lower home values, deteriorating schools, and higher crime. This feeling was reinforced by the fact that Huber was applying for federal assistance. To the suburbanites "federal assistance" meant the same thing as "central city" and "low and moderate income"; they were all euphemisms for black people. Like the Dayton councilmen, the Trotwood and Madison Township officials would soon start advocating that the New Town be annexed to their city or stopped altogether.

Huber played down the situation, counting on his personal relationships with individuals like Mayor McGee and his political influence gained from heavy contributions to both political parties. He felt that the opposition, which in Dayton was still in the minority on the commission, could be halted in informal meetings with key individuals. Over a drink or two they could discuss the matter and reach an agreement. But Andrews and Curran were firm in their opposition and were soon joined by other commissioners, including McGee, who saw Huber's credibility slipping because of his performance on the other federal projects in the area and because his promises varied with whomever he was talking to. Trotwood, with its former mayor now on Huber's staff, was less organized and less vocal in its opposition, but one at a time its councilmen also grew more leary of Huber's promises.

The mounting opposition grew until it became clear that the majority of the Dayton council was taking a firm stand against the New Town with every available opportunity, especially during the local A-95 review process. Dayton's official stand was unmistakable: no annexation, no New Town. Verbal agreements over cocktails would no longer suffice.

Dayton's stand had a direct negative effect on all the official proceedings in progress. The A-95 review could not continue or the HUD application be approved without commitment from Huber, the community authority legislation was stalled without support from the Municipal League lobby of which Dayton was a member, and the zoning process was clouded because of the publicity. Rohrbach decided two courses of action had to be taken. First, because Huber's credibility was slipping, an alternative personality representing the New Town with credibility had to be established. Second, the hostility between the two cities had to be resolved.

Rohrbach became the alternative personality. This could be done successfully because he felt a greater personal commitment to those who would live in and be affected by the New Town, than to his employer. Rohrbach sympathized with the officials of the two cities; they reminded him of most of his clients during his years as a consultant. The situation was the classic one of the small subrural community faced with rapid urbanization and the large central city faced with a dwindling population and tax base. The New Town was being used as a scapegoat, but Rohrbach felt that this was justifiable. The project could hurt both cities, or, with the community authority, it could begin to solve several pressing urban problems facing both communities. Gerwin Rohrbach began to establish his own credibility by keeping a completely open office; telling the same thing to all parties, even though the truth caused some short-range damage; and by taking action that was in the interest of both cities, such as assuring both cities veto power over the community authority during the legislative process.

To resolve the hostility, Rohrbach convinced Huber to hire Herman Pope, president of the Public Administration Service of Chicago, as an outside mediator. The Public Administration Service generally limited its clients to public bodies, but Pope was familiar with Rohrbach's reputation from his work in the Chicago area, so he agreed to take the job. It was easier to convince Pope to be the mediator than it was to convince the cities that they ought to be subjected to mediation. The first meetings in April were between Pope and each of the individual interested parties. After several attempts Pope finally convinced officials of both cities to sit down and discuss the matter. It was no small task, because these rival cities were not accustomed to talking to each other.

Meetings were scheduled for two consecutive Thursdays in May. The first of the direct negotiations between Dayton and Trotwood were held on 4 May behind closed doors at the Miami Valley Golf Club, a plush country club just within Dayton's city limits near Trotwood. Representing the City of Dayton were Mayor McGee, Commissioner Andrews, City Manager James Kunde, and Assistant City Manager Whitney Shartzer. From Trotwood there were Mayor George Van Schaik, Councilman George Bayer, City Attorney Fred Izenson, and City Manager Robert McNay. The first heated meeting resulted in an agreement to meet again.

Before the second meeting, while visiting the HUD office in Washington to see how the application was progressing, Huber found out just how serious Dayton's opposition to the project was. Richard Eckfield, the City of Dayton's lobbyist, had made the city's position as clear to HUD as it had been to Huber and Rohrbach. The federal government was spending a lot of money to make cities like Dayton viable. It seemed counterproductive for it to spend money to create new towns that would sap their vitality. Dayton had no guarantee that the Huber New Town would be tied politically, socially, or economically to the city.[24] Dayton could not and would not support the New Town until it had some guarantees. This position seriously endangered the application and hence the New Town.

On Thursday, 11 May, the second crucial round of negotiations was held between Dayton and Trotwood. For the first few hours of the meeting, each faction argued and shouted until Rohrbach ended the deadlock with an impassioned speech. "You bastards are cutting your own throats," he shouted, slamming his fist to the table. "NCR is moving out, Frigidaire is laying off, half a dozen other industries are moving out or shutting down. And here you are acting like a bunch of goddamn babies while the best thing to come along in the area for years goes down the drain."

Early Friday morning, after an all-night meeting, an "agreement of principle" was reached. The next day the press received a release detailing the agreement. "Major James McGee of Dayton and Mayor George Van Schaik of Trotwood announced an agreement of principle concerning the Brookwood New Town," the release stated. "A resolution is to be presented in the near future to the City of Dayton Commission and the City of Trotwood Council asking for the municipal corporation to look to the future annexation in part to Dayton and in part to Trotwood."[25]

Huber's part of the compromise would be to produce the land for the annexations. Mayor McGee saw the move as an instrument to reverse the declining city population, which, according to the 1970 census, had changed from 262,000 residents to 243,000. Van Schaik, a tall, handsome insurance salesman who was rather unwillingly thrust into the role of mayor when Rausch resigned, said in the release that the agreement would allow Trotwood to grow from a city of 7,000 to one of 40,000, "a very efficient size community which will still allow Trotwood to retain its unique characteristics and community scale."[26]

The release did not indicate which parts of the New Town Dayton and Trotwood would attempt to annex. Both sides did, however, initial a map that outlined the areas for which the two cities would be aiming (map 3). Wolf Creek Pike, which bisected the new community east and west; the Penn Central Railroad tracks, which ran northwest to southeast; and the proposed Dayton circle freeway

I-675, which would run north and south, were the key boundaries.

Trotwood would concentrate its annexation attempt in the area north of Wolf Creek Pike and east of the proposed expressway but north of the railroad tracks. Dayton would attempt to annex the southeastern panhandle of the New Town, land south of Wolf Creek Pike, and the railroad and west of the freeway to Perry Township line at Diamond Mill Road. The land west of Diamond Mill Road in Perry Township was left open because it was not slated for development until the 1980s. After the map was initialed by the city representatives, Rohrbach dubbed the line formed by Wolf Creek Pike, the railroad, and the proposed freeway the "Demilitarized Zone."

The McGee letter to MVRCP was then the city's attempt to guarantee that Huber would fulfill his commitments, that is, to annex the agreed upon section to Dayton. The agreement allowed the New Town application to complete the local A-95 review process with the annexation condition. It also reduced the pressure that had been exerted on HUD by Dayton and had a positive effect on the state A-95 and the community authority legislation. Although individual Madison Township trustees expressed their opposition to the agreement, they

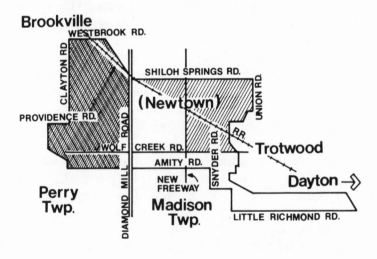

Map 3. New Town Jurisdictional Agreements

LEGEND

☐ City of Dayton Annexation Area
▨ City of Trotwood Annexation Area
▨ Perry Township Area, which was not discussed in annexation agreement between the cities

Scale ———— ⇨
No Scale   N

realized that annexation would still be very difficult to achieve because of the strong sentiment against annexation to Dayton by local residents who would have to sign the annexation petition. Even though the trustees opposed annexation, as did the county commissioners, who in both cases stood to lose power, the positive publicity generated by the agreement, and Rohrbach's openness with both entities, eased some of the pressure on the new community zoning amendment. So the agreement had positive impact on the governmental jurisdictions involved.

Citizen Participation

The HUD application stated, "Every effort will be made by the Community Authority to achieve effective public participation in the development of the new community."[27]

Because the community authority was nonexistent at the time that the application was submitted, it was the responsibility of the private developer and the nonprofit corporation that had been formed to act on behalf of the community authority to achieve public participation. Huber felt, and Rohrbach agreed, that a citizen involvement program was crucial to receive federal approval for the project, because the government was stressing public participation at the time. The community authority would eventually be the conduit for such activities, but what about the early stages of development?

When Huber submitted the preapplication he felt that his involvement with the several black businessmen in the federally-subsidized housing projects, and the "dual-developer concept" would suffice for the early stages. It might have, but Huber's position as the builder of the people was weakened on two occasions in the preapplication stage. First, the black residents of his major Madden subdivision started to criticize his building practices. Then members of the Northwest Advisory Council of the Montgomery Community Action Agency, an Office of Economic Opportunity-sponsored agency, issued a resolution expressing their opposition to the project. The advisory council, representing low- and moderate-income citizens of the area, sent the resolution directly to the HUD Secretary Romney on 6 January 1972.

By the time that Rohrbach arrived, both the premise of effective public participation in the development of the new community and Huber's credibility were on shaky ground with the federal government. With the many tasks facing Rohrbach, he could not devote full time to creating a mechanism for citizen involvement. He decided that his best approach would be to complete the immediate tasks and, while doing so, form personal alliances with individuals who could help implement the citizen participation process. He foresaw three potential groups of citizens that could be involved: the low- and moderate-income group, which had opposed the project; local residents, who would be affected by land acquisition and rezoning; and local elected and appointed officials. A group formed from this base could then begin to effectively participate in the planning and development process.

The first individual from the Northwest Advisory Council whom Rohrbach had to confront was Harlan Johnson, the community's wily young organizer and an idealist left over from the New Frontier. Johnson, who was in his late twenties, employed methods that were similar to those developed by the activists who were involved in the civil rights movement in the South and in the coal regions of Appalachia and by the veteran Appalachian organizer Si Kahn (most of Dayton's poor were black Southerners and white Appalachians). Johnson had entered the community, sized it up, made contacts, brought people together, developed leadership, worked with area organizations, set priorities, developed power tactics, built political power, and worked on self-help strategies (Kahn 1970). His community organization was now ready for its first big confrontation with the local millionaire developer.

Rohrbach, a community organizer himself, understood Johnson and knew that he could make an ally of him if he negotiated correctly. So meetings were arranged, and the tall, bearded Johnson and the stubby, ruffled Rohrbach confronted each other. Through the spring of 1972 a series of meetings were held between representatives from Johnson's group and members of the New Town staff (primarily Huber, whom Johnson distrusted; Rohrbach; and Rausch). Demands were made, compromises reached, and agreements concluded. The two central issues that were raised were those of low-and moderate-income quotas and representation on the community authority. It was finally agreed that the citizen group would ease its opposition to the project while the developer would include a higher number of subsidized housing units, though not nearly so high as demanded, and would give the low- and moderate-income group representation on the Interim Non-Profit Board of Trustees.

Rohrbach had negotiated extremely well. He was so successful that his enthusiasm for the project and especially for the community authority had rubbed off on Johnson, and his group not only ceased their opposition but became lobbyists for the New Town. They formed the ad hoc citizens' New Town committee which traveled at the expense of its members, many of whom were on welfare, to Columbus to testify before the Ohio General Assembly in support of the community authority legislation. The next step was to convince the ad hoc group to work within a framework in which others could be involved to implement a public participation process.

For this task Rohrbach hired Community Services of Yellow Springs, Ohio. Community Services was a nonprofit corporation which had been founded by former Antioch College president, Tennessee Valley Authority director, and Miami Conservancy District organizer Arthur Morgan to help preserve and foster small communities. The philosophy of Community Services was that the best possible human living environments were of a relatively small scale. Although there was concern that a 5,000-acre new town adjacent to an already densely populated metropolitan area was contrary to Community Services' basic philosophy, Griscom Morgan, president of Community Service and son of Arthur Morgan, felt that it offered a realistic alternative to the hodge-podge subdivision development occurring around Dayton. Rohrbach was also able to convince Morgan that his group would have a positive impact on the development of communities within the New Town.

Morgan and Rohrbach began to co-opt all the dissenters and doubters of the area. They took anybody who said anything about the New Town and placed him on a planning task force. The group was forced to meet at the Madison Township Grange Hall in late May in Friday sessions that became progressively longer. Here the group started honing their ideas against reality. It was an odd collection of those who were interested in the New Town phenomenon: members of Johnson's ad hoc committee; citizens from the local area, who had been drawn in through the zoning presentations; local officials from the cities, villages, county, planning boards, townships, villages, zoning boards, school systems, utilities, and police and fire districts; the press; consultants; Interim Non-Profit Board Trustees; New Town staff; and even a HUD representative from Washington. Rohrbach hoped that the planning task force would form the base for an effective public participation forum.

Staff and Consultants

The planning task force meetings were held in the Madison Grange Hall's low-ceilinged basement. With Optimist Club banners and plaques below the exposed pipes that creaked each time the upstairs toilet was flushed, the metal folding chairs and Formica tables were arranged in a semicircle around a chalkboard and four easels laden with a proliferation of New Town maps and charts. It was Gerwin Rohrbach's stage, where he rumbled across the room bringing the group that he and Morgan had assembled up to date on the project's latest accomplishments.

Since the first of February, the HUD application had been completed and submitted; the local A-95 review process had been finished, and the state review was nearing completion. The Community Authority Bill had been drafted, lobbied for, and passed into law. New zoning amendments had also been written and approved in two separate jurisdictions. A major agreement had been reached between two rival municipalities, and an effective citizen participation process had begun. But by late May through the planning task force meetings Rohrbach was trying to lay the groundwork for something more. He was starting to develop the framework for the overall planning process of the New Town.

What had been accomplished thus far had been done with the corporate resources that had been existent in the Donald L. Huber Development Group when Rohrbach arrived. But he was aware of the immense amount of work that lay ahead and of the many weaknesses of the present staff and consultant team. He was convinced that there would have to be many internal changes before any successful process could be developed to complete the New Town.

"Fire people in the morning," Rohrbach once said, with a wry smile, to a junior associate, "you're better geared for it then." That had been exactly what Rohrbach had done. He had gotten rid of all the unnecessary staff members and had forced the remainder into a structure by which things could be accomplished. Several of the students had left; those who remained were placed in the newly formed graphics department to produce the mapping necessary for the environmental impact statement and zoning. Several of the secretaries left, and those who remained were given strict guidelines to follow for office procedures. Some of the middle managers had been transferred from the New Town staff to other departments of The Donald L. Huber Development Group. Those remaining were given responsibilities that were necessary to the completion of specific tasks.

The planning task force meetings had been used to bring all the various outside parties together with the New Town staff and consultants, and a similar method had been used to bring key persons within the organization together. From the middle of March, Rohrbach held weekly manager's meetings where all the major issues facing the new community were discussed. These meetings were instrumental in the coordination of the A-95 review, state legislation, land acquisition, zoning, governmental relations, and citizen participation.

During the planning task force meetings and the manager's meetings of the spring, after most of the staff adjustments had been made, Rohrbach began to formulate his future staff and consultant needs, keeping them in perspective with the process that he was developing. In April he sent a detailed formal memorandum to corporate financial vice-president Richard Turner that requested from Huber the anticipated employee and consultant needs for the project. The consultants who had been retained before his arrival presented a different type of problem than the staff had. The data that they had produced had been used even though the bulk of it had been faulty. Rohrbach decided to phase out some consultants and put the remainder under strict, binding contracts. New consultants would then be sought to replace those who had been phased out. The submission of the HUD application had brought out the need for new consultants in the key areas of economic and physical planning. HUD had indicated the many discrepancies in the data that had been used for the economic model and the marketing projections; so Rohrbach had sought out a set of figures that was alternative to those of the Battelle Institute from Real Estate Research Corporation. Although Llewelyn-Davies Associates was retained to participate in the planning task force, Rohrbach had started to produce new physical data with his own expertise and that of the graphics department, but he knew that he would have to replace Llewelyn-Davies with another physical design consultant once his process emerged.

Huber's advertising agency presented another problem. It was inept in dealing with even the most basic tasks that the New Town required of a public-relations firm, such as producing the displays, the newsletter, and developing a permanent name for the project. Its staff was accustomed to selling hamburgers and was unable to cope with the complex ideas involved in producing a new type of human living environment. The agency did, however, employ Robert Husted, who had proven to be an efficient state lobbyist. Because his services might prove valuable in the future, it was decided to retain the agency for the time being.

Even though much had been accomplished since Rohrbach's arrival, many new problems had emerged including some difficulties with the staff and consultants. Rohrbach's strict handling of New Town's employees had alienated several individuals. The Donald L. Huber Development Group's operations were divided among three offices: the main corporate office south of Dayton, in Kettering, Ohio; the New Town office in Trotwood; and the Madden office in West Dayton. Because the New Town office was receiving the bulk of the attention in the press, the employees at the other offices, especially the Kettering branch, grew jealous. This was compounded by the fact that the employees at the New Town office were, in most cases, working twice the hours at the same pay.

The poor relations between the two offices were complicated further by Rohrbach's frankly stated opinion about the incompetence of those who had preceded him. Rohrbach's dismissal of consultants began to raise questions about the judgment of his employer, Donald Huber, who was beginning to feel less secure because of the attention that Rohrbach was receiving from the press and local officials. The two men's personal relations were strained further because Huber's daughter and son-in-law had been among those employees who had left the New Town staff. The situation became more complicated by Rohrbach's desire to have the financial decisions concerning the New Town made at the Trotwood office. This caused resentment on the part of Huber's financial vice-president, Richard Turner, and his assistant, Roger Berardinis. They saw Rohrbach as a threat to the security of their jobs, so they formed an informal alliance with Hyser that was aimed at undermining Rohrbach's position. Despite all these internal difficulties, Huber was impressed with the dramatic progress that the New Town had made since Rohrbach had arrived, and he restrained any resentment that he might have felt at the time.

There were still many areas that required much attention. The HUD application had to be approved, which required the completion of the state A-95 review, the acceptance of the new environmental impact statement, and other new data needed to be produced to replace that which HUD had found insufficient. The Community Authority Bill was law, but the community authority for the New Town had not been organized. The transition needed to be made from the Interim Non-Profit Board of Trustees to the community authority board. Also, a new community zoning amendment had been passed, but specific zoning had not been applied for or approved. The sticky problem between the cities of Trotwood and Dayton remained. Much effort was still required to keep the peace and fulfill the commitments for annexation that had been made. The citizen participation process had been initiated, but it was not truly effective. These items had already received considerable attention and were well under way to being completed.

There were many planning and development tasks that had received very little attention. The land had been acquired but there was no program to manage it. There was the Llewelyn-Davies master plan, which had been replaced by a new plan that Rohrbach had produced for the second environmental impact statement, but it would have to be adopted for zoning with a specific plan for the first phase. Specific urban design and engineering standards were also needed for all the various architects, land planners, engineers, developers, and home builders who would be involved in the construction. A workable economic model was needed not only for HUD but for the internal workings of the corporation. And once the whole project was planned and constructed it had to be sold; so a marketing and sales program needed to be developed.

In the early planning effort of the New Town the work had been finished on a task-by-task basis. With the completion of the first crucial areas of the project, the problems that arose plus the many interrelated tasks that had yet to be initiated made Rohrbach all the more aware of the need for an overall system for the New Town to be developed within. For this effort he would draw on his past experience to design a program that would include all the necessary tasks. This process would then be administered by competent managers and knowledgeable consultants.

Rewriting the Rosetta Stone

5 The Process

On Monday, 12 June 1972, assistant secretary of HUD Samuel Jackson visited Dayton to see the New Town. After a breakfast briefing with local government officials, who exchanged subtle jabs about agreements in principle but remained otherwise friendly, Donald Huber gave Jackson a tour of the area. Cruising the city in one of Huber's Cadillacs, followed by another with less important staff members, Huber showed the federal representative all the projects in which his family had been involved. The affable developer was careful to spend more time at developments like the Madden subdivisions and a Dayton Metropolitan Housing Authority complex where federal money or blacks were involved, because the assistant secretary was a black man. Huber had also been careful to invite a large number of local black politicians to the breakfast and was a bit perturbed when his business associate, State Representative C. J. McLin, failed to show up. However, during the day, Huber was able to introduce Jackson to several other black employees, like William Leigh, and some black political allies.

After the tour, Gerwin Rohrbach gave Jackson a presentation of what had been accomplished up to that point towards making the New Town a reality: the HUD application, the A-95 review, the community authority legislation, the new community zoning amendments, the jurisdictional agreements, and the citizen participation efforts. The visit was concluded with a press conference where Jackson announced that Huber's New Town was a "go" project as far as HUD was concerned, and that its request for federal assistance would be given top priority.

The Jackson visit marked a turning point in Rohrbach's approach to the New Town. Before he had concentrated on completing critical tasks that were necessary to ensure the project's survival. Afterward, with some additional administrative and graphic aid, he was able to concentrate on developing a planning process. As a professional city planner, Rohrbach was familiar with the planning process that included collecting data, setting goals and their priorities, investigating resources, analyzing alternatives, developing programs, and finally measuring the effectiveness of the programs. This process would form the basis of Rohrbach's system for the New Town.

The word "process" to Rohrbach, however, had a much deeper meaning than to the professional planner. Because he was educated first in biology, then in landscape architecture, he thought of process in the scientific sense. Rohrbach attended Harvard's Graduate School of Design at a time when there was a concentration of talent at the school because it offered some of the few graduate programs in the fields of environmental design. Walter Gropius and some of the pioneers in city planning and landscape architecture were still teaching there. The program in landscape architecture spawned a school of thought about the manner in which man should approach his environment, which was best articulated by Ian McHarg in *Design with Nature* (1969). McHarg, chairman of the Department of Landscape Architecture and Regional Planning at the University of Pennsylvania, was a contemporary of Rohrbach's at Harvard, and they share a common philosophy about the process of land planning.

McHarg named his method the ecological planning process; it is simply a method of studying the biophysical and sociocultural systems of a region to reveal where a specific land use may best be practiced effectively. The method defines the best areas suitable for a potential land use at the convergence of all or most of the factors deemed propitious for the use in the absence of all or most detrimental conditions. The method involves a number of steps showing the transformation of data at each level, which are: (1) ecological *inventory* of the region, or, defining the parts of the system; (2) *analysis* of the region, or, showing how the parts work; (3) *synthesis*, or, showing the interactions between the parts in an ecological method; (4) *alternatives*, or, presenting different organizations of the environment; (5) *implementation*, or, presenting various strategies, tactics, and processes that could be used to realize a particular design or plan alternative; and (6) *evaluation*, or, gauging the results of the plan over time from criteria elicited from the users.

The area under study determines which factors need to be inven-

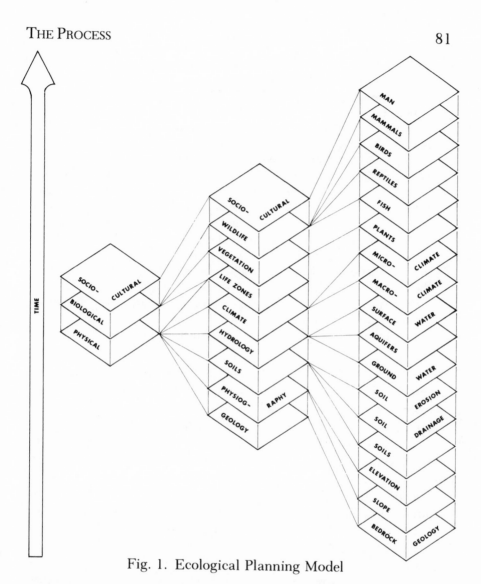

Fig. 1. Ecological Planning Model

toried. McHarg has identified the following factors for consideration: geology, physiography, groundwater hydrology, surface water hydrology, soils, climate, vegetation, wildlife, and land use (fig. 1).

McHarg, whose own firm of Wallace, McHarg, Roberts and Todd became involved in the planning of two Title VII new communities, The Woodlands in Texas and Ponchartrain in Louisiana, has eloquently described this process as similar to the biological structure of people.

A single individual is composed of billions upon billions of cells which emerged from a single fertilized egg. This requires inordinate organization to ensure replication of cells, their specialization as tissues and organs, the processes of growth, reproduction and death, consumption of food, metabolism and waste disposal. It involves predictive and adaptive powers, and above all, cooperative mechanisms to insure coordination. Most of this is involuntary. When man is considered as an ecosystem or in the biosphere, it is clear that there are fewer involuntary mechanisms to insure regulation and we must depend upon that primitive instrument that is reason. Yet we still require predictive powers, adaptive mechanisms to respond to growth and change; we need choices to be made explicit, and these must be related to the capacity to realize them. In all of this the most compelling need is for coordination, and thus for cooperative mechanisms analogous to intercellular cooperation and the regulation of the autonomic nervous system. This process, as old as life itself, is planning. It has no political coloration; it is neither socialist nor capitalist although clearly opposed to anarchy. Planning is the social equivalent to intercellular cooperation; it is the instrument of social symbioses.[1]

Although the direct application of the methods of natural science to social theory has been criticized by some social scientists, it was a way of thinking that affected Rohrbach's actions and was vital to his values. He used the biological process in his philosophic approach to the overall planning process of the New Town, and it would have a more direct impact on the policies he developed for land planning and management.

Rohrbach had spent much of his career in Chicago, St. Louis, and southern Illinois organizing citizen groups that could implement plans that were developed for their communities. In Chicago he became acquainted with Saul Alinsky's methods of community organization, which were similar to those that Harlan Johnson had used with the Northwest Montgomery County Advisory Committee and those of Si Kahn (Alinsky 1946; Kahn 1970). These methods had already been applied by Gerwin Rohrbach. He had entered the Dayton community through the Huber organization, sized it up, made alliances, brought people working on the project together, developed leadership, worked with other organizations interested in the New Town, prioritized the immediate tasks, developed tactics to fulfill tasks, built political power, and was working on self-help strategies for various individuals who had a stake in the action. He would continue to use these techniques to implement his process.

As a businessman and as a planner, Rohrbach also was influenced by new techniques of the social sciences that were developed for a synergistic approach to management, such as the systems approach and organization development.

The systems approach could be more accurately described as the systems approaches. Systems approaches are mathematical and modeling explanations, first presented in the basic scientific communities (physics, chemistry, and biology) as an attempt to unify scientific information to understand natural systems. The concept was broadened to explore man's relationship to an ever increasingly complex base of scientific knowledge. The philosophical groundwork for various systems approaches such as general systems theory, cybernetics and operations research has been laid by Kenneth Boulding, Ludwig von Bertalanffy, Norbert Wiener, Russell Ackoff, and others.[2] These approaches are means of the classification of natural and social systems by the way their components are organized in order to derive typical patterns of their behavior.

Various systems approaches have been utilized by large, complex government agencies like the Department of Defense and NASA. Goals such as reaching the moon in the space program were set, then objectives, and finally tasks were developed that would have to be completed to reach the goals and objectives. These tasks were then arranged into a program.

Organization development is a discipline that evolved from group dynamics as etablished by psychologist Kurt Lewin. Students and followers of Lewin, including Chris Argyris, Warren Bennis, Carl Rogers, Edgar Schein, and other behavioral scientists, differ from traditional social scientists in that their role as practitioners, or change agents, occurs in organizations outside the academic environment, usually in large corporate structures. These practitioners were interested in creating new knowledge about human organizations and change through action research rather than depending on what applied from conventional knowledge.[3]

While systems theories deal primarily with the relationship of man to technology and organization development with the function of human groups, some similarity of concern does exist. For instance, both concentrate on the ability of people to interact in the postindustrial age, and both have influenced the thinking of city planners.

One tool for systems management is the Program Evaluation and

Review Technique (PERT), the critical path method. Unknown to Rohrbach for several months, a PERT chart had already been prepared for the New Town by the McKinsey Company. Rohrbach had begun to design his own program when he discovered the McKinsey chart by accident. Once he had found it, he was able to begin adapting the McKinsey plan to his own process.

Rohrbach's process had started to evolve when he took the job. He had first collected data, then he had set goals. The data that he had collected was used to complete the crucial tasks that had been completed in the early planning efforts. He worked on these tasks, keeping them in perspective with the goals he had set. The seven goals for the project had been set down on a scratch pad in February. The goals were to (1) obtain facts and hard data; (2) establish priorities and strategies; (3) train existing staff members and weld them into a team with clean-cut channels; (4) supplement and/or replace existing staff with unusual talent by instituting a national search for such talent; (5) view each task as being part of an interrelated system; (6) view all physical development and investment as being conducive to positive social change; and (7) all efforts must be part of an open decision-making process with maximum citizen participation and involvement.

Rohrbach attempted to make these goals part of corporate policy by adhering to them and suggesting decisions related to them in his interactions with Huber and others involved in the New Town. With the data collected and the goals set, Rohrbach went about the other steps of the planning process toward designing a development program. The final program was an adaptation of McKinsey's computer-based project plan. The McKinsey plan had listed eleven consolidated subnetworks: land acquisition, zoning, financial analysis, physical planning, the HUD application, the community authority, community services, marketing and sales, construction oversight, utilities, and annexation.[4] These subnetworks were adapted to the needs that had changed and had then been incorporated into a new program with the thirteen following similar categories of planning and urban design, zoning, construction and development, marketing and sales, financial analysis, public utilities, HUD relations, jurisdictional relations, land management and acquisition, community authority legislation, community authority operation, citizen participation, and public relations. These thirteen subnetworks were combined in a "project plan-

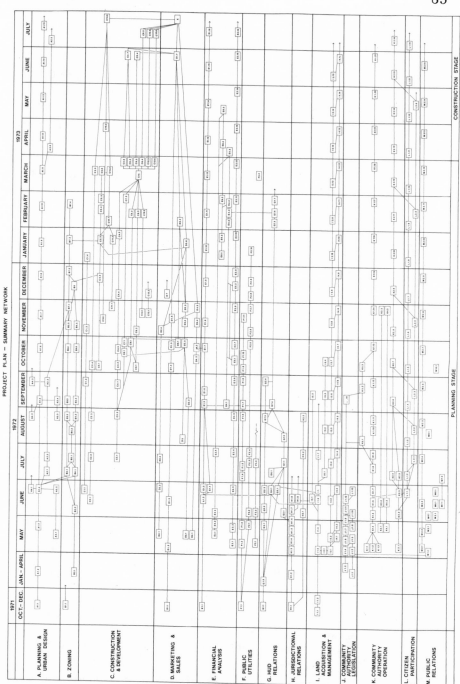

Fig. 2. Project Plan-Summary Network (see Appendix for explanation.)

summary network" that detailed each major task in the critical path method used by McKinsey and other systems management experts (fig. 2).

The project plan formed the basis for the staff and consultant requests that Rohrbach had made of Huber in his memorandum to Richard Turner on 10 April 1972. Attached with the memorandum were a matrix chart illustrating the various needed staff and consultant positions and job descriptions for those positions. The chart showed Donald Huber, corporate president, at the top followed by Gerwin Rohrbach, general manager of the private New Town development corporation, and Edward Rausch, community authority director of operations. Rohrbach and Rausch, directors of the private and public developers, were shown on equal levels supported by a common administrative pool. Below Rohrbach were listed four departments that related to the major subnetworks of planning, marketing, construction, and finance in the summary chart. Each department would be headed by a director who would be supported by a staff. The memorandum listed target dates for filling such positions, those already filled, and the proposed salary of each (fig. 3).[5]

Job descriptions were included for each position. Rohrbach described his own position in the following manner:

> The general manager will be responsible for the planning, organizing and implementing of the development of the new community in a consistent and profitable manner. He shall be responsible for the execution of the basic policies formulated with the ownership group. More specifically, he will develop and recommend for approval project and departmental budgets and goals for the owners. He will supervise department action through his department managers. He will serve on the Community Authority Board of Directors throughout the life of the project and coordinate the planning activities of the Community Authority with the private development group. He will assist in the coordination with local, state and federal government officials, as well as financial negotiations with the owners. He will control procedures both in financial and other areas. He will establish budgets, forecasts, quotas and establish compensation schedules and policies for the staff. He will review and approve the advertising and public relations programs. He will review government reports and develop procedures with builders to determine the level of unsold units and other measurements of space and unsold lots. He will develop potential joint ventures and investigate venture opportunities. He

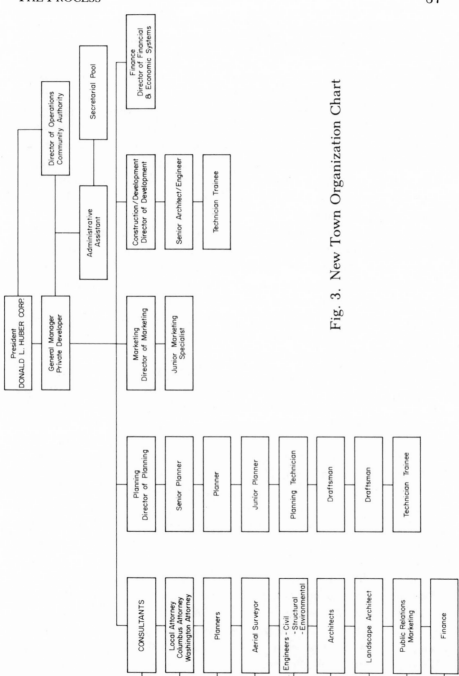

Fig. 3. New Town Organization Chart

will make recommendations with respect to community owners. He will
represent the community activities, where appropriate.[6]

Gerwin Rohrbach saw himself as a vital participant in every activity.
The New Town was more than a job to him, it was the opportunity for
self-fulfillment that few individuals ever realize. It was occurring in
the mature period of his life when he could take full advantage of the
culmination of his years of preparation, and he was investing his
future in the project. He had a verbal agreement with Huber for an
eventual equity share of the private development corporation. So the
owner's group he referred to in his job description applied to more
than Donald Huber. This increase in power frightened Huber, who
was accustomed to wielding power through the use of money. The
manner in which Rohrbach had accumulated power, both within and
outside the organization, was new to Huber. Nevertheless, he tolerated
his general manager because his methods had moved the New Town
closer to reality. Because of this success Huber was forced to commit
more and more of himself until he, too, found himself in a position
where his whole future was invested in the project.

The means for the project's ultimate social, economic, and aesthetic success, as envisioned by Rohrbach, was the effectiveness of
the planning process measured in graphic form by the summary network. He saw himself as an artist and often used the metaphor of a
symphony when referring to the project. The summary network,
which, once complete, covered an entire wall in Rohrbach's office,
was its score. The notes were the little rectangles in the network that
represented crucial tasks. The conductor was Rohrbach. To him, the
New Town, still officially known as Brookwood, in Dayton, Ohio,
represented a major chapter in the history of urban planning. He
believed that if properly executed, the planning process and principles developed for the project could be the blueprint for building
new communities anywhere, at any time in the future.

Each of the subnetworks required a great deal of interaction; yet
the major components can be discussed separately as they occurred
between June and November 1972. This is the clearest way to present the emergence of the process. As each is reviewed, it is important to remember that each was occurring in the same time frame as
the others with multiple interactions.

6 Land Acquisition and Management

The naturalist Aldo Leopold (1949) wrote, "When we see land as a community to which we belong, we may begin to use it with love and respect. There is no other way for the land to survive the impact of mechanized man."

This is the manner in which those environmental, or ecological, planners like Rohrbach and McHarg approach the land. In addition to being trained in the natural sciences themselves, their process was one that recognizes the value of scientists by including their findings in a thorough site analysis. This analysis of the ecosystem provides the core of their process, which is not the case of a process that is imbedded in the design world of aesthetics and push pins. Through a working understanding of the natural sciences, they are able to produce accurate studies of geology, soils, hydrology, physiography, climate, vegetation, and wildlife.

Rohrbach was given a site. It was his responsibility to transform it into a community. But before this could happen the site had to be legally controlled. Originally Huber had felt that a plan for the New Town could be produced, some initial land purchased, part of the community constructed, and then more land purchased. This was the technique that he and his family had always used. But it had become apparent because of the newspaper coverage, which inflated land prices, and because of zoning requirements that a different approach would be necessary. It was decided to use the information program, which would emphasize the benefits of the new community, to persuade residents to sell while at the same time muster their support for zoning. The benefit in this program that was most often emphasized to individuals with a basic rural orientation was the project's potential positive effect on the environment.

Huber actually had started selling the New Town's positive environmental effect in his earliest interactions with government officials, local residents, and the press. Huber had convinced many of his sincerity (on first meeting him it was easy to believe that he was a sincere man). In a lengthy early February article, the *Journal Herald*, the Dayton newspaper that was most diligently covering the story, discussed the new-town concept. The article came at a time when the county planning commission was considering the first attempt for a new zoning amendment, after the first environmental impact statement had been submitted to HUD, and when the new general manager had been on the job barely two weeks. The article was divided into three main parts: the reaction of a local farmer who supported the project, the environmental and land-use impact, and the thoughts of a farmer who opposed Huber.

The farmer who supported the new-town concept was Forest Lightner, a former county commissioner. As a commissioner from 1953 through 1966, Lightner was an advocate of open space, being one of the prime movers behind the establishment of a countywide park district. Huber had contacted Lightner about his seventy-seven-acre farm early in the process. Lightner was easily convinced to grant Huber an option to buy his property, because he was promised that a large portion of the land would remain green. Lightner was so convinced of the project's potential that he spoke in favor of the New Town at several public hearings. "Life is like this—it's tough for us to change, to work through all the bugs and see the light," Lightner said. "I'm selling because they need this place to put together a better package, one which would insure a community with some parks and open areas, not like most developments around here."[1]

The environmental part of the article was based on the first environmental impact statement that had been submitted the previous December. The impact statement had been compiled by Huber's major consultants, the Battelle Institute and Llewelyn-Davies Associates with several local sources that included the Ralph L. Woolpert Company, an engineering and planning firm, and Ralph Scott, an ecologist. The conclusions of the impact statement were that there was no realistic alternative to the site except the New Town, and that the site was doomed to development in any case because of its proximity to the metropolitan area.[2]

The existing physical environment was rated good to excellent in the impact statement. There were a large variety of plant and animal communities. The waterways, Wolf Creek and its tributaries, were generally well off. The air was generally clean, except for some dust pollution from farm operation and odors from farm feedlots. The land was in generally excellent condition.

The social environment also received mostly good-to-excellent grades, although in categories like safety from floods, fires, and traffic, conditions were considered only fair. Social opportunities such as recreation, educational, civil and cultural activities, and the availability of utilities and services were rated poor.[3]

The importance of the existing conditions was considered secondary to what the authors of the report anticipated for the future. Assuming that development was inevitable, a virtual disaster was predicted if a new community were not built. Waterways would be ruined because of channel encroachment, increased runoff would be caused by mindlessly stripping away vegetation, and there would be the eventual pollution from septic tanks. Air pollution would increase drastically because of uncontrolled industrial development and increased automobile traffic. The quality of the land would deteriorate by the indiscriminate stripping of vegetation. Noise pollution would rise because of the added industrial and residential hubbub. Personal well-being would suffer from increasing air, water, land, and noise pollution; greater flooding potentials; increasing traffic hazards; inadequate police and fire protection; and overall degradation of aesthetic factors and poor social opportunities would be worsened by a gathering population.[4]

Not surprisingly, the environmental impact statement predicted a totally different outcome with Huber's new community. A rosy picture of man and nature living in harmony was painted by the report. There were, however, other points of view.

The February newspaper article also sought out someone who was opposed to Huber's proposed development. Everett Arrington was a farmer who wanted to see nothing new around his homestead. Although his land was not inside the New Town's borders, all Arrington would have to do was sit on his front porch to watch its impact. Arrington had seen the impact of suburbanization before, including that for which the Huber family was responsible, and he was convinced Donald Huber would do no better in this case. Partly crippled, the sixty-two-year-old farmer had spent most of his life working for his eighteen-acre tract of land. "I don't care which direction you turn any more, they're building," Arrington told a reporter. "I don't like to see it crowded, because I like to have a little freedom. An' it just won't do to fight a thing like this, because Huber has a big outfit, an' about all you can do is sit back and watch it grow. One of these days there won't be no more open space to play in, nowhere else for the rabbits and birds to go."[5]

There were many farmers like Arrington on the New Town's periphery and within its proposed borders who shared his opinion. And, although they were unorganized, they could refuse to sell their property or oppose zoning in public hearings.

These farmers were joined by another group of skeptics; those who questioned either the environmental impact statement's or the HUD application's methodology and/or Huber's sincerity. This group included the new general manager, Rohrbach; ecologist Ralph Scott; the county planning commission; and several HUD officials. One of the major reasons why Huber hired Rohrbach was because of his background as a land planner. But it was soon apparent to Rohrbach that the environmental information being used was heavily loaded in Huber's favor and that a large portion of the data was incorrect, thus making many of the assumptions incorrect. Scott was known in the area as a renegade anyway. Formerly employed by the Miami Conservancy District, he had left after a dispute to keep his integrity intact. He was hired as a consultant by Huber but disagreed with much that was contained in the original environmental impact statement, especially the use of reservoirs for flood control. The county planning commission expressed its hesitancy by delaying the new community zoning amendment. HUD substantiated the other skeptics' claims by rejecting the first environmental impact statement.

Rohrbach was in such a position that he had to redo the environmental impact statement in a manner that would be acceptable to both HUD and himself, convince zoning officials of his sincerity and bring the necessary land under control, then make good on all the commitments that were made in the process. He had to do this by strengthening the support of allies, like Lightner, and changing the minds of skeptics like Scott.

The essential land acquisition was completed by July. The last key piece of property brought under control was the land owned by Raymond Kitchen. Kitchen was a farmer with opinions similar to those of Everett Arrington. Like Arrington, he had worked all his life for his land, a fifty-acre farm with well-manicured lawns and immaculate white structures surrounded by an even, white, rail fence. He sought to preserve the character of his land. The farm was situated in the middle of the area that was being considered as the prime location for the new community's town center; so the property had to be purchased, or another less desirable site chosen and the application for zoning delayed. It took months of negotiations. The information program of slide presentations and monthly newsletters had some impact. Finally, when the New Town staff was about to give up and select another town center site, an agreement was reached.

Kitchen optioned his property to Huber with several provisions. The most important conditions were a life estate on approximately twenty-two acres where Kitchen, already in his late sixties, could live out his life and an agreement that the option had to be exercised on 1 December 1972 and closed before the end of that year. Huber was also responsible for major repairs to the property. The price was $3,000 per acre, or $150,000 for the fifty-acre tract. It was a good price, but the price had never been a central issue. As Donald Huber stated in a memorandum concerning the agreement, "Mr. Kitchen has a deep and emotional involvement with his property. It has been very difficult for him to make this decision to sell the property, even with the life estate. He is very concerned that we will impose our will on him and that he will not have complete freedom on the land."[6]

With the completion of acquisition, a land ownership statement was able to be submitted to HUD, which had previously commented that the acquisition and control program, as proposed in the application, needed considerable elaboration. This statement was submitted on 31 October 1972. At that time, the Donald L. Huber Development Group owned or controlled by option to purchase 4,429 acres within the project boundary, plus about 48 acres outside the tract, which were owned or controlled for the purpose of land trade, and about 873 additional acres outside the tract, under control but with an indeterminate potential use.

It was anticipated that before the completion of the first development phase in 1978, all of the remaining approximately 200 acres that needed to be owned or controlled, would be. About 914 acres of the holdings were composed of land that was required for the first development phase from 1973 to 1979. All of this acreage was under control at the time of the report.[7]

The land ownership statement also elaborated on the method that would be used to exercise the option on property not owned outright, how utilities would be extended to the area, and it contained a brief rehash of Huber's past land acquisition efforts in Dayton that compared and contrasted them to the New Town.

With the land under control, Rohrbach was faced with fulfilling the promises that had been made to individuals who had sold their property and to HUD. The HUD application stated that, in relation to the environment, "the achievement of a high standard of environmental quality in the new community depends equally on the conservation of attractive natural open areas, and the development of harmonious and aesthetically pleasing man-made surroundings. This entails development which respects rather than destroys local ecological conditions."[8]

Further commitments and promises were made in the environmental impact statement by the developer and on behalf of the community authority. In the impact statement, the private developer promised that

> to achieve a high level of environmental quality throughout, the overall planning will be developed in close collaboration between consultant planners, landscape architects and ecologists to ensure that natural systems are protected as far as possible and that alternatives are evaluated in relation to ecological systems. This will be achieved partly by the example of the private developer and partly by the guidance, regulation and incentives given to participating builders by the Community Authority. Also, a member of the Community Authority staff who is an ecologist will be assigned the responsibility for environmental monitoring, on a full-time basis.[9]

The over four thousand acres under some type of legal control presented a problem. Huber had been using a farm management organization to oversee the property that he owned to reap what profits he could from corn and soybean farming. But if the commitments to HUD and to the local farmers like Lightner and Kitchen were to be kept, a better maintenance program had to be ensured that respected the land in the manner that the rhetoric had projected. Also, in early June, Rohrbach was faced with making several zoning decisions and would soon be selecting urban design, landscape architecture, and architecture consultants. All these decisions would have an impact on the land; so an ecologist was needed as soon as possible. Rohrbach chose Ralph Scott.

Scott's relationship with the Huber Development Group began with the first environmental impact statement, parts of which he strongly disagreed with. When work began on the second environmental impact statement, this time by Rohrbach, Scott was again called in as consultant. He was hesitant. As a naturalist, he had mixed feelings about working for a big developer, especially one with Huber's reputation and especially when his warnings had been disregarded. He found Rohrbach more receptive. A relationship began between them, and Rohrbach began to convince Scott that he could make a difference.

At 10:00 A.M. in the last planning task force meeting on the last Friday in June, Scott, who was a part-time reporter for the *Journal Herald*, found himself in the audience with Rohrbach rambling across the front of the basement room in the Madison Township Farmer's Grange Hall, tossing about carefully constructed colored maps, schematics, charts, and the other paraphernalia that had been produced by the New Town graphics department. Rohrbach was bringing the group up to date on what had been accomplished in the way of legislation that had been passed and deadlines that had been met. Then he started talking about the environment and the promises that the New Town had made to the federal government about the environment. "And believe me," Rohrbach was saying, "it is perhaps one of the more comprehensive commitments made by any developer in this country. A commitment to work with that environment, first of all respecting what you have, and then work with it over the coming decades to not only maintain it, but more likely than not to improve it—in spite of massive urbanization on that tract."

Ralph Scott was there with his friend and fellow *Journal Herald* reporter Pat Fritz, who was busy recording the events. They were hearing Rohrbach say of the New Town's plans for the environment,

"I say improve it, because it ain't all that healthy now.

Oh, it may look rather romantic when you're driving around in an automobile, looking at all the trees and fields. But farming and suburbanization are not necessarily the healthiest things that can happen to an environment with the common practices that occur.

Now you get out of your car and you look up and down the streams and

you will find the last thirty years of detritus of humanity dumped there.
    And most of the houses out there—everytime they flush, flush into the
ground.
    Everytime a field lot gets stuck with cattle, the excrement comes down-
stream.
    Everytime a farmer goes out and sprays his fields with poisons and with
fertilizer it ends up in the streams, the groundwater and the soil.
    So it ain't that good.[10]

Pat Fritz was one of the few who knew that Rohrbach and Scott had
breakfasted together earlier that morning and that Rohrbach had used
the breakfast to culminate a series of meetings between them by offering Scott the position of staff ecologist. Fritz was pondering whether
or not Scott would accept.

Huber had been hesitant about hiring an ecologist, especially one
with Scott's reputation for attracting controversy. But Rohrbach was
convinced that a man like Scott was exactly what was needed and he
convinced Huber of this by pointing out how good it would look to
HUD. Rohrbach continued,

    Now when we come along with development, we've made it worse.
    Because the concentration of poisons increases, man's carelessness in-
    creases, and it becomes a hopeless mess.
        What we're saying is, we are not going to let that happen.
        We are going to pump money back into that environment to, most like-
    ly, improve it.
        Now that means a massive commitment of money and staff. And one of
    our problems is to find the kind of people that one can rely on to do that
    kind of job. And we are in that process right now—and we hope that we
    are in the successful process of talking to the right people.[11]

Scott was convinced. He would take the job. He and Rohrbach discussed the potential of what they hoped could be accomplished.
Rohrbach romanticized about forests. "Every European city has its
own forest and many of the smaller European cities are financed primarily from their forest industry. We have the land to produce
Christmas trees. People, I think, would like to cut their own Christmas
trees in their own town. And Christmas trees are useful in controlling
soil erosion. And if we can farm trees, why not be in the fish business?
Fish farming has a viable economic base and also keeps the lakes

clear."[12] (This idea is similar to Ebenezer Howard's garden cities, where agricultural production was interwoven through the developed areas.)

Scott talked of preservation as a form of management. "There has to be some form of preservation not for preservation's sake but for the fact of preserving the natural environment to have it function as naturally as possible as a monitor so we can understand what may go wrong with man-managed systems."[13]

The two men continued discussing other possibilities: a system that would distribute the New Town's sewage to the open space as fertilizer, a school system that would be integrated into the natural environment, arboretums, and so on. (Again, it is interesting to note that Ebenezer Howard also proposed that the refuse of the town be utilized in the surrounding agricultural areas.)

At the time he joined the New Town staff, Scott was thirty-six years old, he had a degree in biology from Ohio University, he had been the ecologist for the Miami Conservancy District, the chief naturalist for the county park district, and the curator of conservation and wildlife for the Dayton Museum of Natural History. He was, at the time of his appointment, a staff writer on the *Journal Herald*. Scott's new title was ecologist and land-management specialist. His duties were to conduct natural ecological surveys of the land and aquatic environment, to monitor environmental systems as they related to the increasing urbanization of the area, and to develop a land-management program to make the area productive recreationally and economically.

Scott was to collect data concerning the site's natural ecology. He would then set goals for the site that would accommodate its transformation from a rural to an urban landscape. To fulfill these goals he would seek out the available resources within the corporation and the existing governmental structure and investigate the potential resources of the community authority. Based on those resources he would analyze his alternatives to set the priority of his goals, then develop programs for the successful completion of those goals. Afterwards, as areas of the new community were developed, he would measure the effectiveness of his programs by continually monitoring the environment.

With the employment of Scott and the formation of a land-management program, Rohrbach was beginning to develop his own overall plan. He was now in a position to obtain additional facts and hard data about the physical environment. With this information, priorities and strategies could be established. He had supplemented his staff with an individual with wide-ranging talents in science, writing, and illustration who fit into the emerging New Town team. Rohrbach viewed Scott's programs as a vital part of the overall interrelated system and saw them as being conducive to positive social change. He planned that Scott's work would be part of an open decision-making process that would stimulate knowledge and involvement from the citizen's involvement group that had started to function with the planning task force.

Rohrbach was certain that Scott would fit into an open system. He had been the Miami Conservancy District's ecologist for more than three years until he and his assistant were laid off the previous September. L. Bennett Coy, conservancy general manager, had described the layoffs to the local press as a reduction in force caused by financial problems. But they came less than a week after Coy had publicly censured Scott for criticizing the Wildlife Division of the Ohio Department of Natural Resources.[14] The confrontation had culminated in repeated clashes over what Scott felt was too much secrecy in a public institution. In this case, Rohrbach was running a private endeavor in an unexpected open manner. Scott was an individual who could be trusted as a watchdog for the New Town's natural environment. He was an individual who, like Rohrbach, saw the land as a community.

7 Zoning

New York City enacted the first comprehensive zoning ordinance in 1916. A Cincinnati attorney, Alfred Bettman, was instrumental in its adoption and the publication of a model zoning ordinance for use throughout the United States, including Ohio. The purpose of zoning was to promote public "health, safety and morals." But zoning laws have come under the severe attack of many urban critics who claim that zoning is responsible for many of the same social ills it was meant to correct.

Planning historian John Reps said, "Zoning is seriously ill and its physicians—the planners—are mainly to blame. We have unnecessarily prolonged the existence of a land use control device conceived in another era when the true and frightening complexity of urban life was barely appreciated. We have, through heroic efforts and with massive doses of legislative remedies, managed to preserve what was once a lusty infant not only past retirement age but well into senility. What is called for is legal euthanasia, a respectful requiem, and a search for a new legislative substitute sturdy enough to survive in the modern world" (1964, p. 56).

Zoning laws have been used by the attorneys of large oil corporations to proliferate gasoline stations to the point where one can be found on about every corner of every major intersection of every metropolitan area. Zoning has been used by large food franchise operations to line major roadways with giant cowboy hats, neon fried chickens, and plastic double-deck hamburgers. Zoning has been used by home and subdivision builders to turn acres of "undeveloped" farmland into rows of flimsy ranch homes with the life expectancy of a moth, while the central cities decay and rot. As a result, in a nation with an abundance of land there is the ever-increasing possibility of land shortage. This possibility has prompted

99

much discussion about managed growth and various state and federal environmental mandates. One approach offered for managed growth was the New Community Development Act, HUD Title VII.

New community developers, like Donald Huber, though, were still faced with working within existing zoning laws. Realizing this, Huber had begun wooing the responsible officials early in his planning efforts. These efforts were stalled primarily because of the mistrust that appointed planning officials had for Huber and of the fear that elected officials felt for the possible political ramifications that would result in rezoning between four and five thousand acres. Rohrbach was able to neutralize the mistrust of the planners by using their professional jargon in meetings to build trust. By informing local residents about the project, negative political ramifications were avoided. The information program was supplemented by meetings with the officials to answer questions and to solicit suggestions. As a result of these efforts a new community zoning amendment was recommended to the appropriate zoning officials by the county planning commission and then passed into law by the township trustees and the county commissioners.

While the new zoning amendment gave Huber a potentially advantageous regional marketing position, there were many requirements that had to be met before the project could be approved. Then the specific zoning request would have to go through the same process as had the amendments. Included in those requirements were a general plan that showed the whole area to be developed and a specific plan that showed the section to be developed immediately. The general plan could be amended from time to time when specific "phase" plans were submitted. Once a phase plan was approved, only slight modifications could be made when the specific subdivision plat plans were submitted for the review by the responsible administrators.

Other provisions specified that land use could not be changed within 300 feet of another person's land; that at least 40 percent of the land had to be used for residential purposes, between 2 and 15 percent for office and business, 5 percent for industry, and 20 percent for open space; that an average of four dwelling units per acre would be required; that before applying for new community zoning, the developer had to have a minimum 4,000-acre planning area and

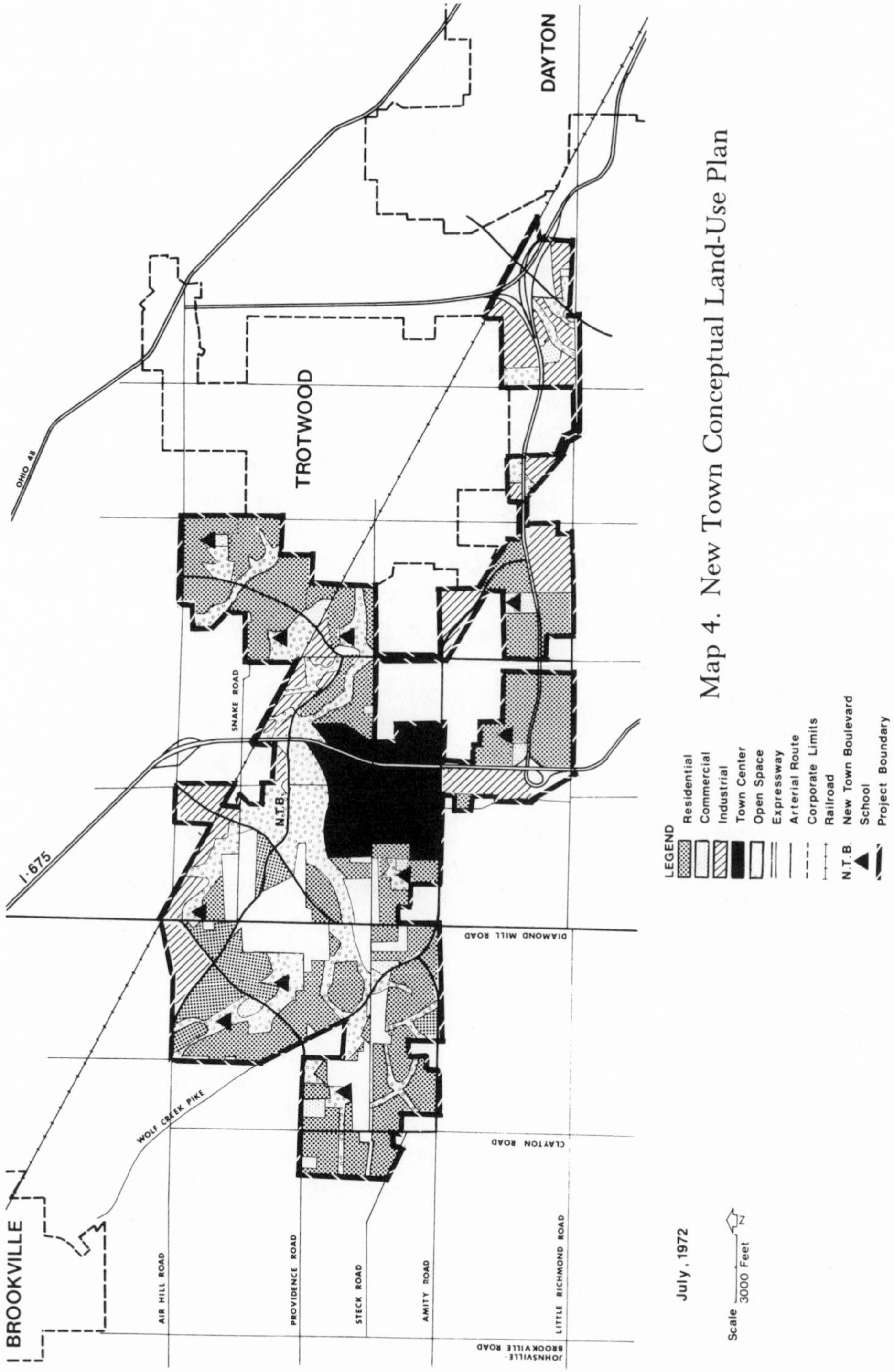
BROOKVILLE
DAYTON
TROTWOOD
OHIO 48
I-675
SNAKE ROAD
N.T.B.
DIAMOND MILL ROAD
CLAYTON ROAD
WOLF CREEK PIKE
AIR HILL ROAD
PROVIDENCE ROAD
STECK ROAD
AMITY ROAD
LITTLE RICHMOND ROAD
JOHNSVILLE-BROOKVILLE ROAD
LEGEND
Residential
Commercial
Industrial
Town Center
Open Space
Expressway
Arterial Route
Corporate Limits
Railroad
N.T.B. New Town Boulevard
School
Project Boundary
July, 1972
Scale 3000 Feet
N

Map 4. New Town Conceptual Land-Use Plan

own at least 2,000 acres; and that all utilities, with the exception of high-tension lines, had to be underground.

With the appropriate zoning law and the land controlled, the New Town was ready to develop a proposal that would meet the legal requirements.

The central element for zoning was the master plan, which would include the general plan and form the basis for the phase plans. The master plan that existed and that had been submitted with the HUD application and the original environmental impact statement had become obsolete once new data was produced by Rohrbach. He had decided to generate a new "concept" plan that would meet both zoning requirements and could be used for the second environmental impact statement. Rohrbach preferred using the word "concept" instead of "master," because he thought that it more aptly described the true nature of such comprehensive physical plans. In the spring he had decided that the best way to design this plan was to use the combined talents of the staff, consultants, elected and appointed officials, and the interested citizens assembled at the planning task force meetings. In this way he was able to again neutralize potential opposition by incorporating skeptics into the decision-making process. It also enabled a plan to be produced that was familiar to zoning and planning officials who had actually taken part in its design.

By late spring such a concept plan was produced and first used for the second environmental impact statement, then it was readied for the zoning request that was pending on the acquisition of the last few parcels of necessary land. The proposed concept plan that evolved from this process called for the construction over a twenty-year period of a comprehensively planned community for approximately forty thousand persons (map 4). The total cost, including all expenditures for community space, roads, utilities, and structures was estimated to be in excess of $500 million. Projected land use was planned to consist of 2,629 acres (53 percent) residential; 1,000 acres (20 percent) open space; 400 acres (8 percent) industrial; 93 acres (2 percent) commercial and office; 230 acres (5 percent) community facilities; 378 acres (7 percent) major roadways, including parking areas, collector, secondary and primary roads; and 240 acres (5 percent) reserved use. Upon completion the project would contain in excess of 11,900 total dwelling units, designed to accommodate all income groups, family sizes, and ages.[1]

In the environmental impact statement, Rohrbach stated that the concept plan was influenced by four broad areas of concern:

1. That the New Town would provide all residents of the community with a wide range of choice in terms of size, style, type, and price of dwellings as well as relationship of each residential unit to other facilities;
2. That the development must achieve an exceptionally high standard of environmental design;
3. That the plan would provide opportunities for residents outside the New Town to make use of the high quality of project services and facilities provided within the new community, thus having the new community considered an integral part of the greater Dayton area and not as an isolated subdivision development; and
4. That the plan be so designed that it would be flexible enough to accept changes in emphasis or direction as development proceeded.[2]

These four concerns acted as the basic goals of the concept plan and the program for zoning. In many ways the concept plan was unrevolutionary and quite similar to other new-town plans like those of Columbia and Reston as well as other federally assisted projects such as Jonathan, Minnesota. It utilized most of the traditional land-planning techniques that had been developed by city planners and landscape architects. The floodplain and slope areas were used for open space, flat areas for commercial and residential, and areas with easy access to rail and highway for industry. Like other new towns it proposed the use of pathways connecting schools and shopping areas to residences.

There were several innovative features of Rohrbach's concept plan that separated it from those that preceded it. First, though, it utilized many traditional techniques, it was referred to as a "concept" plan rather than a "master" plan, implying more flexibility in its execution. As Mumford pointed out, flexibility and the ability to adapt to changes from one generation to the next was one of the secrets of the successful planning of such cities as Rome, Venice, and Amsterdam (1961).

Here it is important to understand how Rohrbach hoped his plan would be implemented. Although the bulk of the concept plan had been developed by himself with Huber, key staff members like Rausch and Scott, and consultants like the Real Estate Research Corporation and The Ralph Woolpert Company, the input provided by the planning task force, which included various officials and private citizens, was considered a vital part of the plan's development. Rohrbach saw the plan as a base to work from that would be fixed as far as natural conditions and human alterations and proposals were concerned but flexible as far as the needs of those who would be the community were concerned. The concept plan represented the ground rules, and how those rules would be performed would be up to those who played the game. The inclusion of local government officials and a variety of citizens in the future decision making was a central part of the process that Rohrbach was developing.

There were other innovations proposed by Rohrbach that were somewhat revolutionary. The master plans of other new towns had relied heavily on the village concept, which was a plan where several villages would make up the whole community. In fact, the original Llewelyn-Davies plan for Brookwood had been based on this concept. It had been derived in the planning profession from the British approach to new towns as first advocated by Ebenezer Howard and reinforced by the middle-class, white American's romantic notion of rural and small-town life. Rohrbach believed that this approach was obsolete in urban, metropolitan America. There was too much plurality and mobility for it to be realistic. If the New Town was truly going to be a new town, it had to reckon with this reality. Instead of villages Rohrbach proposed the use of "neighborhood" or "convenience" service centers with easy access to residential areas as well as access to the greater metropolitan area. Also, the residential areas would be located near convenience centers and local schools but would be open to the larger metropolitan area. Thus, instead of being isolated in a contrived village, the resident would be offered more choice.

Rohrbach also differed from other new-town planners by advocating concentrations with higher densities of structures and residents, like that in the multipurpose town center area. The basis for this approach was his study of other urban areas both in Europe and the United States. He had witnessed many times the effective use of high-density areas concentrated near key transportation routes or other strategic locations in an urban area. Near his own home in St. Louis he watched Clayton, Missouri, become the center of the St. Louis metropolitan area in the 1960s. Clayton included a similar mix of high-rise commercial and residential buildings mixed with specialty shops, single-family homes, and open space that Rohrbach was proposing for the town center. He also thought that by concentrating density, more land could be left open, which, he believed, was one of the main reasons for new towns in the first place.

Another departure from the original Llewelyn-Davies plan and from other new-town plans was the exclusion of a large central lake. On this matter he heeded the criticism raised by ecologist Ralph Scott, who felt that the damming of creeks caused much more damage in the long run than the floods that it was supposed to prevent.

The concept plan relied heavily on the automobile for its transportation network. Where other new towns proposed elaborate mass-transit programs, Rohrbach felt the reality of the automobile as part of the American way of life was a fact for the immediate future and one that had to be accepted and worked with. But he also felt the plan had to be flexible enough to be adapted to mass transit in the future if there were to come a time when it would be a more integral part of the American way of life. So he proposed that the right-of-way for the major expressways running through the New Town be left wide enough to accommodate mass transit. Because the key areas of the concept plan, like the town center, were oriented to the expressway, if mass transit were to become a reality the community could adapt with minimum effort.

Because of these variances, Rohrbach was criticized by several others involved with the New Town, including his employer Donald Huber. Huber had originally approached the New Town in terms of the village concept. This was based on his exposure to other new towns like those he had visited in Europe, Columbia, Reston, and Jonathan. Huber felt comfortable with the concept of villages because it lent itself to his experience as a single-family home developer, which also made him leery of Rohrbach's proposal for high-density areas. Huber had also strongly supported the idea of a large lake, because he felt that a lake would be a marketable amenity. But probably what unnerved Huber most about Rohrbach's concept plan was the method in which he had solicited suggestions from citizens, many of whom were in the low-income category. This was completely foreign to Huber's experience as a developer. Although he grew to accept (at least on the surface) Rohrbach's use of service centers rather than villages, the issue of density and citizen participation became constant sources of first disagreement and then conflict between the two.

So far as the issue of the lake was concerned, Rohrbach found himself criticized from two sides by Huber, who wanted a big lake or

lakes, and Scott, who wanted none. The compromise position was the
construction of several small lakes that accommodated Huber's
marketing ideas while reckoning with the ecological sensitivity of the
area. But like most compromises it left neither side fully satisfied. The
approach to transportation and density was criticized by several
groups, the most vocal being the citizen group that Griscom Morgan
and Harlan Johnson had mobilized. The citizens felt that an all-out
commitment had to be made to mass transit, which was a position
that Rohrbach believed would be detrimental to the New Town's
potential for success. The citizens, especially those directly involved
with Community Services, also were convinced that density was one
of the roots of all evils in urban America.

With this criticism the concept plan began to evolve further. Alternatives were discussed and the fine points refined. Concept Plan One,
used for the environmental impact statement, grew into Concept Plan
Two, which was used for the basis of the zoning proposal that was
submitted to the appropriate jurisdictions in June 1972. The submission of the actual request was delayed several weeks because of the
negotiations with Raymond Kitchen, whose property was located in
the middle of the town center. Once Kitchen agreed to option his
property, which fronted Wolf Creek Pike just east of the proposed
I-675 right-of-way, the land-acquisition efforts ended, and the zoning
request was made to the Montgomery County Planning Commission,
who had to review the proposal before it could be approved by the
county and township officials.

On the evening that Kitchen sold his property, Rohrbach was driving his battered Volkswagen down Wolf Creek Pike that ran by Kitch-
en's solid, white farmhouse. He was on his way back to the New Town
office in Trotwood from a meeting that had been called in a local
church to line up support for zoning, when he spotted the farmer. "He
was just leaning on a fence post watching the sun set," Rohrbach said.
"He looked sad, real sad. Everything he's worked for all his life has
been yanked out from under him. Oh, he's going to live out his life
there, but it just won't be the same. The land won't belong to him.
We've got a commitment to these people who've lived their whole life
with the land. We can't just come out here and rape it."

On 17 July, the formal request for zoning, which included the concept plan and a detailed development plan for the first phase, was
made by Huber to a joint meeting of the Montgomery County Rural

Zoning Commission and the Madison Township Zoning Board. The boards set their public hearings for August, anticipating a positive recommendation from the Montgomery County Planning Commission. The documents that were submitted asked for the rezoning of 1,325 acres in Perry Township and of 3,023 acres in Madison Township, almost all of which were at the time agriculturally zoned and all owned or controlled by Huber, to new community zoning under the recently passed amendment.[3]

Rohrbach decided to use the same strategy that had been used to get the zoning amendment approved. Potential opposition would be neutralized by flooding the area with information about the project. The New Town staff contacted every resident on the perimeter of the project and arranged meetings in neighborhood houses. At each meeting, Rohrbach, Rausch, Deddens, and Scott presented all the data concerning the project that had been collected to that time: technical reports, maps, charts, newsclippings, letters of support, and slides. They then tried to answer honestly all the questions that were raised. Many of the individuals were old Dunker Germans with whom Rohrbach spoke in fluent German about the New Town. The meetings in the homes were supplemented by information in the newsletter that was mailed to every resident in the two townships as a matter of course and by larger gatherings with interested parties in the local schools and churches.

There had been a fear in most developers and home builders, including Donald Huber, of publicizing their plans near the time when zoning was being considered. Rohrbach believed that with a project the size of the New Town, citizens would turn out in mass at any public hearing just out of curiosity, and that if there was a large gathering at a zoning hearing the potential for people to be negative was greater if they knew little or nothing about the project. He felt that by employing community organizing and planning techniques, he could answer questions before a public hearing and decrease the possibility of large numbers showing up by supplying those attending the hearing with information and bolstering alliances with persons like Forest Lightner, who could be used to speak in favor of the project at hearings.

On 10 August the Montgomery County Planning Commission approved the rezoning. On 16 August the Madison Township Zoning Board voted four to one, with one abstention, to recommend the adoption of the zoning plan for the 3,023 acres in the township. About fifty persons, mostly New Town staff, friends, and reporters, attended the public hearing; no one spoke against the plan. For more than two hours Rohrbach and his staff answered questions on concerns such as road rights-of-way, future zoning changes, public services, possible annexation, sequence of development, the economic base for taxation, rent supplements, citizen participation in planning, and other items.

On August 21 the Montgomery County Rural Zoning Commission held its public hearing in the county courthouse. Across the hearing room every available easel had been stacked with maps and charts concerning the New Town. The courtroom was packed, but mostly with citizens who were interested in the other case on the docket that was to be presented first. It involved a developer who wanted to rezone about twenty acres for a planned unit development in the southern portion of the county. The developer's staff in bright, double-knit suits ineptly tried to explain their proposal to the angry crowd that had come out to oppose the project. The citizens were upset about possible damage to a local nature preserve and were concerned about flash flooding caused by the additional runoff that the development would produce. The developers tried to explain the benefits of the proposed project but the request was soundly defeated.

Following the first case, the courtroom virtually emptied and moments later, after a few questions were answered by Rohrbach and Scott, the request for rezoning of the 1,300 acres in Perry Township was approved unanimously.

In September the county commissioners passed the New Town plan, and on 14 October the township trustees gave final approval to it. Thus, almost forty-five hundred acres were rezoned with practically no opposition. The only zoning left to be approved would be related to the four remaining specific phase plans, which would require public hearings, and the detailed subdivision plat plans for each phase, which would require administrative actions.

The approval of zoning had been obtained by Rohrbach through the utilization of the techniques and methods of the planning process and community organization, in relation to the overall project goals. He had collected the necessary data to comply with the new community zoning amendment. Then he proceeded to get zoning passed with a minimum of opposition in both local governments using the four broad concerns expressed in the environmental impact statement as goals for the zoning plan. The concept plan was developed into the zoning program, which was able to be presented in a manner that illustrated its relationship to everything else connected with the New Town and to the greater metropolitan area. The zoning program was presented to the community and to the officials as one that would help positive social and environmental change in the area. Once approved its effect could be measured and what was learned could be applied to other development phases and other new communities in the area, the state, and the nation.

8 The Community Authority

Donald Huber and Gerwin Rohrbach saw the purpose of the community authority differently. Huber felt that the success of the New Town depended largely on its ability to market itself. He conceived the community authority to provide an entity that could alleviate some of the pressures on new-community developers that resulted from residents' complaints arising from an extended development period. At the same time, by being responsible for public improvements and human services, it could offer an attractive amenity package to potential residents and make the project application more attractive to the federal government.

Rohrbach felt that the success of the New Town depended largely on the ability of its residents to control their own destiny. He saw the community authority as a mechanism that would provide the ordinary citizen with the power to dictate his own future by offering him a democratic entity that could act as an intermediary between business and government. In a larger sense, he believed that if the community authority could work in the New Town, the principle could be applied to other situations. For instance, one stumbling block to regional government is the potential loss of power by local community leaders. The community authority concept applied to this non-new community situation could offer a means where vital services could be centralized in a metropolitan area, while individual communities could maintain their character with certain powers.

This difference in opinion affected the way each man felt that the community authority should be operated, which was also influenced by the way each viewed citizen participation. The New Community Interim Non-Profit Corporation had been organized for the HUD application. Its trustees were the interim policy makers, and director of operations Edward Rausch was its administrator. Huber saw the Interim Board of Trustees as a blue-ribbon committee comprised of substantial members of the community. This is the way that the board was organized, and it was the way it would have functioned if two things had not happened.

There was the opposition that arose to the project from the Northwest Advisory Council and the hiring of Gerwin Rohrbach as general manager. Headed by Harlan Johnson and its chairperson, Edward Duffy, the council had directed a resolution to HUD secretary Romney during the preapplication stage opposing the project until certain conditions were met. The resolution began, "Whereas, in the new town of Brookwood, in Montgomery County, citizens have been excluded from any planning . . ." and continued by quoting an unidentified Huber representative as saying, "Nobody will be able to override Huber until the community is completed." The resolution concluded with two demands, one for more low-income housing and the other for "official representation with real power, not just token representation, on Phase One planning by low income people, black people, present residents of the projected new town area, the Northwest Montgomery County Advisory Council, youth and other people traditionally excluded from the decision-making process."[1]

This resolution presented a major problem to the project's application and review process. The issue was resolved by Rohrbach in his negotiations on Huber's behalf with the advisory council. These negotiations resulted in the ad hoc Citizens New Town Committee, which lobbied for the Community Authority Bill in Columbus and participated with other citizens drawn in by Rohrbach and Morgan in the planning task force that helped compile the concept plan for zoning. One of the conditions of the negotiations that related to one of the demands in the resolution was the assignment of a public representative to the Interim Board of Trustees. The condition was reluctantly agreed on by Huber.

Huber retained the power to determine the manner in which this representative would be selected. Several names were to be submitted by the ad hoc committee, from which Huber would then choose one to recommend to the county commissioners. In April three names were submitted to Huber, who chose Brookville farmer Ralph Dull, the least vocal and controversial of the group, to be recommended to the Montgomery County Commission. In May 1972 Dull was appointed as the seventh member of the Interim Board of Trustees, which met monthly.

He joined the three public representatives (Dillman, Leiber, and Swank) and the three development representatives (Huber, Rohrbach, and Leigh).

As stated in its articles of incorporation, it was the original purpose of the New Community Interim Non-Profit corporation to facilitate the orderly transfer of public responsibility of planning and development to the community authority or to act as an alternative if the enabling legislation had not been approved.[2] Because the legislation had been enacted, it became the corporation's chief purpose to act for the community authority until it could be organized under the new state law, making certain that the criteria for eligibility were followed. Those included a petition to the county commission; approval by the cities of Dayton, which was the largest city in the county, and Trotwood, which was contiguous to the New Town; and the formation of "a Community Authority district" that had to encompass at least one thousand acres and had to be zoned for comprehensive development. To handle the legal matters connected with the petition to the county and the transfer of power, the board, on Huber's suggestion, hired the bill's sponsor, State Representative Frederick Young.

Before the petition could be submitted, four main problems had to be resolved. First, there was Edward Rausch's potential conflict of interest. He had resigned his position as mayor of Trotwood but remained on the city council. This could endanger the community authority's position with Dayton. Then there was the matter of who had employed Rausch and where his loyalties were. Second, there was a problem with the very close working relationship between the public and private developers, as exemplified by the hirings of Rausch and Young. This was compounded by the fact that all of the trustees had been suggested at some point to the county commissioners by Huber. The third major problem was how to incorporate the citizen participation program into the workings of the interim Non-Profit Corporation during the transition period. The last problem facing the establishment of the community authority was how to fulfill annexation commitments while in the petitioning process to avoid vetoes from either city.

Because the resources of the private developer were being used until the community authority became an entity, the New Town staff was used to supplement the board and Rausch's efforts. Rohrbach, the private developer's general manager, was responsible for the allocation of those resources. Working within his process, the goals for this program had been set by the state law. The community authority would have to be established within that framework and with the purposes that the law intended. Those purposes were to establish a means for citizen participation in planning and development, provide a way for human services and community facilities to be financed, and enable the new community to make maximum use of Title VII financing and pass the savings from such financing on to residents.[3] With these goals set, the necessary data and resources were assembled for the petition, while the problems were simultaneously addressed.

As the individual programs in the planning process progressed, Rohrbach began to distinguish each activity as to what involved the interests of the community authority and what involved the Huber Development Group. The authority was crucial to the development of Ralph Scott's land-management and monitoring program. It played a key part of the concept and zoning plan, because it would be responsible for at least 20 percent of the total land area as part of the open-space system. The community authority was a vital part of the relationship with HUD concerning the request for assistance. Because of the veto power possessed by Dayton and Trotwood, jurisdictional relations had a direct impact on the community authority petition to the county. Because one of Rohrbach's goals for the project was for all efforts to be a part of an open decision-making process with maximum citizen involvement, the remaining programs, planning and urban design, citizen participation, financial analysis, marketing and sales, and construction and development, were all linked to the community authority.

Edward Rausch was a reasonable man who looked considerably younger than his fifty years. Aware of the complexity of his situation, he submitted his resignations to the Trotwood council (effective in September 1972) and to the Interim Board. He was then rehired by the Donald Huber Development Group as the director of operations for the New Town.

During the transition stage before the petition was submitted and for a while after its approval, Rausch was also to act as a liaison between the private and public developers to lend additional support in that orderly transfer. By July the potential issue of Rausch's conflict of interest was cleared up, but the board was left without an administrative officer; so the interim trustees began to search for a new director.

Meanwhile Huber grew uneasy about the autonomy that Rohrbach was advocating for the community authority and about the fact that he had lost some control over the public developer with the resignation of Rausch. A series of pointed memoranda and emotional meetings resulted between Huber and Rohrbach, during which the general manager threatened his own resignation. By August Huber made a tentative agreement for a separate operating budget for the Interim Corporation that would be administered by the new director. Rohrbach believed that if the community authority was to truly represent the public's interests, it had to be a separate and equal entity during the entire planning and development process. Huber felt reluctant about his loss of power and accused Rohrbach of trying to take over control of the New Town. These feelings were reinforced by the opinion of Warren Hyser, Huber's executive assistant.

At the time Huber agreed to provide separate operating budgets, Rohrbach recommended that Carlton Laird, whom he had worked with as a consultant when Laird was city manager of Lombard, Illinois, be considered either as the director of the construction department or the interim community authority manager. Huber did not respond negatively to this suggestion, although he said to Rohrbach that he wondered whether Laird had enough "builder experience" to be the New Town's director of construction. Because most of the New Town construction would be in the area of heavy public works such as roads, utilities, and grading while individual builders would be building subdivisions, Rohrbach felt that Laird did have extensive experience in successfully planning and constructing major public works in a number of communities, but he did not press the issue with Huber.

Carlton Laird was the editor of *American City* magazine, a municipal publication of management, planning, and engineering that is circulated to most municipal officials, department heads, and consulting engineers and planners. He had been the city manager of three other municipalities beside Lombard: Whitehall, Michigan; Wood River, Illinois; and Ossining, New York. In each of those four cities, Laird developed effective municipal management systems, planning programs, and financing to promote new development and improve the quality of public services. Before entering public administration he had been employed in private industry as an engineer. He had a combined degree in civil engineering and law from the University of Wisconsin.

To aid the trustees, Huber and Rohrbach agreed to use the services of the same executive search firm that had recommended Rohrbach and the eventual director of planning and urban design, Edward Kreines. It was agreed that Laird's name would be submitted for consideration by the impartial search firm. On 16 August Peter Lauer of that firm completed an independent report that was issued to the trustees. The report recommended several candidates, and Laird was among them.

The trustees decided to interview two candidates, John Stainton and Laird. Stainton had been brought into consideration in early August after Lauer had almost completed his report by Reuben Clark of Huber's Washington law firm. Stainton immediately became Huber's choice for the position. Before Stainton had been brought into consideration, Huber had insisted that a thorough check on the background of each candidate should be instituted. Lauer checked on Laird and the others being considered but had not checked on Stainton, because no information about him had been available until early August. Through numerous phone calls Kreines and Rohrbach were able to substantiate that Stainton did have a good reputation and was well respected. This information was presented to the trustees.

The trustees, after interviewing the two candidates and studying the reports on them and the others that had been submitted by Lauer, unanimously chose Laird at their 16 August meeting in an open discussion with citizen representatives present. Rohrbach thought the decision was a healthy one because it had been made independently. But Huber became embittered because his choice was not hired. He grew more convinced that Rohrbach was out to take over the project.

The approval of Laird provided the public with a watchdog function similar to that of Ralph Scott in his relationship with the natural environment. Because, in spite of Huber's belief that Laird was Rohrbach's man, his only allegiance was to the public.

The personality problem between Huber and Rohrbach grew more serious. But there were more immediate problems facing the trustees in their transformation from a nonprofit corporation to a public developer of a more than four-thousand acre New Town that would house around forty thousand individuals. Before the petition could be submitted, the annexation issue had to be resolved, and questions concerning its independence and how effective citizen participation could be incorporated had to be answered.

9 HUD Relations

On Friday, 26 May 1972, Spencel Lengyel of HUD's Office of New Communities attended a planning task force meeting at the Madison Grange Hall. At the end of the meeting he offered several comments concerning HUD's position on the New Town.

He told Rohrbach that he sensed that the developer's motives in creating a better living environment were sincere. He noted that the developer's contract with HUD was an important one that would last well beyond the development period of twenty years, but that the informal relationship between the developer and the community was an even more important one. He went on to say that he was satisfied with the degree of cooperation that had come to pass between the developer and the community to that point. He noted that the concept plan was to be used as a guide in establishing parameters, and that the plan and the outcome of the project in twenty years were not likely to be identical. Lengyel let Rohrbach know that the Office of New Communities Development was favorably impressed by Huber's organization and that the office was willing to consider the developer's application, although their final decision would not be the end of the process but the beginning of the overall operation, because once the office has made a decision to move forward, that signals the beginning of negotiations, which is where the real work begins. Rohrbach was pleased. The planning task force was just the type of involvement that HUD had advocated under Secretary Romney's leadership. While Rohrbach was busy with the planning task force, Donald Huber was busy strengthening his political alliances. Because he had contributed financially to Governor John J. Gilligan's successful campaign in 1970, he had little difficulty in securing an appointment to the governor's advisory commission on housing and community development. In August the governor named Huber a trustee of Bowling Green

University, though Huber admitted to having little knowledge about educational affairs. These two appointments gave Huber a lot of power on the state level in the areas of housing, community development, and higher education.[1]

While Huber fostered his Democratic contacts, who were in power on the state level, he began cultivating relationships with Republicans in power in Washington. One of the first employees whom Huber had hired in his early planning efforts was graduate student Ron Morrison, who had worked on Ohio Senator Robert Taft's 1970 campaign. The relationship between Huber and the Republicans grew productive. As a favor to Huber, Senator Taft requested that the HUD assistant secretary Jackson meet with Huber in his office to review the Brookwood project. On 1 June Jackson arrived with Ted Lamont, director of the Office of New Communities, to meet with Taft, Huber, and Charles Ross, the Ohio state chairman of the Nixon reelection campaign.

Senator Taft began the meeting by stating, "This project and one or two others are the most important to the State of Ohio." During the meeting, Charles Ross also indicated the importance of the project to Ohio, and to his position as state chairman of the Nixon reelection campaign.[2] Huber explained several issues connected with the project. There was the problem of options expiring, which already involved an investment of approximately $3 million; the Dayton-Trotwood agreement; the dual developer approach; the participation by the future residents in the planning process; and the Community Authority Bill, as it passed the Ohio General Assembly. At the end of Huber's presentation Jackson stated, "We believe in the concept, and will bend things to make it work." He also stated that he was looking forward to visiting the site himself later in the month.[3]

On 9 June Governor Gilligan wrote a letter in support of the project to HUD Secretary George Romney.

> This is the first proposed New Town to submit an application in Ohio. I have been following the progress of the development and strongly support the project. I would hope your review can be expedited since land options are expiring in the very near future.
>
> The involvement of local citizens as trustees for the future residents to plan, implement, and manage those facilities that most vitally affect their lives promises significantly to improve the quality of this New Town. The involvement of all income levels from the beginning of the project assures broader participation and eliminates many transition problems. I am very

interested in the dual developer guarantee approach which offers great hope in significantly widening the availability of housing of low and moderate income families.

Gilligan then mentioned the passage of the Community Authority Bill in the Ohio General Assembly and the agreement between the cities of Trotwood and Dayton to jointly annex the New Town and cooperate in the development of this project. He called the agreement a "milestone of cooperation." The governor concluded by stating that he was "hopeful that the Department of Housing and Urban Development will see fit to select Ohio as a site of this New Town in the very near future."[4]

On 12 June Secretary Jackson visited the site and announced to the local press that the New Town was a "go" project as far as HUD was concerned. This period marked a high point in the relationship between Huber and Rohrbach. Huber was wary of Rohrbach's involving so many citizens in an open decision-making process, but he did not hesitate to point out these efforts as proof of his commitment to the public in his communications with state and federal officials. Even though Rohrbach felt that Huber's relationships with politicians were a bit shady, he liked the optimism that had been generated and hastened to point to the support of the governor and the senator in the planning task force meetings or to the press. The good relationship between Huber and Rohrbach was bolstered by the news from informed sources, like Reuben Clark, that the Dayton project had been catapulted to the first in line of the new communities that were being considered by HUD.

Because the success of the New Town was based on HUD approval, the relationship with HUD was central to all other programs. So the approval of the HUD application was the primary goal of Rohrbach's "project plan-summary network" and all other activities were keyed to it. To achieve this goal there were several activities that required attention. Though the second environmental impact statement had been submitted, it had to be approved by HUD, then released for a ninety-day public review period before the project would be approved. The state A-95 review had to be completed, and a land-ownership statement submitted.

After the draft of the second environmental impact statement was submitted in April, it was reviewed by HUD and the planning task force and then resubmitted in June. The Gilligan letter was one attempt to prompt HUD to release the environmental impact statement as soon as possible, because a three-month delay would follow whenever it was released and Huber wanted approval as soon as possible. The state A-95 was completed on 27 July after Rohrbach had responded to questions raised by the state in his May letter to Andris Priede, the state deputy director of development planning, and after other questions concerning the community authority legislation and the environmental impact statement were answered in separate actions.

Also in July the good relationship between Huber and Rohrbach began to deteriorate steadily. Employee dissatisfaction and rivalry (which affected Huber's own family) and different viewpoints concerning citizen participation, the concept plan, and the community authority operation strained the relationship between the two individuals. This was further complicated by HUD's delay, after its expressed optimism, in releasing the environmental impact statement.

The delay resulted partly because HUD was very much concerned about the scandals that arose in the 235 and 236 housing programs where large windfall profits had accrued to developers from collusive appraisals. Therefore, land appraisals on the New Town could conceivably be made that would not reflect potential windfall profits to the developer. This was a major concern of Jay Kane on the HUD staff. When he saw the first appraisal report submitted as part of the HUD application in February he pointed out that this section was "deficient in that it does not conform." This was as much as saying that the appraisals reflected, in his opinion, windfall profits accruing to the developer. A further comment was made that the question of security that was related to appraisal value "may prove to be one of the most serious deficiencies in the Application."[5] Huber was in an especially sensitive position because he had been involved in the 235 program in his Madden Hills development.

In April, when the land control and ownership pattern became relatively fixed, Rohrbach recommended to Huber that they get a competent firm to make a new appraisal following HUD guidelines rather than the dictates of the developer. In return, Rohrbach was informed several times not to deal with or respond to Jay Kane, but to let Reuben Clark handle Kane with the appraiser whom Huber had engaged in December 1971.

Rohrbach had been concerned about the economic planning since his arrival. He had managed to get most of the New Town staff centralized in the Trotwood office to work on the HUD application, community authority legislation, zoning, governmental jurisdictions, and public participation. However, certain key staff members were not transferred to the Trotwood office. They were responsible for the economic model and other economic systems. Their function was kept under Donald Huber's watchful eye in the Kettering accounting office on Far Hills Avenue.

In April, when Rohrbach submitted his detailed staffing memorandum, which related to the process developed in the project plan, he recommended to Huber certain staffing priorities and specifically stated that the existing staff was not competent to handle the economic systems functions. He suggested that an outstanding director of finance be selected immediately.[6] The corporate vice president of finance, Richard Turner, who was a friend of Warren Hyser, repeatedly emphasized that the economic systems function had to be retained in the Kettering office. This increasingly distressed Rohrbach, who felt that there was little or no relationship existing between what was being done on the economic model in Kettering and what planning was being done in Trotwood during the summer months.

HUD's staff concerns were supported by Secretary Romney on 10 July in his response to Governor Gilligan. Romney's letter stated, "Although the application was submitted on February 29, problems in both government approval and environmental areas were such as to prevent processing of the numerous exhibits comprising the submission." Romney acknowledged that the community authority legislation, the agreement between Trotwood and Dayton, the new environmental impact statement, and Assistant Secretary Jackson's visit had all stimulated the New Town's progress. But he concluded that "within the limits of the Office of New Communities Development staff constraints and the summer vacation schedule we anticipate being able to release the Environmental Impact Statement in the near future. In accordance to the Council on Environmental Quality Guidelines, the Community Development Corporation Board will be unable to consider the project until the required review time has run its course. Consequently, it is not anticipated that the Board will consider the Brookwood new town proposal until the November or December meeting at the earliest."[7]

The delay angered Huber, who had counted on his political connections to get the project considered at the September meeting. He was worried about the dates on which options would start to expire on the property. In spite of the fact that Rohrbach was directly responsible for almost everything that had spurred the application on up to that point, Huber began to blame him for further delays.

The issue of appraisals also threatened to delay the HUD review past the November or December date that Romney had indicated in his letter, because Jay Kane was still insisting that an acceptable appraisal report be submitted following HUD guidelines. Because the appraisal value of the land was an essential factor in the economic model, which would have to be approved by Kane and others in the review during the ninety-day period following the release of the impact statement, Rohrbach finally had to make a strong recommendation on 4 October that the Real Estate Research Corporation be engaged quickly to produce an appraisal report that would be acceptable to HUD guidelines.

Meanwhile, Huber had used Senator Taft's office to arrange another meeting between Huber and Assistant Secretary Jackson. At this meeting, with Charles Ross again present, Huber discovered through Spencel Lengyel that there was another problem, a power struggle between blacks and whites within HUD, that was delaying the release of the environmental impact statement. This staff problem had been compounded by Secretary Romney's resignation, the Nixon reelection campaign, and the moving of the Office of New Communities' staff offices.

Jackson was perturbed by Huber's use of Senator Taft's office. Jackson felt that he should not be involved in politics, especially because it was widely being speculated that he, one of the most powerful blacks in the Nixon administration, might be named HUD secretary. Nevertheless, Jackson did assure Huber that the environmental impact statement would be released on 15 September, and that the board would consider the application at its December meeting and then release its statement at the end of the ninety-day period, which would be 15 December.

At the meeting with Jackson, Huber explained the problems of meeting a 1 March deadline for exercising options on the project. Jackson indicated that the New Town could concurrently, with the offer of commitment from HUD, start work on the project agreement and trust indentures. In other words, project financial agreements relating to bond sales could be well under negotiation in December, assuring Huber the cash necessary to exercise his options.[8]

Jackson's decision to give assurances to Huber was influenced by the White House. 1972 was an election year. Nixon was seeking reelection. Huber was known to be a generous political contributor. Huber's representatives had contacted the White House and, in turn, the word had come down from the assistant to the president for domestic affairs, John D. Ehrlichman, for the matter to be expedited.

On 6 October, a month before the election, after several more internal delays within HUD and after the Real Estate Research Corporation had begun its work on a new appraisal, HUD released the Brookwood Environmental Impact Statement.

10 Public Relations

Everything that happened in the New Town office was, to some extent, public relations. The operation was geared to the selling of the idea that a better human living environment could be planned that respected the site's ecology while soliciting public participation with a private corporation and while cooperating with local, state, and federal officials.

Much of the salesmanship was done by Gerwin Rohrbach, who by midsummer had emerged as the central figure in the New Town's development. There were many reasons why Rohrbach had eclipsed Huber as the main personality, and this caused serious repercussions in the relationship between the two men. It was during the annexation negotiations that Rohrbach had first sought to establish an alternate personality to represent the New Town because of Huber's lack of credibility with many of the local officials. The general manager's intent was to establish himself as the working representative of the New Town to those in the area, while Huber, as president of the corporation, would represent the project in an official capacity of formal gatherings and on the national level.

Rohrbach was more interesting and more colorful to the local press than Huber. Rohrbach's control of dialect, body motion, and profanity interested and amused reporters, citizens, and the local officials. Huber was a developer, and this made him suspect. Some of his actions in Madden Hills and in his dealings with several government officials had some convinced that there were substantial grounds for suspicion. Rohrbach was not a developer. People trusted him. They believed in the competency that his organization exhibited.

Rohrbach felt that the best public-relations program was no official public-relations program. Public relations was best done by staff members in a manner where data were continually collected about every facet of the project and then made available in an informative way to whomever was interested.

This type of program began to evolve in the information effort, which had to be used for land acquisition and zoning. The information program utilized the monthly newsletter, neighborhood presentations, and displays in the Trotwood office. Rohrbach, who was skeptical of "PR types," was dissatisfied with the performance of Huber's advertising agency, Kircher, Helton, and Collett, which had been responsible for these tasks. His dissatisfaction was expressed in an April memorandum to Huber that pointed out several recommendations concerning the advertising agency and the public relations program in general.[1] Subsequently, the Donald Huber Development Group undertook a search for a national graphic design firm to develop an identity program and name for the project. This search reflected Rohrbach's misgivings about the ability of advertising agencies to cope with a project like the New Town. They were reinforced by the opinions of some members of the staff, several of whom were young designers, who wanted to do away with an ad agency approach altogether. Once, when an advertising executive remarked during a presentation that "the New Town could be sold like hamburgers," several of the designers burst into laughter.

Possibly the best public relations that the New Town received was in the local press. One particular, thorough series of articles ran in the *Journal Herald* during the late summer of 1972. In the series, reporter Denise Goodman investigated other new towns and discussed their racial composition ("mostly salt, with a sprinkling of pepper"), housing costs ("too expensive for Archie Bunker"), and the issue of control ("trying to fulfill the American dream with slightly un-American governments"). Goodman summed up some of the major accomplishments and reviewed the major problems of new towns, contrasting the promises that had been made with the realities. For example, in the cases of the other new towns' attempts to integrate low- and moderate-income families into an upper-middle-class community, Goodman believed that Columbia and Reston were winning the battle concerning physical integration but were losing the war so far as social and psychological integration were concerned.[2]

At the time that the article was written, Columbia, when compared to most affluent suburbs, including those around Dayton, was accepting a healthy share of federally subsidized housing. About six percent of the town's then 7,000 occupied housing units were subsidized, which was twice the rate of Dayton's suburbs that were *most* active in that effort. Also, the Rouse Company had pledged that ten percent of Columbia's housing would be subsidized when the town was complete, which was twice the rate recommended for most Dayton area suburbs by the Miami Valley Regional Planning Council (this was a rate that was considered liberal by both those within the metropolitan area and those in other areas).

Reston had, in 1972, 200 subsidized units for low-income families and 138 for the elderly. Gulf planned 650 more such units. But while those families can live in such innovative cities, Goodman felt that they paid the price of their dignity, because this subsidized housing was easily identified as "where the poor people live."[3]

Goodman asked Melvin Tumin, a professor of sociology and anthropology at Princeton University who specialized in examining the sources of mid-twentieth-century conflicts between young and old, black and white, and rich and poor, if the new-town concept could work. Tumin echoed many of the same conclusions as Gans did concerning plurality in communities. Tumin stated that the more people have in common, the less likely they are to have conflict. Likewise, he observed, the more differences in a human mix, the more likelihood there is for situations where people do not get along. New-town attempts to mix people of different racial, economic, and social backgrounds may seem morally good, he concluded, but they are contrary to sociological history that says it will not work. "I do not think new towns are the way towards a mass solution of black poverty or white poverty or of class hostility," Tumin said.

On the other hand, people talk of building 50 such new towns of 100,000 people each. If Reston and Columbia and some other places can show up with some viable patterns, they may set a model for those "new towns." If they come up with a record of success, it will be a way to sell these other places. It may mean there will be much more federal support the next time out.

I see new towns being related to central city problems the same way I see half-way houses being related to prisons. I know the evaluation of half-way houses. There isn't one that is working . . . and yet, because it's an attractive idea, because it sounds right, the big thing now from the law enforcement agencies, the federal government is investing massive sums of money in half-way houses.

I think new towns are like that. They divert attention to apparently attractive ideas that don't have any fundamental relation to the central ger-
minating problem of jobs and education.

For symptomatic, remedial relief for small numbers of people, they may
work. But they're hardly the way you go after the major institutions any
more than bright shiny new housing in the slums has ever really made a
difference in slum behavior.[4]

Even though most of what Tumin said and much of what she found
out about other new towns was pessimistic, Goodman was still attracted to the idea. As Tumin said, it sounded right. She still held out
hope for Huber's New Town because she believed it would benefit
from the mistakes that had been made in the past. She believed this
because she had been convinced by Rohrbach, who believed it. She in
turn tried to convince others through a mechanism that was much
more effective than anything any advertising agency could conjure
up. In the final article of her series she explored why she felt the
Dayton New Town would be different.

The biggest difference, Rohrbach had convinced her, was the community authority, which would involve citizens during all phases of
the planning and development process. By doing this, it would affect
the problems that other new towns had encountered in government,
housing, and racial tensions. "Every other new town in the United
States is a company town," Rohrbach said. "If you want a bucket of
paint in Columbia, you have to go, hat in hand, to Rouse." The difference in the Dayton New Town, according to Rohrbach, would be that
the community authority would be controlled by citizens. Rohrbach
felt that problems of stereotyped, subsidized housing could be solved
by learning from the mistakes of Columbia and Reston. He believed
that the federal government could help by instituting a housing allow-
ance program, so that low- and moderate-income families could get
direct grants to buy or rent on the open market. He felt that racial tensions could not be avoided but could be eased by involving early
citizen participation in planning and subsequent participation
through the community authority. This process would provide a
framework in which understanding could begin to take place. "You're
not going to find a racial solution by social manipulation or by social
theory," Rohrbach said, quoting from Gunnar Myrdal's classic study,
An American Dilemma (1944), "but by constant contact, by constant
listening to others talk and finding out that things aren't that much

different between people of different races."

"We're learning from others. And others are going to learn from our mistakes," he said, summing up the evolution of new towns to Goodman.[5]

Goodman believed that history seemed to bear this out. From her examination of Columbia and Reston, she found that Columbia had learned from the previous financial and social mistakes of other new communities, and she believed that Rohrbach and his company had learned from theirs. "We're applying the process from the beginning that other new towns learned late," Rohrbach stated. "We can't go to a textbook. We can't go to somebody and say, 'Look what's been your experience.' It's just not possible yet."[6]

11 Jurisdictional Relations

The New Town had a direct impact on six local government bodies: Dayton, Trotwood, Brookville, Madison Township, Perry Township, and Montgomery County. Besides these governments the New Town also directly affected two school districts: Trotwood-Madison and Brookville Local, and it would probably affect the Dayton Public School System. Each had a certain amount of power at stake and each reacted in a different manner.

Several City of Dayton commissioners had openly opposed the New Town, one dubbing it a "nirvana." During the state A-95 review of the HUD application the city had opposed the project unless there was annexation and certain other demands were met. The City of Dayton had power, because it controlled water and sewer services to the New Town and made decisions concerning vital transportation routes, such as the Wolf Creek Expressway.

Trotwood was not so aware of its power from the offset as was Dayton. Anyway, it was inclined to look favorably on the project because of the involvement of its former mayor. As the plans developed, the project's impact became more clear; and when Dayton expressed its opposition, Trotwood began to take a closer look at its own position. Its council was split in its views. One faction sought to preserve Trotwood's semirural small-town atmosphere, and another saw the city with the potential to become one of the largest, most powerful suburbs in the metropolitan area.[1] Either way, because of the New Town's proximity to Trotwood, the council saw it as a vital part of the city's future. Mayor George Van Schaik, speaking for the Trotwood Council, said the New Town was viewed as a "logical and orderly expansion and growth of Trotwood."[2]

Both Trotwood and Dayton gained added power over the New Town with the passage of the Community Authority Bill because of the veto power over its petition. Also, because of the community authority, both or either city could be responsible for providing police and fire protection and controlling zoning and subdivision regulations if all or part of the project were annexed to both or either city. If not, these powers would be retained by the county and/or the townships. Because of the community authority law, which prevented the establishment of a separate school district, educational services would have to be provided by one of the existing governments.

The power of the Madison Township officials over the New Town rested in zoning. Because Madison was a small community, the township trustees and zoning officers were in close day-to-day contact with their constituents, who possessed a strong anti-Dayton feeling and were uneasy about annexation. Madison Township was composed primarily of large farms and small one- or two-acre plots of land for which individuals had saved all their lives in order to escape the central city. The farmers disliked Dayton, because it represented the urbanization that was contrary to their way of life. Those who lived on smaller tracts disliked Dayton because it represented what they had moved away from: black people, crime, violence, visual blight, pollution, traffic congestion, and so on. The influx of federal money during the 1960s that was designed to alleviate these problems tended to complicate them. As neighborhoods were torn apart for highways, more people left the city. As urban renewal and model cities programs spent thousands, then millions of dollars, the middle class that had fled the city grew more discontented about the way that they saw their tax dollars being spent.

The best way to describe the reaction of the Trotwood-Madison school administration is ineptitude. Already beset with major school financing problems, they were fearful of the New Town from the beginning. Donald Huber promised schools through the community authority. Nevertheless, the school board advertised that one of the reasons for one of their many attempted bond issues was to finance New Town schools. This caused a predictable negative response from voters who were skeptical of both the developer and the school administration, which had unsuccessfully tried nine previous times to get a bond issue passed for various other reasons. Instead of trying to work with the New Town staff to solve problems (Huber's offer to provide schools potentially could have solved many of the board's problems), the board reacted with fear and mistrust. Out of desperation it finally hired an elderly consultant from Ohio State University to work on its problems, including the New Town. He produced several charts and a plan for a plan to plan, but he answered no crucial problems.

Schools were also a hot issue relative to annexation, because residents were fearful that if the area were annexed, it would become a part of Dayton Public School System, which meant more black students.

The reaction in Brookville, Perry Township, and the Brookville Local school system was much more passive. Ray Shock, president of the Perry Township trustees, thought that because the county rural zoning commission handled the zoning jurisdiction, there was not much use getting involved. Besides, he stated that the trustees "hadn't had any inquiries about the plans" from local residents. Likewise, the Brookville Village Council did not take a position on the plans.[3] The reason for this inaction was best summarized by Carl Hammond, superintendent of Brookville schools, who said, referring to the New Town, "Its effect on Brookville will not be felt for six, eight or even ten years."[4] This is the kind of thinking that prevails in small communities before they are hit with the impact of change. Then, when it is too late, the local officials panic, or as in the case of the Trotwood-Madison school, administrators respond ineptly.

The county's power rested in zoning, the establishment of the community authority, and the appointment of its directors. In some cases, such as the appointment of trustees to the Interim Non-Profit Corporation Board, the county sought to help Huber as much as possible. In other matters, like zoning, the county was more cautious. The county officials were also skeptical about the possibility of annexation to either Dayton or Trotwood; in both cases they stood to lose power, and in the unincorporated areas of the county annexation was an extremely volatile political issue.

Administrators of the Dayton Public School System took wait-and-see attitudes. They followed the development of the project, and from time to time they met with representatives of the New Town for the clarification of certain issues but did not become directly involved.

After several months of growing hostility between Dayton and Trotwood, Gerwin Rohrbach and Herman Pope arranged a meeting between representatives of the two feuding jurisdictions at the Miami Valley Golf Club. At that meeting, it was decided to meet again. As a result of action taken by the City of Dayton in Washington, it was decided that at the second meeting all the commissioners of Dayton and all of the Trotwood council would be present to determine once and for all if a New Town was to be built. This heated meeting lasted till three A.M. and was adjourned after a preliminary "agreement of principle" had been reached. All the parties initialed a map, upon which a line had been drawn and agreed upon as indicating limits to both Dayton's and Trotwood's annexation interests. In addition, the Donald Huber Development Group agreed to assist Dayton in establishing a corridor extending from the city limits to the section of the New Town that in the future could be annexed.[5]

Acting on the preliminary agreement of principle, the Donald Huber Development Group began the acquisition of land in the corridor, much of which was on a rock base that made it marginally developable. Concurrently, the City of Dayton lessened its pressure on federal authorities by passing the project through the local A-95 with the annexation condition attached. City Manager Kunde and Mayor McGee also wrote letters in support of the Community Authority Bill to state legislators and the governor when the bill was being considered by the General Assembly.

But even though the preliminary agreement had been reached, the road to annexation was bumpy. First, there were the residents of Madison Township who would oppose any annexation effort by the City of Dayton. Second, there was the opposition to the building of the Wolf Creek Expressway by the Model Cities organization. (There was a feeling that the building of the expressway could compromise some of the opposition in Madison Township and Trotwood). Third, there was the general mistrust of Huber and the project by Dayton officials. This mistrust was so great that Huber's attorney James Gould believed that "Dayton's prejudice against the project will be overcome only by a tremendous display of hard work and a substantial amount of accomplishment towards annexation."[6]

As with the other programs, Rohrbach attempted to coordinate the government jurisdictions with other activities on his project plan-summary network, and he tried to utilize the planning process to complete the necessary tasks. There was a great deal of interplay between governments and the zoning, community authority, and HUD relations programs. Also, the impact of the agreement that had been reached between Dayton and Trotwood played an important part in the image that was being projected to the press. How this agreement was fulfilled would play a vital part in other programs like planning and urban design, the financial analysis, public utilities, and construction.

Rohrbach along with consultant Pope had been able to get officials from Dayton and Trotwood to sit down to talk. In those meetings he was able to get each side to clarify its own goals and priorities. Then facts were presented to show how the New Town, and how the alternative of no New Town, would realistically affect those goals and what were the predictable outcomes of both alternatives. The officials were able to discuss both alternatives in relation to reality and their own preferences. They could then conclude that the best situation was to work with each other and with the New Town staff. This agreement was then translated by Rohrbach into a program by which both municipalities could achieve their goals. The effect could then be measured only by each party once commitments were kept.

Rohrbach's program was designed to keep the promises that the New Town developer had made. The program had been developed in conjunction with other affected activities, like zoning. Zoning was controlled by Madison Township and county officials. Though both jurisdictions stood to lose power because of the New Town, the issue was more controversial in Madison Township because of the immediacy of development in that area.

Rohrbach handled relations with Madison Township officials in an honest, open manner. On 21 June a meeting was held in the New Town office between those officials and representatives of the Donald L. Huber Development Group. As expected, the topic of annexation took the most time and generated some frank expressions of irritation from most of the trustees and zoning commissioners.

The township officials displayed the most animosity toward the City of Dayton and less toward Trotwood. They were, however, sympathetic to the New Town's position in the middle and were impressed by the amount of work that had gone into the HUD application, the environmental impact statement, and zoning. They also expressed disappointment at not being included in the Dayton-Trotwood meetings. Rohrbach was candid on this subject. Relating the series of events that had preceded the Miami Valley Golf Club agreement, Rohrbach felt that the township officials were typical of the better informed and reasonably well-off white residents of Madison Township. Accordingly, he believed that their attitudes were those that would likely be encountered when annexation petitions were circulated.[7] After the meeting Rohrbach listed these attitudes in a memorandum to Huber. Referring to the officials, he stated that

1. They appeared to understand the crisis situation which Dayton is facing. They also appeared to feel that it was not their problem.
2. They had accumulated a large amount of ill-will toward Dayton officials.
3. There was also a certain amount of latent prejudice against blacks and poor people in general.
4. They were deeply resentful of the fact that the City of Dayton had apparently not wanted to cooperate in problem solving or even conferring with them. They had never been contacted on the annexation request by anyone from Dayton, except in casual conversation. They felt that a meeting should be held, but expected Dayton to make the first move.
5. Although not directly expressed, they did not attempt to conceal their determination to fight against annexation in every possible way. This applied both to the Dayton and the Trotwood annexation efforts.
6. The above attitude did not auger well for large-scale annexation activity in the township.[8]

By establishing a working relationship with the officials, Rohrbach was able to separate the issue of annexation, to which the township was opposed; and that of zoning, which they favored because of the master plan approach. In this way, with the aid of positive public-relations efforts in the community, zoning was approved with no opposition.

Because of zoning, the timing for annexation had to be handled very cautiously. Closed meetings were held to keep both Dayton and Trotwood posted of the project's progress. But Huber could take no firm action, except for purchasing some additional land in the corridor, until after zoning was approved. One such meeting took place in the New Town office on 14 June between Rohrbach, his assistant; the City of Dayton's administrator responsible for annexation, Tony

Char; and realtor Pharon Denlinger, who, having completed initial land-acquisition efforts, was put in charge of mustering support for annexation in the corridor area. At this meeting a strategy and timetable were tentatively agreed upon. Rohrbach suggested, because of that strong antiannexation sentiment in Madison Township, that the best strategy would be to start with a small section of land, deleting several sections where known opposition existed, and concentrating on areas of land that Huber controlled or where known support existed. A target date was set for 2 October to file the necessary annexation petition.[9]

On 22 June a luncheon meeting at the downtown Dayton Inn was held in a private room to enable the New Town staff to explain what progress had been made on annexation as well as on the balance of the project. The veto power over the community authority by the City of Dayton was clearly indicated, plus the possibility that Trotwood could exercise its extraterritorial powers. The zoning program, then in progress, was reviewed. It was explained that it would be more tactful for Dayton's annexation to take place in such a manner as to allow zoning to proceed as programmed. Finally, the strategy upon which Rohrbach and Char had agreed was discussed.[10] After that the city reiterated its position clearly: no annexation, no New Town.

Zoning dragged on through the summer till it became obvious that the target date would have to be extended beyond 2 October. In the meantime, the New Town staff with the aid of the Public Administration Service of Chicago produced a fiscal impact statement to comply with federal guidelines. This statement was another of those sections of the original HUD application that had been found insufficient and had to be redone so that once the environmental impact statement was released the Community Development Corporation Board could have a completed application on which to base its review. The fiscal impact statement detailed the New Town's projected impact on each of the affected governments (fig. 4). In every case the fisacl impact statement projected that the New Town development would have an overall favorable fiscal impact upon the community in question. The New Town tax base of residential, industrial, and commercial property offered a more economical mix than did typical suburban bedroom communities. The latter type of development historically overburdened services and contributed only a por-

Fig. 4. New Town Fiscal Impact on the Operations of Local Governments

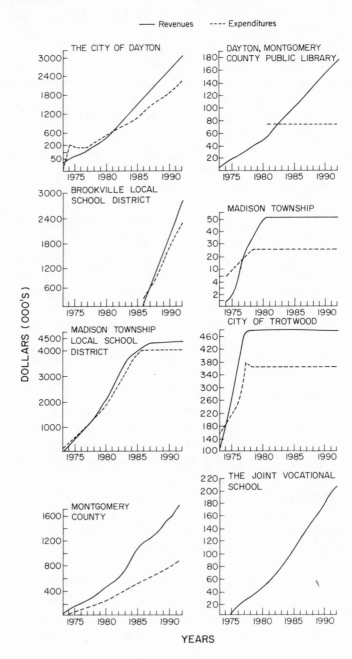

tion of the cost of services. It was shown in the fiscal impact statement that the New Town would have the ability to more than support itself, based on the levels of services and taxes existing during the planning periods (fig. 5). This projection represented a source of increased revenues to the area in addition to enhancing social values.[11]

In late September, with the City of Dayton growing increasingly anxious and the zoning program in the process of being approved by the final governments, the New Town staff met to begin some definite efforts at annexation. An annexation task force was formed that included Rohrbach, Rausch, and Kreines from the New Town staff; Roger Berardinis, one of Huber's accountants; attorneys James Gould and Robert Deddens; an attorney from Columbus, Robert Albright, who had extensive experience in successful annexation efforts; lobbyist Robert Husted; Tony Char of the City of Dayton; Carlton Laird of the community authority; Pharon Denlinger; and a local resident who had been selected as the field captain.

At the 28 September meeting of the task force, various issues, concerns, and strategies were discussed. Included in the discussion were the political situation in the area because of the coming election in

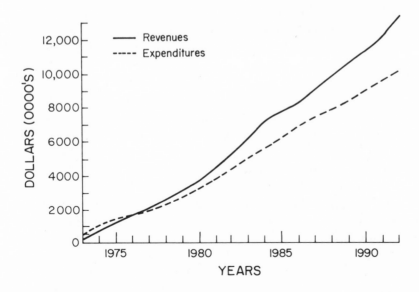

Fig. 5. Total Fiscal Impact of the New Town on all Existing Governments

November. It was decided that it might be a better strategy to delay
the submission of the annexation petition until after the elections to
avoid making the New Town a political issue. Rausch believed that
the task force should be prepared to proceed on collecting at least
seventy percent of the land owners' signatures in the annexation corridor immediately after the November election. Rausch also thought
that Dayton had to offer inducements, such as free water or sewer
lines, to get land owners to sign the annexation petition.[12] "According
to the Fiscal Impact Study," Berardinis commented during the
meeting, "It will cost the city one million dollars to annex the area
which will only provide $37,000 in annual revenues. It will have to
pay out more than it will receive from the New Town till 1981. Don't
you think it'll discourage Dayton?" "No," Rausch answered. "City
Manager Kunde feels that the New Town is essential to the growth of
the City. Without it, Dayton has little hope for physical expansion and
the recovery of tax revenues lost during the 1960's." Another potential
political issue that was discussed at the meeting was Donald Huber's
political contributions. Rohrbach felt that because of the crucial state
of the negotiations that were going on both locally and with the
federal government, it was important to know the amounts and the
recipients of the contributions.[13]

Denlinger and the field captain, who was to be paid on a bonus per
landowner signature, were given the assignment of lining up possible
supporters in the area. Husted and Kreines were placed in charge of
compiling a demographic profile on the residents in the area so that
the task force could be prepared to answer potential opposition and to
offer services that residents might feel were needed in the area.

On 3 October another meeting was held. This time more specific
strategies were investigated. Robert Albright suggested from experience that the best approach was to annex in small sections and in that
way avoid widespread opposition. This approach had been opposed
by Huber who preferred one large annexation of 3,000 acres, because
he felt it would better please City of Dayton officials who had
historically attempted annexations in large sections (those attempts
had been unsuccessful). But once all the alternatives were explored it
was agreed by Huber and Char that the incremental approach would
be wiser.

Husted and Kreines discovered that the biggest concern of the people in the corridor area was schools. A major reason of their opposi-

tion to annexation to Dayton was that if the area were annexed it would become a part of the Dayton Public School System. Albright pointed out that though it was historically true in Ohio that school system expansions did follow annexations, it was not required by law. He showed how in Columbus agreements had been made between the city and the school system that the school system would not be expanded into areas where it was unwanted. What was needed, he concluded, was an agreement with the Dayton Public School System not to follow Dayton annexations into the area.

A subsequent meeting was held between the New Town staff and the City Commission. Rohrbach and Char were able to convince them that the incremental approach was best, that the task force was moving, and that the first results would be evident following the election. Thus the New Town was beginning to fulfill commitments made to the City of Dayton.

In the meantime, however, Trotwood had grown uneasy. Those on the council who advocated retaining a small community atmosphere had been overpowered by those who advocated growth through the New Town. Seeing the statistics in the fiscal impact statement made these council members more convinced that they had a lot to gain by getting as much control as possible over New Town territory. They followed Dayton's example and decided the best way to get what they wanted was to oppose the project. Soon after the environmental impact statement was released for review, on 24 October, Trotwood expressed its official opposition to the project in a letter to HUD. "THE CITY OF TROTWOOD, OHIO, CANNOT GRANT ITS APPROVAL OF THE PROJECT KNOWN AS BROOKWOOD." All that in capital letters followed by four reasons why the letter claimed the project was being opposed. The reasons listed were the insufficient transportation system to and from Trotwood, the indefinite plans for schools, the "high" percentage of low- and moderate-income housing to be built, and the lack of a guarantee on the 1,700 acres that Trotwood wanted to annex. "FOR THESE REASONS, THE CITY OF TROTWOOD CANNOT GRANT ITS AP- PROVAL OF BROOKWOOD AND URGENTLY RECOMMENDS TO HUD THAT THE ABOVE FOUR CONDITIONS BE INCORPORATED AS CONDITIONS UPON WHICH HUD'S APPROVAL OF BROOKWOOOD BE GRANTED."[14]

There were answers to the questions that Trotwood raised concerning transportation, educational planning, low- and moderate- income housing, and annexation. For instance, Huber had repeatedly offered through Rausch the same aid to Trotwood that the New Town staff had given to Dayton with annexation. Also, Rohrbach had been attempting to work for several months with the aging educational consultant from Ohio State University who had been hired by the Trotwood-Madison school system. The primary reason for Trotwood's letter was fear. The council, representing the feelings of many of its constituents, was afraid of the New Town. The more ambitious members of council saw an opportunity for Trotwood's expansion; the more traditional members were afraid of losing their small-town atmosphere forever, so they wrote the letter to HUD.

Rohrbach stated to the press that he could understand Trotwood's concerns. "They're feeling frustrated, confused. . . . These are all problems that are difficult to grasp. If I was in their place I'd react the same way," he said. "To them it's like coping with a monster."[15]

12 Planning and Urban Design

Initial New Town physical planning had been done by Llewelyn-Davies Associates. Rohrbach had found these efforts unsatisfactory, because the planning was based on incorrect environmental data, they had excluded citizens in the planning process, and they depended on village centers.

From the task force a physical plan and preliminary urban design program was developed as part of the overall project plan. The majority of the hard data had been collected for the environmental impact statement and zoning program and had been incorporated into the concept plan. It was a flexible plan upon which future efforts were to be based but not dictated by it.

The responsibility for implementing this program was with the director of planning and urban design. He would work with the other New Town managers, the community authority, citizens, and design consultants to set goals; investigate resources; analyze alternatives; and set priorities of goals. Associated with the director of planning and urban design would be an urban design consultant whose responsibility it would be to devise a set of overall design standards working with the New Town planning staff, other consultants, the community authority, government officials, and the citizen group. These overall guidelines could then be applied to specific situations by individual developers, architects, landscape architects, and engineers.

The preliminary planning and urban design program had been set by the completion of the HUD application, the A-95 review, and zoning. The program became further defined with the submission of the environmental and fiscal impact statements, the land ownership statement and the innovative features report. The innovative features report was a compilation of all the various unique features of the project that had been proposed up to that point. It was presented in Washington at the HUD New Communities Office on 26 and 27 June by Huber, Rohrbach, and Rausch.

> "It is the intent of the New Town Management to consider this project as a legacy for future generations," the report began. The New Town land is now in a state of agricultural use. It should be intelligently converted for the permanent benefit of the region. The New Town social system and institutions are non-existent at present. They have been discussed but they have not been established. *The shapes in which these social elements are formed over the next twelve months will set a pattern for the long term future.*
>
> Thus, the New Town management recognizes a challenge and a responsibility in their development process. They are determined that this project will not be just another large scale real estate venture. It will not be a duplication of some other new community which has been transplanted to the Ohio countryside. This New Town will be as new in every sense of the word.[1]

Listed in the report as advances in design and technology were the process for land-use planning, the potential use of innovative materials for and methods of construction, and the dispersal of low-income housing. Included as innovations concerning the provision of community facilities and services were the dual developer concept, the formalization of the community authority, citizen participation in community design, and a proposed resident information system. What was considered to be a major innovation was the participation of two separate developers: one private and profit making, the other public and nonprofit.

The community authority was an innovation that held much fascination for HUD. The formalization of the community authority by Ohio law also offered several innovations in governmental power. First in the petition process; then in the review and veto power of proximate municipalities and other jurisdictions; and finally in the control of the board of trustees as its governing board, in which case the private developer never had a majority representation.[2] The community authority was a unique quasi government with certain powers that attempted to give new community residents a greater role in the decision-making process.

Another innovation that was initiated with the planning task force meetings was citizen participation in community design. By the time the innovative features report was submitted a larger group of citizens was being organized to work with the New Town staff and consultants, the community authority, and local officials in the design of the community. Rohrbach's hope was to create a body early in the planning process that was based on the idea of participatory democracy, which had been the foundation of New England town meetings; a process that would permit objectors and advocates alike to have a voice in the community planning process and to thrash out their differences in a public forum.

The last innovation covered in the report was the administration of the New Town's planning and development, the "critical-path" method of task scheduling that was used for the project plan-summary network. Following the PERT principle, the task scheduling was necessary because of the multiplicity of activities. It was also proposed that there be a computerized data processing system developed for long-range administration and coordination.[3]

Early in his administrative planning, Rohrbach had requested that the position of the director of planning and urban design be filled by June. In late spring, he began advertising such a position in the various professional planning publications. It was also his hope during the same time period to supplement the existing graphics staff with some additional junior-level planners and/or designers, because of the anticipated increase in work load as the New Town moved steadily closer to the construction stage.

By mid June over one hundred applications had been received for the director of planning position, an indication of the interest in new communities. The number of applications especially pleased Rohrbach. It was his goal to develop a model process that could be used for the building of other American urban environments. To accomplish this he sought to involve young talent, realizing though that much practical experience would be needed to complete the project.

By July the list of possibilities had been narrowed to three possible candidates who would be interviewed for the position. All three were white and male. Edward Kreines was chosen for the position. He was a young man in his early thirties who had joint masters degrees in city planning and communications from the University of Pennsylvania in addition to an undergraduate degree in urban planning. Kreines had served in the Peace Corps and as a consultant for the Rouse Company, the developers of Columbia. As director of planning and urban design, Kreines would be directly responsible for the graphics department, for Ralph Scott (until that time when the environmental monitoring responsibilities could be shifted to the community authority), and the various design consultants who would be involved in the project.

On 11 September Kreines arrived to begin his work with the New Town. When Rohrbach assumed his responsibilities seven months before he was given a site and a concept. When Kreines arrived he was given a conceptual land-use plan, general social and physical design criteria that had been established in the course of the evolution of the project, and an overall project plan. A key task that faced him immediately was the completion of zoning approvals. Although by the time he arrived the successful completion of zoning was well under way, it would be a continual responsibility to complete the ongoing zoning negotiations that involved, for instance, the submission of phase plans and specific plat plans and requests for variances.

For the three months before Kreines arrived, the Donald Huber Group had been searching for an urban design consultant who would be responsible for developing the specific criteria and guidelines by which the New Town would be developed. The urban design consultant would also be responsible for the ongoing monitoring of those guidelines with the director of planning and urban design. These guidelines would be a refinement of those already developed in the innovative features report. This would fulfill HUD's requirement that innovative features be constantly readjusted and evaluated.

Ten firms with national and international reputations were selected to be considered for the urban design position. They were a combination of architecture, landscape architecture, and land-planning firms with offices in the East, Midwest and Southwest. The initial contact with each firm was handled in the same manner: the firm's representative would be met at the Dayton airport, and a quick tour of the area and the New Town followed. On the tour various topics were discussed that related to the project: the metropolitan region, the Miami Conservancy District, Donald Huber's background, his family's background, the relationship of the project to the cities of Dayton and Trotwood, the first phase area, the environmental aspects of the area, the I-675 and Wolf Creek expressways, the HUD application, the community reaction to the project, and the other consultants who were involved.[4] At the New Town office, after the tour, Rohrbach would begin by giving an extensive outline of the background and the status of the New Town, covering many of the same topics discussed casually on the tour but in greater depth. He would then explain the history of the community authority and its potential ramifications. After a period of questions and discussion Rohrbach would review the other firms being considered as urban design consultants, then he would close by outlining what the New Town group wanted in the proposal from the prospects being interviewed. First, it wanted an overall urban design concept for the entire area, including guidelines for the developer and the other architects and land planners. Next, it wanted a proposal providing for continuing urban design construction and review. Lastly, a proposal was wanted for the coordination of all design and architectural services. A September deadline was set for the final decision on the urban design consultant, and it was requested that each firm make a formal presentation of its proposal before that time.[5]

Once each firm had visited the site the first round of proposals was submitted and presentations began. This occurred in August 1972. During this period Rohrbach grew increasingly uncertain about the project's potential because of the increasing internal problems that he was having with Huber concerning the delay in the HUD application, the developer's commitment to citizen participation, and the economic model. Rohrbach was also disappointed by the proposals that were submitted by the various firms that had been interviewed. He had hoped for a "grand" concept, the development of a practical system of physical and social design for the growth of human living environments. The proposals from what were considered among the most "outstanding" architecture, landscape architecture, and planning firms in the nation fell short of this goal. The consultants who were interviewed identified first with their own discipline and attempted to apply what they considered to be the accepted professional approach rather than identifying specifically with the problem of the specific new community on the edge of the Dayton, Ohio, urban area.

The problems with the urban design presentations is one that is inherent in the profession. As S. Dillon Ripley concluded from the series of papers that were delivered at the 1967 Smithsonian Institution Annual Symposium and later incorporated into the book, *The Fitness of Man's Environment*, architects, like many intellectuals, are literate persons who feel themselves to be members of the educated minority.

How often such an elite suffers from less than valid claims to superiority. How often superiority produces what Hoffer describes as a "colonial official" mentality. In New Mexico and nearby areas the Pueblo Indians have developed an indigenous and adaptive architectural style. However, the Federal Housing Administration standards lack cultural reportage; this prevents the Pueblo from constructing what they would like. "As nonintellectuals they presumably have to take what they can get" (Ripley 1968, p. 10). Designers for the masses tend not to see people, only prizes from other architects and planners. Ripley is joined by many other critics of physical planning (Jacobs 1961, Gans 1968, Goodman 1971, Caro 1974).

The last firm to make a proposal presentation was Hellmuth, Obata, and Kassabaum of St. Louis. A few moments after their representatives, Gyo Obata and Neil Porterfield, began to outline their approach, they were abruptly interrupted by Rohrbach, who told them, "Never mind." The architect and landscape architect who had just flown in from their largest current project, the multimillion dollar-Dallas–Fort Worth International Airport, for the Dayton presentation looked bewilderedly at each other. "You're presenting nothing new," Rohrbach continued. "We have called in what we felt were the most brilliant environmental designers in the nation and we've seen absolutely nothing new. Frankly, I'm disappointed with all the firms. They all have attacked the New Town concept in the same manner as a large structural or land use project. What we need is a whole new language."[6] Rohrbach then asked the representatives of Hellmuth, Obata, and Kassabaum; the New Town staff members participating in the interview process; and Richard Levin, a Dayton architect who was also participating, to follow him into an adjoining room where the project plan-summary work flow network was being revised.

There is a complicated multiplicity in the scope of tasks involved in building a city and those tasks need proper orchestration. The physical design is just one component area, though it's an important one as it relates to all the other programs. For instance, coordination is necessary between the urban design concept and the subdivision regulations and if we're going to start construction next spring and it's almost September now—we better get moving.

All the firms which have made presentations have been 'task' or 'product' rather than 'process' oriented. I want Brains, I want creative Brains that I can put on the New Town site so they can interact with our staff, other consultants and citizens. The building of cities is a process and a whole new language must be written to give future direction to urban growth. There are already such vocabularies on the structural and regional levels, but nothing has yet been developed on the city scale. It's like rewriting the Rosetta Stone.[7]

Neil Porterfield, looking somewhat dismayed, responded that his proposal had missed the point and that his firm would respond immediately.

The New Town project excited Porterfield's interest. He wanted to become involved. So, returning to St. Louis after the presentation on Friday, he went directly to work on a new proposal over the weekend. He cancelled several days of his vacation and submitted a new proposal to the New Town group in less than a week. The new proposal called for HOK Associates, the planning subsidiary of Hellmuth, Obata, and Kassabaum under the direction of Porterfield to form a think-tank urban design group. The group was to be known as the New Town Environmental Planning Group (the name New Town was to be changed when the new name was developed). Porterfield's group was to be composed of individuals whose personalities, areas of expertise, creativity, and ability to communicate would provide individual and collective insights into the problems of developing human environments. This group would address itself to the wide spectrum of interrelated problems that could be understood in terms of human ecology and physical urban design.

It would be the specific task of HOK Associates' group to reconcile the realities of what was achievable with the dreams of the impossible. Its intent was to provide implicit yet flexible urban design concepts, criteria, and guidelines for the New Town. The New Town Environmental Planning Group (NEPG) would be developed in two stages: the first would be a large group that would establish the initial guidelines and direction, and the second would be a smaller core group that would police the standards in the future. The larger group would be made up of a combination of participants, while the smaller would be composed of specific individuals involved in the larger groups. NEPG's team leader would be Neil Porterfield.

Porterfield suggested that the individuals who would be involved in the think tank be persons of national and international reputations who had proven themselves to be creative thinkers and effective participants in their particular fields of expertise. These individuals would represent the fields of urban design, sociology, landscape architecture, zoology, political science, architecture, psychology, planning, geography, journalism, construction, medicine, law, and history. Because assembling the most outstanding individuals in these fields would be a difficult logistical task, Porterfield suggested that some individuals could be brought in for short brainstorming sessions with the larger group. Also, to be included in the initial NEPG team would be other consultants like Ivan Chermayeff, who had been retained to develop a name and a graphics program; and Harold Malt, who had been hired by the community authority to develop a street furniture system (that is, designs for street poles, lighting, signs, and so on).

Although the proposal was impressive, Rohrbach felt that the choice of the urban design consultant, who would have a most vital role in the image of the New Town, should not be selected in a vacuum. He believed that it was crucial to have input from the Huber organization, the other design consultants, the interim community authority, and the emerging citizens' group. So he decided to have the choice made in an open forum with all the interested parties participating. Three of the firms that had given proposals were invited to return to give their presentation to a reconvened planning task force session. The chosen firm would then be given the contract as the urban design consultant, with Donald Huber's approval. The other firms that were not selected could be involved in other projects in the New Town so that their investment in the proposal would not be wasted.

The presentations were held in the Madison Township Grange Hall on 1 September. Three firms made presentations: HOKA, Harry Weese and Associates from Chicago, and The Architects Collaborative from Cambridge, Massachusetts. While the other two firms stuck primarily to the "task" approach, HOKA's New Town Environmental Planning Group opened many possibilities for a wide range of citizen and consultant input. HOKA was the overwhelming selection of the assembled staff, consultants, citizens, and community authority representatives.

In his presentation, Porterfield disclosed the names of several of the experts from whom he had received commitments. Making up the basic planning team that Porterfield had assembled were Paul Sears, internationally known ecologist, botanist, and conservationist; Julian

Wolpert, professor of regional science and geography at the University of Pennsylvania; David Niddrie, professor of geography at the University of Florida; Daniel Carson, sociologist-planner and architecture professor at the University of Wisconsin; David Stea, psychologist and environmental designer who was a visiting professor at the University of California School of Architecture and Urban Planning; William Widdowson, professor of architecture at the University of Cincinnati; and Thomas Jenkins, professor of sociology and community planning at the University of Cincinnati. Completing the group were Charles Reay and architect Bernard Bortnick of HOKA.[8]

Porterfield's team began its work on 15 September 1972. As NEPG began its work, other design consultants simultaneously started work on specific projects, mostly in the first phase area. This work would be reviewed by NEPG and meshed with their guidelines. In addition to Chermayeff-Geismar Associates and H. L. Malt Associates, The Architects Collaborative was retained to design the first convenience center that would include a shopping complex, community center, and school; Dayton architect Richard Levin was hired to design several multifamily dwelling complexes; landscape architect James Basset was hired to do the site planning for the first phase; and several engineering firms were contracted for road, sewage, and lake design. By late September, actual design on the New Town had begun.

13 Citizen Participation

The New Town office in Trotwood, Ohio, in September 1972 must have had many similarities to the European Allied Command Headquarters in May of 1944. The walls, which had been temporarily constructed of plywood and corkboard, were filled with maps, charts, and diagrams. Empty spaces had been converted into display areas that were used for a seemingly endless stream of meetings and presentations. A receptionist was constantly busy answering the phone and directing visitors to the appropriate cubicle. Typewriters pounded, coffee perked, draftsmen magic-markered fresh blueprints, and orders were flung back and forth through the corridors and from room to room. It was a source of contagious energy that affected whoever entered.

At the eye of this cyclone of energy was Gerwin Rohrbach, whose office had no door to close out what was happening in the rest of the office. He sat in his corkboard enclosure, surrounded by maps and charts and by the project plan-summary network and backed by a wall of books. When he sat at his desk puffing on his pipe, he gave the impression of a gruff Buddha backed by all the knowledge that existed in those books. They were books that did, in fact, contain the bulk of the important work on city planning, landscape architecture, and new-town planning. There was also a sprinkling of books about management, ecology, law, and community organization. A quote was tacked to one side of the corkboard: "Take each of you charge of some village and organize it. Educate the villagers and show them how to put forward their united strength. Look not for fame or praise . . . do not expect even the gratitude of those for whom you would give your life, but be prepared rather for their opposition." Its author was Rabindranath Tagore, the Indian poet.

Title VII did not specifically require that a new-town developer, either public or private, assure citizen participation to be a part of the planning or development process of the new community in order to be eligible to participate in the program. It was felt that during the initial planning stages, the developer's obligation to keep the public adequately advised of the new community's program would be met as he carried out his negotiations with elected officials and bureaucrats with whom he had to deal in the course of gaining the required government approvals (Mields 1973).

During the course of these negotiations for the Dayton New Town, it became apparent that an effective citizen participation program had to be adopted for several reasons. There was first the letter from the Office of Economic Opportunity-sponsored Northwest Advisory Council of Montgomery County to George Romney in January 1972. The letter began, "Whereas, in the new town of Brookwood, in Montgomery County, citizens have been excluded from any planning," and ended with the demand for "official representation with real power, not just token representation, on phase one planning by low income people, black people, present residents of the project New Town area, the Northwest Montgomery County Advisory Council, youth and other people who have been traditionally excluded from the decision-making process."[1]

Second, there was the obstacle of local residents' potential opposition to zoning. With the massive dispersal by the news media of information concerning the New Town, and with the connection of the name Huber with Huber Heights, local elected officials were skeptical of early zoning plans. Before action could be taken on zoning, opposition had to be compromised and some grassroots support mustered for the project.

Third, there was the demand by affected governing bodies that they and the citizens be directly involved in the planning efforts. Those demands came most dramatically from the cities of Dayton and Trotwood. As stated in Mayor James McGee's letter to the regional planning council, "Without political participation and representation by New Town residents, we are convinced that New Town will result in the accelerated decline of the center city in a physical, social and economic sense."[2]

The New Town group responded to this opposition by making several commitments to initiate an effective citizen participation process. The first such commitment came in the HUD application.

"Every effort will be made by the Community Authority to achieve effective public participation in the development of the new community. This community involvement in the planning and management of Brookwood's development and operation will be particularly oriented toward encouraging the participation of minority groups. It is essential to the purposes of developing a self-determining new community, which will have its own system of community government to promote public interest and participation in local affairs at all levels and in all sections of the population living and working in Brookwood."[3]

Next there was a commitment made through the community authority law. As presented to the state legislature, one of the primary purposes of the community authority was to "establish a means for citizen participation in planning and development."[4]

Further commitments were made in both the environmental impact statement and the innovative features report. The environmental impact statement reaffirmed the commitment made in the HUD application by once again stating that "every effort was being made to achieve effective public participation in the development of the new community."[5] The innovative features report went further by proposing a broad citizen participation program "that would provide a unique opportunity for members of the public to have something to say *in advance* regarding the accommodations to be provided by the community in which they later may wish to live."[6]

The envisioned program was summed up in the innovative features report in the following manner: "This program represents a return to the idea of participatory democracy which was the foundation for New England town meetings. It will permit objectors and advocates alike to have a voice in the community planning process and to thrash out their differences in a public forum. This citizen participation program is obviously an area where the developer should not participate in an overt manner, if a true representation of public opinion is to emerge."[7]

These commitments were made by the Donald Huber Development Group, authored largely by Rohrbach with the full knowledge and approval of Huber. Action on them began with the initiation of the communication program, which was designed to convince landowners to sell their property and to quell potential opposition to zoning by local residents. Through an active public-relations program in the local homes, churches, schools, and fraternal lodges, a large group of interested, middle-income citizens were gathered that would eventually help to form an effective citizen involvement body.

The other large groups of individuals that would compose this body would come from public officials and low-income citizens with an interest in the New Town. The public officials were drawn in through the series of official reviews and negotiations. The low-income citizens were involved through Gerwin Rohrbach's personal efforts with their leaders. Both groups were instrumental in the passage of the community authority legislation, and both groups gained some power over the functioning and the emergence of the community authority. The low-income citizens sought and were granted representation on the Interim Non-Profit Board of Trustees, while local municipal officials were given the veto power over the community authority petition.

All these people were brought together by Rohrbach and the consultants of Community Service in the planning task force meetings. These meetings produced the conceptual land-use plan that was used for zoning and the environmental impact statement. This core was envisioned to represent "the initial application of the citizen participation process in new community design." A much larger group of interested citizens was to be formed to provide the platform for a "major on-going participation effort."[8]

As it developed, the citizen participation program utilized both the planning process and community organization techniques. Following the planning process, the New Town management team had collected data that was available about the necessity of citizen participation, set goals, investigated available resources in the area like Community Services, analyzed alternatives, made commitments through various interactions and negotiations, and developed a program that was consistent with and a part of the overall project plan. To fulfill those commitments, Rohrbach had hired a consultant to organize the citizens. The consultant had made entry into the larger community, sized it up, made allegiances, brought people together at planning task force meetings, developed leadership, and started to work with other public and private organizations that were involved. By midsummer the fledgling citizen's group with its new leaders was ready to begin to investigate the tasks involved, develop tactics to fulfill those tasks, build additional political power, and develop self-help strategies that would make the body independent from the Huber organization.

The most immediate task, the group decided, was to organize itself. This period was described by Gerwin Rohrbach in a July memorandum to Huber. The memorandum noted that the tempo of the citizen participation effort was beginning to build. Rohrbach stated that he felt Huber should be aware of the encouraging progress that had been made to that point. Rohrbach had first noticed the participation of interested citizens in the planning task force. He felt that it had been impressive and that the regularity of their attendance and their degree of involvement was unusual in view of the technical nature of much of the discussion at the meetings. Many of those who attended those planning sessions indicated that their interest would carry over to the long-range citizen participation program.[9]

There had been an effort to seek federal funding for the program, but Rohrbach had been notified that no such funds were available. Rohrbach and Huber had discussed the possibility of hiring a staff member to coordinate the program but both agreed that the hiring of such an individual could jeopardize the credibility of the results of the program. Accordingly, the New Town staff convened two additional meetings with the small group of concerned citizens in an effort to encourage the spontaneous growth of a program and the emergence of an unpaid natural leader within this group. This phase of the group organization process was vital, because the selection of the wrong type of leader could either kill or cripple the program. Rohrbach stated in the memorandum that he would continue to delicately guide and maneuver the group, but in a decidedly "arm's-length fashion."[10]

By early August, this core group had held several independent meetings, collected among its members a small operating budget (it is important to remember that many of these people had low, fixed, or moderate incomes), and was ready to advertise its first mass meeting. The group was left to evolve on its own. Rausch and Rohrbach's assistant attended a few of these meetings but did so in an open manner, making it clear that they had no desire to interfere with the proceedings and, rather, that they sought to act as resources.

Several things became apparent from these early meetings. First, no clear leader emerged. Griscom Morgan declined because he had been employed by the developer, while Harlan Johnson alienated many of the middle-class citizens, and Non-Profit Board Trustee

Ralph Dull failed to assert himself. The most likely candidates seemed to be Betty Devers, a Trotwood civic leader, or one of several pastors of area churches. Second, the citizens respected and feared the New Town organization as "a very sophisticated management team" that they felt was "trying to work behind the scenes." Third, the citizens were idealistic. Fourth, there was a great deal of confusion about Donald Huber's personal stand concerning their group. Dull suggested that Huber attend a meeting to explain his feelings about the New Town and about people in general (a suggestion that Huber ignored).[11]

After contacting a wide variety of people from the metropolitan area such as politicians, governmental agency employees, students, reporters, housewives, farmers, chamber of commerce members, and welfare mothers; the first mass citizens' meeting was held at the large Salem Mall complex in Trotwood on 10 August 1972. At that meeting, with well over a hundred people in attendance, the citizens decided to call themselves the Joint Citizens New Town Planning Council of Montgomery County (JCNTPC). They then voted to incorporate as a nonprofit entity "so that they could be recognized as a legitimate force."[12] The meeting was open to any area resident with an interest in New Town and drew a cross section of young and old and white and black from as diverse sources as staff members from Dayton Model Cities to the couple who owned the small Trotwood diner.

Gerwin Rohrbach commented to a reporter following the meeting that he was "extremely pleased" with the meeting and that "the commitment to maintain the citizen participation process by the people of the Dayton area is one of the most valuable contributions to the New Town's planning."[13]

The meeting was greeted much less enthusiastically by Huber, who made no public comment but was greatly disturbed with the appointment of Reginald Dunn as JCNTPC coordination committee chairman. Dunn was the administrative assistant for the Model Cities Planning Council of Dayton, and Huber considered him to be a threat. Because Dunn was black, and because he was the only leader to emerge from the first meeting, Huber feared a black takeover of his project. Rohrbach tried to convince Huber that the meeting had been a positive step and that letting citizens organize would be a beneficial rather than a harmful strategy. According to

Edmund Burke (1968), there are two major premises that underline what he terms "behavioral change strategy." First, it has been found that it is easier to change the behavior of persons when they are members of a group than when they are approached individually. Second, individuals and groups resist decisions that are imposed upon them. They are more likely to support a decision and equally important, more likely to assist in carrying it out if they have a part in discovering the need for change and if they share in the decision-making process.

Subsequent JCNTPC meetings were held, each drawing several hundred participants. Committees were formed and officers elected (a white man, the Reverend David Schneider, pastor of a church on the New Town site, was elected chairperson, much to Huber's relief). This emergence of the citizens' group coincided, by Rohrbach's design, with the selection process of the urban design consultant. The two programs were thus linked together when Porterfield's NEPG was chosen, a contract drawn and signed, and work begun according to Porterfield's proposed work schedule.

Concurrently, Schneider and the other leaders of JCNTPC sought to gain recognition of their group as the official citizens' lobby for the New Town. They first sent a letter to HUD secretary George Romney stating that its purpose was to "officially let it be known that the Joint Citizens New Town Planning Council, Inc. was the official body for maximum feasible citizen participation in the New Town planning and decision making."[14] The letter stated further that JCNTPC was independent of the Donald Huber Development Group and all other public and private agencies, that it represented a broad base of citizens from the metropolitan area, and that it had been organized under state law. Copies of this letter were then sent to all the involved federal, state, regional, and local officials. Enclosed with the latter were copies of JCNTPC's articles of incorporation, its bylaws, and a copy of the general agreement with the Huber Development Group.

The general agreement enclosed by the citizens' group in the letter to Romney referred to its effort to gain official recognition by the Huber Development Group. They had asked Donald Huber to sign a simple, one-page request for agreement on two items: that JCNTPC be known as the "official body for maximum feasible citizen participation"; and that JCNTPC be informed of all matters pertaining to administrative, operation, financial, and legal responsibility for the New Town.[15] Although JCNTPC was a creation of his own corporation's planning effort; it had been programmed to come into existence for months according to the project plan; and commitments had been made to local, state, and federal officials for months; Donald Huber refused to sign the agreement. The citizens accepted Rohrbach's signature as a compromise.

The NEPG think-tank sessions began the second week of September. They were held on the New Town site at a local Girl Scout camp and were to be devoted to setting goals. The sessions began amidst a great deal of confusion, disagreement, and mistrust. Porterfield and his team were confused. There was growing disagreement among the New Town staff members because of internal problems that were developing with the corporation. And there was the mistrust of the citizens toward Rohrbach; Porterfield; and, above all, the always absent, inaccessible Huber. When the weather became too cold for the Girl Scout camp, the meetings were moved to the local junior high school. The few results that had been produced were greatly overshadowed by frustration and a growing sense of disillusionment.

At this point Rohrbach abandoned his arm's-length approach and attempted to manipulate the process more directly. He was moved to sway from what he believed by his growing feeling that he had no real power. He felt that he was being manipulated by Huber to get the HUD application and zoning approved, after which he and his programs would be discarded. His feelings were aroused primarily because of what appeared to be Huber's increasingly irrational behavior. Huber was making a variety of conflicting commitments to certain persons that were also in conflict with what was being promoted by the New Town office. Some support for his sense of powerlessness came from feedback that Rohrbach was receiving from government officials. Huber had told them, "He [Rohrbach] won't be around forever" and had made comments to the effect that certain commitments were being made only for the sake of expediting official negotiations. Rohrbach was deeply disturbed by Huber's opposition to the urban design and citizen-participation programs. A series of conflicts between Rohrbach and Huber resulted over marketing, financial planning, control of the community authority, and delays in the HUD application approval that caused Rohrbach to entertain seriously the prospect of his resignation over the Labor Day weekend.

Rohrbach was worried about the HUD delays and Huber's be-

Fig. 6. Citizen Participation in the New Town Design Process

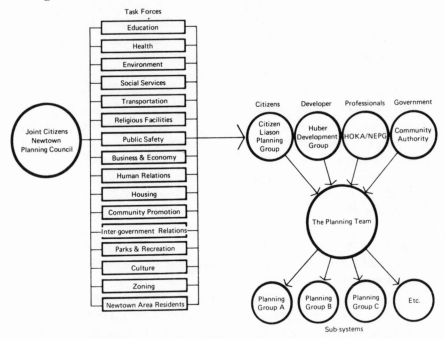

havior. Huber had, on several occasions, mentioned scrapping the whole project and had openly tried to coerce the activity of the community authority by threatening Carlton Laird with holding back operating funds. So Rohrbach pushed harder to establish the citizens' group in the planning process.

The citizens were divided by the NEPG team into task forces. These worked at developing goals and objectives during the last week of September and the first of October (fig. 6).

In the second week of October a different method was used to begin to apply these goals to the urban design program. The method selected by Porterfield and Rohrbach was that of the "charette." Porterfield felt that the charette technique was one that could involve a large, heterogeneous group of people in the design process. The term is derived from the French beaux arts period. A charette was a small cart on which paintings were taken to the galleries. The paintings were criticized by citizens along the way.

At the charette meeting Neil Porterfield said, "Our first meetings have been very strained, I hope that can change and we can begin to trust ourselves more. Tonight's format has been changed to involve the Joint Citizens Council representatives more directly in the planning process. What we're going to do is jointly design the first year plan based on the preliminary social goals we have collected in our first sessions and the environmental, planning and marketing data collected by Mr. Rohrbach and his staff."[16] Porterfield then reviewed them for the meeting. Edward Kreines, Ralph Scott, and Robert Spicer (a recently hired sales consultant) would each review his program. A break would follow, then the charette. What would separate this session from the previous think tanks and task forces was that the group would be dealing in a specific plan for a real area.

First, Kreines reviewed the planning efforts for the New Town by the Donald Huber Group up to that point and examined the implications of the first phase. Ralph Scott then discussed the natural features of the first-year site in relation to the opportunities and constraints for development. As an example, he described how the initial plan for one large, twenty-three-acre lake had been abandoned in favor of a series of smaller lakes. "The history of lake construction in the United States has proven that artificial lakes collect nutrients from chemicals in both urban and rural areas which produce unmanageable algae," Scott said. "This problem can be reduced to a manageable scale, although it can't be completely eliminated, by smaller lakes." Harlan Johnson asked if the lake sites were fixed. "By the natural features," Scott answered, "yes, the sites are fixed, but there is flexibility in the specific design and engineering of each." Finally, Robert Spicer discussed the marketing aspects for the first year. He said that the elements that would be considered included a commercial center, a school, a community center, housing and open space. Spicer suggested that the commercial center be considered first and read a list of what the center should ideally include. David Schneider commented that the list was rather long for a convenience, village type of center. "That's because," the sales consultant answered, "it is planned to service an area larger than the first year development. That is, areas outside the New Town. A center this size is needed to make it economically viable for year one."

After a short coffee break, the planning efforts began. Paper squares that represented the various first-year New Town elements were cut and then distributed along with a variety of colored markers. A base map with mylar overlays was hung at the front of the school room and the citizens were invited to design the plan. Various combinations for the school, the commercial center and the community center were discussed by the NEPG members, JCNTPC representatives and the New Town staff. Through the evening each physical element was discussed in relation to the social goals that had been developed by citizens, the economic objectives of the private developer, and the environmental constraints that the site offered. Each decision was evaluated and recorded by NEPG as it related to the conventional wisdom in environmental design. Professors Jenkins and Widdowson from the University of Cincinnati and Porterfield were especially helpful in illustrating how things that both the New Town staff and the citizens considered problems, like large parking lots, could be managed. At the end of the evening a plan had been produced. "What NEPG will do now is compile a report based on tonight's plan to present back to the citizens, the Donald Huber Development Group and the Community Authority," Porterfield concluded. The meeting was adjourned in an air of optimism.

The next week NEPG concentrated on reviewing the work of other design consultants such as the architects of the first commercial center, the street furniture designer, the graphic designer, and the land planner, making sure that all the efforts would be coordinated. These consultant reviews had begun in September and were planned to be an ongoing activity of NEPG. Porterfield and his team also prepared the first-year planning report, which was to be a prelude to their overall urban design standards.

On 16 October NEPG made the presentation of its report for the planning for the New Town's first-year development to the Donald Huber Development Group, the community authority, and the JCNTPC. In that presentation, Neil Porterfield summarized what had happened that far.

> Our urban design plan is a process of people working together. We started out doubting and in a hurry. There were three of us—developer, citizen and consultant. Each of us had our own needs and wants and we knew we had to understand the other two groups who had different needs and wants. The one need we have finally agreed upon as necessary for our working together is communication.
>
> We are now working together for the first time since we started. On October 21, after struggling with planning jargon like "mix" and "land

use" and "density," we decided to understand the New Town through its first year development on 249 acres of land. We talked and we wrote on the chalkboard, and we drew colors on a map. The result is presented in this report for the design of the first phase. We must try to keep remembering that our plan for urban design is a process of people working together.

The questions that we answered will be used by specialists—engineers, architects, landscape architects and so on—to come up with more detailed designs, buildings, streets, play areas and ponds. If we have begun to understand the first year's development, we can begin to understand all of New Town.[17]

Porterfield and his team, with Rohrbach and his staff, were attempting a form of "action research" for urban planning. Rather than using an applied research or a conventional design consulting approach, they were attempting to create a new base of knowledge for the design of cities based on an idealistic notion of American participatory democracy.

14 Financial Analysis

The programs discussed thus far resulted in a flow of money from the development corporation. These were the project's front-end costs. The financial analysis program was to organize those costs so that they could be recouped and profit realized.

The largest amount of front-end costs came in the acquisition of the land. The purchase of 5,000 acres of land adjacent to a busy metropolitan area is a significant expenditure. Huber's initial plan to acquire land tract by tract, as needed, had been abandoned. Various other methods from outright purchase to options to buy property were used instead to bring the necessary acreage under control (the bulk of the land was controlled by options).

Loans were secured by mortgages on substantially all the land (approximately one thousand acres) that was purchased outright. These loans bore interest of between 6 and 8 percent and were due $15,730 in 1972, $122,292 in 1973, $83,596 annually from 1974 through 1977, $75,679 in 1978, $63,379 in 1979, $33,708 in 1980, and $85,000 in 1981. The additional land, 4,391 acres on which the development corporation obtained options to purchase, would cost an aggregate price of $9,642,697. The options on this land would expire from 28 June 1972 through 15 July 1976, and option payments were to be forfeited if not exercised. The terms of these options called for cash payments aggregating approximately $5,431,530 when exercised and the balance in purchase money mortgaged at 6 to 8 percent over periods up to eight years.[1] The necessary investment in the approximately five-thousand-acre site was approximately $10,375,373 from 1972 to 1998, which meant that the development corporation would be paying almost $2,100 per acre.

To request first a change in zoning laws and then the rezoning of these over five-thousand acres was also an expensive venture. There were legal and technical expenses required from the process of amending and creating laws through the approval of master-plan zoning to the many phase, subdivision, and variance requests. In addition, there was the continuing cost of the communication effort (the presentations, monthly newsletter, and office displays).

The fee to submit the HUD application alone was $10,000, and this was only the beginning of the expenses linked with relations with HUD. The many technical engineering, design, and planning reports plus again the legal fees and the public relations necessary to get the application process moving made it one of the more costly programs.

But there were many lucrative financial benefits to the developer once the application was approved. The Urban Growth and New Community Development Act of 1970, which was Title VII of the Housing and Urban Development Act of 1970, authorized the HUD secretary, acting through the Community Development Corporation, to guarantee obligations issued by public and private developers to help finance new community development projects. Proceeds from the sale of obligations guaranteed under Title VII could be used only to finance land acquisition and land development. As defined by Title VII, land development was generally limited to grading; to providing water, sewer, and other utility installations; to installing roads, sidewalks, and storm drainage; to constructing public facilities; and to other installations or work that the secretary could deem necessary or desirable to prepare land for residential, commercial, industrial, or other uses or to provide facilities for public or common use. However, Title VII also provided priority treatment in obtaining federal grants and a possible new community supplementary grant that was available for certain facilities and services.

In the HUD application, the Huber Development Group and the interim community authority requested guarantees amounting to $14 and $17 million respectively. The private developer intended to issue $12 million of the authorized $14 million of debentures to finance land acquisition and development. The public developer, acting at an "arm's-length" from the private developer, would issue its guaranteed debentures for public facilities.

It was Rohrbach's responsibility as general manager to coordinate all the activities connected with the New Town, and the financial analysis program was a crucial segment of the overall process. As stated in his job description, the general manager would "control procedures both in financial and other areas. He would establish budgets, forecasts, quotas and establish compensation schedules and policies for the staff."[2] To fulfill this responsibility Rohrbach developed the financial analysis program as part of the overall project plan. There were four principal components of this program: the economic model, which was the continual financial analysis of the project and conceptual land-use plans as they evolved; HUD relations in financial affairs; the development and ongoing monitoring of an operating budget; and the search for an equity partner.[3]

Much work was done by Rohrbach in the spring, summer, and fall of 1972 to develop this program. The project and concept plan were analyzed for their financial implications. HUD's staff raised some serious questions about the land appraisal and other financial matters that were responded to by the New Town staff. A budget was completed and revised as the project developed. In the summer of 1972 the search for an equity partner commenced. As stated in the proposal that was developed in that search, "The Donald L. Huber Corporation wishes to enter into an equity participation arrangement, whereby the participant will receive a thirty percent equity ownership position in the New Town land development project in exchange for a three million dollar cash investment."[4] The proposal further stated the joint venture's primary function was for the acquisition of land for the project and the development of land for sale to purchasers, which may include entities controlled by or affiliated with the venture, who would then construct improvements. It was proposed that the project be constructed as a joint venture partnership with the New Town development corporation (which would be a wholly owned subsidiary of the Donald L. Huber Corporation) being a seventy percent general partner and the outside investor, being a thirty percent united partner. The partnership form of ownership would then allow both the immediate realization of federal income tax benefits and subsequent distribution of profits and equity investment from the venture. This partnership structure would also permit consolidation of all earnings generated by the project into the partner's financial statement.

There were several attractive features about the New Town from the point of view of a potential investor, but these features were risky and hinged, to some extent, on federal approval. According to the project's early economic model, the New Town's ability to finance the purchase of land, develop and create value in that land in order to repay a partner's investment began in the fourth year and returned to the thirty percent equity partner an average annual 25 percent return on investment. In addition to the land-development project, the New Town would provide an opportunity for other real estate equity investment. The Donald L. Huber Corporation was to participate in the construction and operation of commercial, industrial, and multifamily buildings. The total estimated value of these units, in 1972 dollars, was as follows:

Commercial . . . . $ 20,000,000
Industrial . . . . $ 90,000,000
Multifamily . . . . $100,000,000.[5]

The equity proposal noted that because all land would be controlled and developed by the land-development company, financed with government-guaranteed debentures, it was possible to create a "monopolistic situation." Therefore, the proposal concluded, the potential opportunities to a partner were unlimited.[6]

There were serious problems developing in the management of the New Town. What was developed and suggested by Gerwin Rohrbach and what was practiced and listened to by Donald Huber were seldom similar. This was especially true in the financial analysis program.

On 18 April Rohrbach submitted a memorandum to Huber. In it he recommended certain staffing priorities and specifically stated that the existing staff was not competent to handle the economic systems function and that an experienced, highly competent economic analyst/ urban land-use economist with accounting experience be hired to fill the position of director of finance.[7] Rohrbach never received a response to this memorandum directly from Huber. However, vice-president of finance Turner repeatedly emphasized orally that the economic systems function had to be retained in the corporate office in Kettering; that the staff, made up of accountants with local building experience, that had been assigned this task was competent; and that, in any case, it would be unwise to change horses in midstream because the HUD review was imminent.

As the summer months passed, it became increasingly obvious that little or no relationship existed between what was being done on the economic model in Kettering and what was being done in the New

Town office. The primary difference was that the accountants in the corporate office were oriented to tasks as compared to those in the New Town office who were oriented to process.

By the end of July Rohrbach felt that the situation was reaching a crisis. He requested a meeting with Huber that became a very emotional session. Rohrbach insisted that the staff working on the economic model be transferred to Trotwood, or he would resign, because he was beginning to realize at that time that a failure to produce viable economic models for the private developer and the community authority would be made to be his fault, even though he lacked real power in this area.

On 13 August the staff senior accountant, Roger Berardinis, was assigned to the New Town office. Immediately, Rohrbach requested in writing that Berardinis develop a detailed subtask network with manpower allocations so that it could be determined what assistance was needed to accomplish the financial work task and so that those tasks could be better defined. They included the development of the fiscal impact statement and the continual adjustment of the economic model through the ongoing financial analysis of the project plan as well as other tasks in the program like the operating budget.[8] Though he disliked working at the Trotwood office, the major fiscal impact study was completed by Berardinis and the New Town staff with the consulting assistance of the Public Administration Service of Chicago and submitted to HUD in October.

On 5 October Berardinis sent a letter of resignation to Huber, giving his last day of work as 20 October. Rohrbach was not informed of this resignation until the evening of 11 October, which left him seven working days to find a replacement. This period was a delicate time because of the negotiations that were going on with HUD concerning the release of the environmental impact statement for review and the consideration of the HUD application by the Community Development Corporation Board. The outcome of these vital negotiations hinged to a large extent on the content of the economic model.

In mid-October Rohrbach found himself in an awkward position. The application was his responsibility, but though he had requested a thorough economic program and competent staff for months, he lacked the real power in the decision that had been made relative to financing and marketing for the economic model. And, in spite of the successful programs that had been completed by the New Town staff from the submission of planning reports and successful governmental negotiation to the development of an active citizen participation program and the emergence of construction guidelines and standards, the success of the project relied on an area over which the planning staff had no real control.

15 Marketing and Sales

In the project plan the marketing and sales program was separated from public relations in that public relations sold the New Town concept, while marketing and sales was to sell the real estate. Marketing was considered as an intellectual function of research and planning. Sales was considered to be the function of implementation.

The New Town had several potential marketing advantages over its competition in the Dayton metropolitan area. They arose from the density allowed by zoning, the expenses that would be incurred by the community authority, and the federal guaranteed loans and grants. Master plan zoning allowed for a gross density of only four dwelling units per acre but a net of up to forty in some multifamily areas. By concentrating the areas of development, the situation was created whereby Huber could recoup substantial front-end costs by selling undeveloped land to the community authority for its open space system. The community authority could also provide an amenity package at no cost to the private New Town development corporation that could not be equaled by any other area developer. Furthermore, the loans and grants provided through the federal approval could provide the physical infrastructure of the community at little or no cost to the private developer, thus alleviating one of the heaviest normal front-end costs.

The New Town's marketing and sales program began to emerge in April and June of 1972 as Rohrbach completed his project and staff plan. Research was compiled about the market area from which goals for the New Town were projected. These marketing goals were then prioritized in relationship to the economic model and the concept plan, and finally sales programs were developed for the first phase. The effectiveness of the sales program would then be measured and revised for subsequent phases. Rohrbach requested that a director of marketing and research be hired to manage this program with a staff that would include a sales director, research assistant, and the necessary consultants.

There had been dual sets of research that had been compiled for the New Town. The first report on the market potential for the project was done by the Battelle Memorial Institute for the HUD application. After these projects were rejected by the HUD staff, a second report was completed in April by the Real Estate Research Corporation (RERC). The most important element of the second report, the one on which Rohrbach based his planning, was the projection of overall growth of the market area. The market area of the New Town, as defined by RERC, was basically Montgomery and western Green counties. Since most of the Dayton Standard Metropolitan Statistical Area (SMSA) growth was contemplated to take place in these counties, the projection of the total SMSA growth could determine the magnitude of the housing market from which the New Town could draw its share.[1]

This share was computed by first determining the regional supply and demand for housing. Demand for housing units was derived from projections developed both by Battelle and RERC that considered two main factors: household formation and replacement and vacancy rates. Battelle projected the formation of 73,531 households during the twenty-year marketing period of the New Town, or 3,700 households per year. The growth trend would slow with population growth declining markedly after 1985. Battelle projected that the Dayton SMSA would virtually stop growing by 1990 because of declining birth rates and out-migration. RERC, assuming a decline in the birthrate and out-migration but not a complete stop in growth, arrived at a projected total household formation of 106,741 over the twenty-year marketing period.

To further translate these household formulation figures into projections of housing demand for the Dayton SMSA, it was necessary to add the demand created by demolition, fire, and abandonment of existing units and by the vacancy factor in existing and new units. Using local records, RERC estimated that the demolitions at the time of their study amounted to some twelve hundred units annually. They felt that this rate should increase because of urban growth until 1990, when the effects of the projected slowdown in growth of the SMSA could be expected to stabilize the demolition rate.

Vacancy of housing units was another factor that could influence the overall demand for housing. In 1960 the United States census showed a vacancy rate of 4.8 percent. In 1970 this had fallen to 3.35 percent, which RERC felt indicated a somewhat tight market reflecting a slight shortage of supply because of the inavailability of resident mortgage funds during the late 1960s. RERC projected, however, a rise in the overall vacancy rate because of the increase in rental units into the housing supply.[2]

Using these factors, RERC computed the demand for the Dayton SMSA. The census indicated that 49,388 housing units had been created in the Dayton SMSA as compared with total population increase of 155,643 during the decade between 1960 and 1970. Thus, both housing and population increased by 22 percent (or, a unit was built for every 3.1 persons). Because RERC projected that in the long run vacancy in new units would rise and persons per household would continue to decrease, they also projected housing units to increase at a faster rate than population.

With Battelle's assumptions, there would be a projected twenty-year demand of 104,195 units for a population increase of 215,652. Housing would grow by 27 percent, while population would increase by 24 percent. Alternatively, a unit would be built for every 2.8 persons. RERC's projections yielded a twenty-year demand of 138,788 units. The net increase would be 111,188 units for a population increase of 320,707. A unit would then be built for every 2.9 persons.

RERC found while computing the supply in the area that there was a significant trend towards multifamily units. (In 1966, multifamily units consisted of 28.5 percent of the housing market, while in 1971 they accounted for 58.8 percent.) As in most metropolitan areas, this trend reflected a number of changes not only in patterns of living and taste, but also in the cost of producing single-family housing (townhouses and other types of single-family detached housing were considered multifamily by RERC).[3]

There were several reasons why multifamily housing was capturing a larger share of the residential housing market. First, land development and construction cost increases pushed single-family housing out of the reach of a significant portion of American families. There were the increases in the variety of design available in the multifamily field. There was also the introduction of the condominium and townhouse ownership concepts that broadened the marketing appeal of these types of units. In addition, apartments became more desirable because they featured the avoidance of maintenance and security problems. Finally, the amenity packages offered with multifamily developments were in many cases superior to those of single-family home subdivisions.

This trend had been evident nationwide, and Dayton was following it. RERC expected that the proportion of multifamily units would not rise as fast over the twenty-year period from 1972 to 1992 as it had done over the previous ten years. However, RERC did believe that it was reasonable to assume that approximately 60 percent of the dwelling units constructed in the Dayton SMSA during that period would be multifamily units.

The evaluation of the New Town's share of this housing market was made extremely difficult by the fact that the concept was untested. The developer and HUD believed that a well-located and well-planned New Town could offer enough attractions in the form of recreation and opportunities for open space, planned residential environments, and proximity to schools and shops to attract substantial shares of the regional housing market. However, to arrive at specific market conclusions from this general point of departure was strictly an exercise in judgment.

The New Town was not a residential development; it was a community. It would not be offering only expensive townhouses or inexpensive apartments or subsidized apartments or detached houses, but all of these and more at a variety of price and rents. This was to be a program of simultaneous residential marketing unlike any existing development in the Dayton SMSA.

RERC made a number of general assumptions that it considered to be essential to the judgments that had been made regarding resident growth and capture rates. These assumptions concerned the general economy, the local economy, and any number of contingencies. However, RERC felt that it was necessary to state only two assumptions that were basic to their projections. The first was that the Wolf Creek Expressway had to be built at an early date so that easy access could be made available to downtown Dayton by 1980 at the latest. The second was the RERC felt that Route 35 had to be completed westward from Dayton to Union Road by the mid-1970s (see map 2).[4]

Given these assumptions, projections were made for the estimated growth capture rate of each township in the two-county area for the period from 1975 to 1995, which were to some extent based on growth patterns that had been established in the decade from 1960 to 1970. Through these calculations, it was determined that Madison Township was not expected to be one of the strongest growth areas; it was projected to capture 5.8 percent of the total SMSA growth. Concentrating on what was considered to be the main drawing area for the New Town, Montgomery County plus the three western townships of Greene County, Madison was expected to receive 6.7 percent of this growth.

The double attraction of an early completion of high-grade access to Dayton and the creation of the New Town was certain to increase these capture rates substantially. It should be then possible for Madison Township to capture twelve percent of the total SMSA growth once good access had been established. This would bring its experience in line with the townships of the area that exhibited high growth from 1960 through 1970. RERC figured that the New Town could be expected to account for some 85 percent of the Madison Township growth.

The growth outlined by RERC was of a much more concentrated nature than that envisioned by Battelle. This was precisely what new communities were designed to do, that is, concentrate growth into a smaller area than would have otherwise been the case. Once the New Town was under way and access had been established, RERC anticipated that the New Town could capture at least ten percent of the total SMSA growth. RERC used capture rates of this magnitude for the post-1980 years. Under Battelle's assumption of dwindling growth, the post-1980 capture rates ran at twelve percent. If Dayton did, in fact, what was projected by Battelle, the competitive situation would certainly not be as strong as otherwise. RERC projected that before the 1980s the capture rates would be much lower, on the order of seven percent. The combined effect of this prognosis was an overall capture of 8.6 percent of the total SMSA growth expected between 1973 and 1992.[5]

Rohrbach used RERC's report for the basis of the conceptual land-use plan that was submitted to HUD as part of the environmental impact statement, part of the zoning program, and for calculations concerning the financial analysis and review of the economic model.

Rohrbach continued to request a director of marketing and research to develop and implement this program. In early July, Huber decided to appoint Rohrbach's adversary Warren Hyser acting director of marketing and research. In many ways this caused more problems than it solved. Rohrbach and Hyser were constantly at odds. After about a month, Hyser began to spend less time at the New Town office and more at the Kettering office. Nevertheless, by early September a marketing plan and sales program began to emerge. Robert Spicer, who had been on the sales staff at Columbia, Maryland, was retained as a sales consultant. Together with Rohrbach and Berardinis, Hyser and Spicer developed a marketing plan for the first phase. On 1 August the New Town's local advertising agency was terminated and Ivan Chermayeff was hired simultaneously to develop a name and graphics standards for the project, and a local public-relations firm was hired to implement those standards. These efforts were then to be coordinated with the New Town Environmental Planning Group and meshed into a sales program. Chermayeff was asked to present the criteria that he had developed first to the New Town staff then to a joint urban design team-citizen's meeting.

On 27 October Ivan Chermayeff and an associate editor of *Saturday Review* flew in from New York to present his proposed standards. The first meeting in the afternoon with the New Town staff included Huber, Laird, Rohrbach, Rausch, Kreines, and Rohrbach's assistant.

"First of all I don't think the name should be controversial," commented Donald Huber. "I'd like my name to be connected with this town's name in some way, I mean I don't think it should be like Huber Heights or Huberville, it should be more like how an artist signs a painting. You know, Brookwood or whatever *by* Donald Huber, with Don Huber in script. I've seen other developers use this quite effectively, it adds a real personal touch." The graphic designer just nodded.

That evening a presentation was made to a joint NEPG/JCNTPC meeting. Chermayeff presented the following criteria as both positive and negative considerations for the process that would determine the final selection of the name for the new community:

1. One single, simple, spellable, pronounceable, name.
2. A special name. One which will not be confused or associated with other towns in the area or state.

3. A name which brings to mind pleasant associations or images appropriate to the goals and aspirations which exist in the minds of the people considering a community and a home in which to spend a major portion of their lives.
4. A name which is neither misleading nor pretentious. In other words, a name which does not suggest qualities which might exist but in fact do not. The town must live up to its name.
5. The name when heard or seen must within reason set the imagination to work, yet the name cannot be fashionable. It must be timeless in order that it not become somebody else's yesterday.
6. The name should lend itself to a strong visual identity. It must be promotable efficiently and consistently. It would be valuable but not essential if editors, writers, journalists and copywriters were able to do something with the selected name.
7. The name should be explainable. The more related the name is to people or places already known or understood, the easier and better and more convincing such an explanation could be.
8. The name does not stand alone but it should be able to, with or without an explanation.[6]

Chermayeff was accustomed to developing names and logos for large corporations, and the subrural Ohio schoolhouse packed with citizens was quite a departure from the New York boardrooms. Nevertheless, it became apparent to those involved that the expertise of a graphic designer and a magazine editor could play a vital role in creating the image of their city. After all, much of urban design is concerned with the visual image of place, and the name of a place plays an essential role in creating an image. What was derived from the meeting was that for the New Town to be truly a "new" town, its name had to be at least partly generated by those who might live in and around it and those consultants involved in designing the perimeters in which it was to be built.

Meanwhile, in early September, Rohrbach recommended to Huber that Hyser be transferred back to the Kettering office because of what Rohrbach termed both his "unsuitability to the tasks which needed to be done and because of his disruptive tactics." At the same time he had also requested that Berardinis be transferred back and that new people be hired to fill both spots. Huber compromised and Hyser returned to the corporate office to become Huber's administrative assistant.

In late October, Rohrbach learned that Huber had assigned Hyser and to the Kettering office the task of recalculating the land and housing unit absorption rates as well as the housing mix. Hyser used Battelle data, which Rohrbach and others had not been able to verify, and techniques from Huber's local experience for the new projections. For several months, Huber had indicated that he did not agree with RERC's estimates that projected, as the years went by, an increasing number of dwelling units in the multifamily or apartment categories. Donald Huber was convinced that there would be a swing back to single-family occupancy.

The RERC report, however, recommended a 60 percent multifamily and 40 percent detached single-family overall mix for the New Town by 1992. It projected a certain number of units to be marketed each year through 1992 with a total of 11,900 units for a population of approximately 40,000, depending on what family size was used for planning. This projected mix would provide at least a sound basis to plan and build a community with a broad range of life-styles and housing opportunities for the widest possible range of families and incomes. It could also provide the basis for a physical arrangement of types of housing on the land that would relate to the environmental constraints as well as provide a community that could develop on a sound economic base whereby the cost of services could be supported by an income assessment. This factor of density was an extremely crucial factor in the concept of new towns as opposed to the typical suburban low-density pattern that had been prevalent.

The RERC report had been accepted by Huber at the time of its completion and had formed the basis for the revised concept plan developed during the planning task force meetings that was submitted as part of the environmental impact statement. This plan was subsequently accepted by HUD as the New Town's land-use plan. It was also used as the basis for the conceptual land-use zoning plan that was approved by both Montgomery County and Madison Township. Previously, it had provided the basis for the housing plan submitted to MVRPC and the State of Ohio as part of the A-95 review process. Both the regional planning agency and the state accepted these plans, and Huber himself had used the data for various presentations and speeches. It was, therefore, assumed by Rohrbach that the general housing mix and the rates of land and unit absorption were generally acceptable and could form the basis of sound input into the economic model.

But during the autumn of 1972 Huber increasingly questioned the total number of units projected by RERC as being marketable as well as the mix and other aspects of the housing market that had been suggested. Huber implied that the mix might be reversed, that is, 60 percent be single-family detached and 40 percent be multifamily with 40 percent of the single-family units built being retained as rentals. These suggestions were at variance with what experienced professionals in the field were recommending. Rohrbach felt that if Huber's suggestions were used in making basic marketing and sales decisions on the New Town, it could prevent a real new community from emerging on the outskirts of Dayton.

As with the other programs, by October the marketing and sales program was emerging into a viable process that had been planned by Rohrbach. But with its emergence, another direction was being taken by the project's owner that negated the process development.

16 Utilities and Construction

Ian McHarg has stated, "A plumber is a most important member of society—our civilization could not endure long without his services" (1969, p. 32). In the case of the New Town near Dayton, Ohio, the plumber was indeed a crucial part of the process. Before the project construction could be commenced the infrastructure had to be designed and built.

As with planning, finance, and marketing, Rohrbach had requested a director of construction and development in his April staffing memorandum.[1] As with the positions of director of finance and marketing, action on the hiring of a director of construction had been delayed by Huber though several well qualified candidates, including Carlton Laird, who had extensive experience in the area of public utilities, were contacted and interviewed. The responsibility for the various work tasks necessary for completing these programs fell again on Rohrbach and the increasingly overburdened New Town staff.

The utilities and construction program was interrelated with all the other programs. Ralph Scott's environmental monitoring and land-management programs were directly related to the effect of the installation of utilities and the construction of facilities. The zoning plan fixed, to a certain extent, where all the physical structures would be located. The community authority could greatly assist in absorbing land costs and would be responsible for the construction of public facilities. With HUD approval the construction costs of those facilities and of the major private developments would be financed through both guaranteed loans and direct grants. Public relations, as the selling of the concept, and marketing, as the selling of the real estate, were related in the determination of types of individuals who would be attracted to the project and the kind of structures that would be built. The jurisdictional relations played a vital role in the manner in which services would be provided to the New Town. Although certain items were fixed by zoning, they were refined through the planning and urban design program. Planning criteria were developed by the urban design consultant with the citizen's group. These criteria enabled other land-planning consultants, architects, and the New Town staff to begin detailed design. Finally the cost of construction and the sources of those funds to pay for it were a vital part of the financial analysis of the economic model.

The utilities program began in May after the agreement had been reached between the cities of Dayton and Trotwood. Before commitment was made by the private developer to annex part of the project to Dayton, the city had threatened not to extend water or sewer lines to the New Town. With this agreement the city agreed to extend services, with the provision that if annexation commitment was not followed then there would be no services.

The City of Dayton had, during the high-growth periods of the 1950s and the 1960s, extended trunk lines to any area of the county that had requested them. This policy changed in the early 1970s under the leadership of city administrator Anthony Char. The city had adopted a policy of no annexation, no water or sewer. The New Town became its first opportunity to test this policy. Even with city approval, certain actions had to be taken to insure water and sewer, telephone and electrical services to the New Town. Telephone service and electricity were items that had to be negotiated for directly with the public corporations that were responsible for the area, which were General Telephone and Dayton Power and Light. In the case of water, negotiations had to be made directly with the city. Water services were already available to the first phase area and a major portion of the annexation corridor, so water was not a priority consideration.

No sewage services existed in any section of the New Town; the residents who were already there depended on septic tanks. In order to provide sewer services, new districts had to be formed to extend trunk lines to the project. A strategy was developed to form two districts to avoid possible controversy in the New Town area. The first, which was to be called the North Branch Sewer District, would serve the first phase area. The formation of this district could be accomplished with little controversy, because sewer line already extended to the City of Trotwood and because land in the North Branch Sewer District was controlled by Huber and by other developers interested in obtaining sewer service. Action on the second, which was to be called the Wolf Creek Sewer District, could be delayed until after the project was under way.

Other innovative types of services, like cable television and solar heating, were discussed intermittently by Huber, Rohrbach, and Laird. But because of inadequate staffing and lack of time, serious efforts in these areas were delayed.

Through the summer several candidates had been interviewed for the position of director of construction, and no action had been taken. Still, Rohrbach pushed for a March 1973, groundbreaking, which would depend on several crucial factors, including HUD approval.

Negotiations for telephone, electrical, and water proceeded to a point where by October those services were reasonably assured for at least the first phase area. The formation of the North Branch Sewer District was delayed for a time because of some uncertainty about the size of the area it should encompass, but by late October these services were also reasonably assured. Preliminary utility planning had been completed by the Ralph Woolpert Company for the environmental impact statement and, as items became fixed by zoning, other consultants, and the New Town planning staff, more detailed engineering began to evolve by the autumn of 1972.

This process was repeated for each specific item of the New Town. For instance, engineering studies were done for possible lake sites for the first phase area in June. These studies were developed for zoning and then refined by Scott, Kreines, Rohrbach, and the project landscape architect. Once the lake plans reached this point they were reviewed by the NEPG team and citizens and refined further. Final lake sites were then determined for phase-one zoning plans and given to the convenience center architect. At this point the architect assembled not only the physical data that had been collected but also all the pertinent information from related programs. The convenience center was to be used also for a sales center, so efforts had to be coordinated with the marketing and sales program. It would also be used by the community authority, so input by Carlton Laird and the interim trustees was essential. A similar process was used for transportation and housing planning, the location of schools and convenience centers, and the routes of water and sewer lines.

By November 1972, final engineering and design on the first phase was well under way, and engineering had begun for the total project. But still the March groundbreaking depended on the resolution of many issues.

17 Summary

Perhaps the best summation of the New Town's planning process is an analysis of how the project's key participants, Donald Huber and Gerwin Rohrbach, viewed each program in relationship to the total process.

Huber's initial approach to land acquisition was to use the same method that his family had always used in the Dayton area. New Town development, however, was different from typical subdivision development. This difference included both the necessary governmental negotiations and requirements plus the more rapid inflation of land values. Rohrbach had developed a team approach, using both real estate and legal consultants with the New Town staff to bring the land under control. The team was assisted by an informative communications program that sold the concept to the public.

Once the land was controlled, Huber had attempted to manage the over five thousand acres through the use of a farm-management company that he had used with much smaller developments. When this company proved inadequate to manage a project the size of the New Town, Rohrbach suggested hiring Ralph Scott. Scott then began to develop a comprehensive land-management and ecological monitoring program.

The initial zoning strategy had been to attempt to convince specific responsible officials that the new community was a good idea. This was tried through private presentations and by flying the officials to Columbia, Reston, and Jonathan. Rohrbach realized that if zoning was to be approved, more than the officials had to be convinced of the project's validity. It would take no grass-roots opposition and some support. The cultivation of this support was done in conjunction with the information effort used for the acquisition of the land. These supporters were then later incorporated into the citizen participation process.

Donald Huber conceived the community authority as an entity to alleviate some of the pressures on new-community developers that resulted from residents' complaints arising during the extended development periods that new towns required. Concurrently, by being responsible for public improvements and human services, it could offer an attractive package of amenities to potential residents and make the project application more attractive to federal officials.

Rohrbach saw the community authority as a mechanism that would provide the ordinary citizen with the power to dictate his own future by being a democratic entity that could act as an intermediary between business and government. He also believed that if the community authority could work in the New Town, its principles could be applied to other urban situations.

Initially, under the direction of Huber and Hyser, it was felt that the HUD application would be approved in a matter of a few months through the influence of friendly politicians and the use of consultants who had political influence with the Office of New Communities. This approach continued to persist in the Kettering office after Rohrbach was functioning as general manager. Rohrbach's approach to the HUD application was to use competent consultants and staff with honest, direct dealing in the various negotiations.

Before Rohrbach's arrival, public relations were handled by Huber's small-city advertising agency, which had little or no competence in dealing with the New Town, and the skeleton staff of students who worked intermittently at the Trotwood office. Rohrbach's public relations consisted of operating an open office that was accessible to any interested individual or group. This was supplemented by the informative communications program. The open system produced positive results in the local press, which was continually featuring favorable stories about the New Town.

The manner in which relations were handled with existing local governments prior to Rohrbach's arrival was similar to the way that zoning and HUD relations were approached. Huber depended on his personal relationship with local officials to carry the project. But skepticism on the part of old allies arising from other federally assisted projects, the hiring of Rausch, and the variance of promises that Huber made to different officials placed the situation in turmoil in the midst of the A-95 review process. To resolve the problems in this area Rohrbach suggested the use of an impartial interventionist who was able to help the involved parties find some solutions. From that point, it was Rohrbach and the New Town staff who spearheaded the effort to insure that the commitments made concerning those solutions were met.

At the time when potential urban design consultants were being interviewed, Donald Huber wrote a memorandum to Gerwin Rohrbach that summed up how he viewed urban design and planning. "In reviewing the correspondence to the various consultants on urban design," the third-generation Dayton builder wrote, "I note very few references to the development of an urban design map. I am curious if you [Rohrbach] are planning to use the urban design consultant for this purpose. It would seem fairly important to the project. Perhaps the reference you have made to sketches, drawings and plans includes the overall master urban design map."[1]

Many planners, like Gans, believed that one problem of the planning profession was the production of master plans that had no way of being implemented or, in the case of some programs like urban renewal, were damaging to the social and physical environments. Rohrbach felt that urban design had to go beyond the mere production of master-plan maps and reports that were completed unilaterally by professionals for sponsors. Planners had to begin to create a broader criteria for urban design that were based not only on their own expertise and that of architects and engineers, but also that of social scientists, ecologists, and ordinary citizens. Furthermore, the power of implementation was needed.

Huber viewed citizen participation as the use of blue-ribbon, select citizen types of committees, where Rohrbach viewed citizen involvement as developing from a much more diverse base. Huber saw citizen-involvement groups as impotent bodies removed from the decision-making process. Rohrbach sought to involve citizens as an intricate part of the whole process.

Genevieve Carter reviewed several motivations for action research that affect the nature of the research as well as its utilization (1952). These motivators are similar to those of the New Town's key participants, in relation to how citizen involvement was viewed. The first category Carter detailed was persuasive involvement, which at one point in the process motivated Rohrbach. Rohrbach persuaded Neil

Porterfield of the use of a citizen participation model that sought the objective of substantiating decisions that Rohrbach had already made in several official reports regarding how public involvement should evolve.

Carter's second category was escape involvement, which was Huber's prime motivation. Huber requested participation to delay and avoid action and controversy. Involvement was not intended to lead to action but to preclude it. He was interested in finding the "right people," with little involvement from minorities or low-income people except in a superficial way.

Carter's third category was involvement that led to intelligent social action. Except for when Rohrbach was using persuasive tactics to substantiate his own position, during a period of heavy stress, this type of involvement was his primary motivator, as it was for Neil Porterfield and those involved in the NEPG team. Both Rohrbach and Porterfield saw the need for a different approach to environmental design but realized that there was not the necessary existing process. So they devised a process that would create new knowledge and new skills that could be applied to the New Town and then to other situations.

When Huber appointed Hyser acting director of marketing and research he stated in a memorandum to Rohrbach that he was uncertain of what Rohrbach had in mind for research. This question in many ways exemplified the difference in not only how each viewed the marketing program, but the whole project. Huber recognized the importance of each task but failed to see the relationship of one to the other. To Rohrbach every task was a part of the overall planning process. He felt that marketing research was a vital part of the data base for both the specific marketing and sales program and the entire project plan.

Huber's attitude about the project was further exemplified by how he perceived its naming. He had a paternalistic view of the project: it would be the New Town *by* Donald Huber. To Rohrbach the naming was an integral part of the overall process that affected its visual image, its sales potential, and its livableness.

Rohrbach also believed that financial planning should be coordinated with the total planning effort by those decisions. This was prevented by Donald Huber who insisted on controlling financial planning and forced it to evolve in a different direction than the rest of the project. Though he supported the New Town staff's efforts in planning and in successful negotiations with various bodies, Huber chose to ignore the essential qualities of what was planned and communicated.

Huber was not an unintelligent man. He could and did see the importance of singular tasks, like those decisions involved in the provision of utilities to the project and in construction. He did fail to grasp the many interrelationships between tasks. Rohrbach did understand the process and attempted to make it a part of corporate policy through official reports, correspondence, conversation, and other action. But the manner in which each viewed the process was of secondary importance to the values that motivated his involvement. Huber was a shrewd businessman. His business was building houses. He saw the new-town concept, coupled with HUD Title VII support, as a reasonable business venture and a personal legacy. Huber was a "nice," soft-spoken man who used his political savvy to the benefit of his business. By late 1971 Huber the businessman realized that he badly needed a manager to get the project moving. Gerwin Rohrbach appeared to have all the skills necessary to get the New Town off the ground. And during his tenure with the project incredible progress was made. What Huber did not expect was Rohrbach's commitment to involving local citizens in the decision-making process. This commitment was especially threatening to Huber.

Rohrbach was attempting a synthesis, or a series of syntheses, between the naturalistic idealism of British garden cities and the pragmatic realism of American greenbelt new towns. A synthesis between the McHarg type of ecological planning and the Gans type of socially oriented planning. A synthesis between organizing the poor, nonrepresented people and systems management. A synthesis between a federal program and private industry that was sensitive to both the site's ecosystem and its proximity to a large metropolitan area as well as to that region's major black community.

Because of the differences in how each viewed the process, and in the values of each point of view, by November 1972 the wealthy home builder and the intellectual general manager had created and nurtured two separate images of the New Town.

Donnybrook

18 The Resignations

On Tuesday, 28 November 1972, in his barren Trotwood apartment three blocks from the New Town office, Gerwin Rohrbach reflected on the New Town experience as it had evolved to that point.[1] He had returned from his home in St. Louis to pick up his few remaining belongings from the interim lodging. He spoke casually. "When I started my work in Dayton, the McKinsey project plan which had been prepared for Don in October, 1971, was little more than a sheet of paper. Almost all the work tasks contained in the plan were delinquent, many were overdue by months. I wasn't going to take the job. But I liked Don. He was saying all the right things when I first met him back in the autumn of 1971. But I never realized what a mess the project was in till I arrived in February."

As of 1 February 1972, when Rohrbach arrived as general manager of the New Town, land acquisition for both the first phase and the whole project was running behind, and the HUD land ownership statement was incomplete, because land acquisition was incomplete. Zoning resolutions had not been submitted to either Madison Township or Montgomery County, a zoning master plan had not been finished, and only casual presentations had been made to local officials concerning zoning. The HUD application had not been submitted, and much of the research for the application that had been completed was of such poor quality that it would have to be redone once it was reviewed by HUD. The environmental impact statement had been submitted to HUD in December, but it was of such a poor quality that it was totally rejected in March. Not only had the Community Authority Bill not been submitted to the Ohio General Assembly, but no workable draft had been produced nor had any worthwhile lobbying been started. In addition, work tasks related to community services,

marketing and sales, construction, utilities, and annexation were
seriously behind schedule.

The New Town office had been officially opened in Trotwood but it
was certainly not organized to function. There was very little furniture, no file system, and no displays. There were no contracts with any
consultants, only vague letters of agreement; no budgets or cost control procedures; and no records of correspondence. The staff that had
been accumulated was without leadership or professional training in
planning or large-scale development. To complicate matters there was
a growing mistrust of the developer, Donald Huber, by local officials
and low- and moderate-income citizens' groups.

When Rohrbach arrived there was a staggering number of tasks
that needed doing; some had to be done within a month or two, a significant number within a matter of weeks. First, the massive HUD
application was compiled, produced, and delivered within a two-and-
a-half-week period in February. Continual improvements and corrections were then made. The environmental impact statement was completely rewritten. The A-95 review approval was requested and was
secured both at the local and state levels by spring 1972. Land-management and acquisition programs were structured. A land ownership
statement was completed for HUD. A new community zoning amendment was drafted, submitted to local officials, explained at many
public meetings, subjected to public hearings, and unanimously
passed in both the township and county. Then a conceptual land-use
zoning plan was put through the same process and also unanimously
approved. So the 4,500-acre project was zoned for new-town development by autumn. An annexation program was devised and generally
agreed upon by various political bodies in May. The Community Authority Bill was drafted, lobbied for, and passed into law in June by
the Ohio General Assembly. Subsequently an interim director was
hired by the interim board of trustees. The planning task force, the
Joint Citizens New Town Planning Council, and other citizen-
participation groups were assisted in organization. Position descriptions were written; searches were conducted on a national level; and
key staff positions such as ecologist, director of planning, sales consultant, and graphics manager were filled. Other positions for director
of marketing, senior planner, director of construction and others were
in the interview stage by late autumn. Consultants were brought
under cost control and management procedures, while new and better

consultants replaced those who proved to be incompetent. Architects, a landscape architect, a street furniture designer and an urban design team were interviewed and selected with citizens participating in the selection process. A new fiscal impact statement was undertaken in August and was published and submitted to HUD in October after lengthy coordination with local governments. New appraisals meeting HUD guidelines were undertaken in October and nearly completed by the Real Estate Research Corporation by mid-November. A major public information program was organized and implemented with well-received presentations held at service clubs, churches, schools, and other public meeting places. A graphic design consultant was engaged to devise a name and graphics system for the New Town. Budgets were prepared and, with the use of cost control systems, incurred costs were kept at or below budget figures. A conceptual land-use plan was devised on accurate field data, market projections, regional planning goals, and intensive professional and citizen input. Finally marketing plans and sales programs were beginning to be devised to meet 1973 construction and sales goals, anticipating a March groundbreaking with the site planning for that first-year construction program well under way by November.

"The planning of a New Town is an extremely complex task." Rohrbach explained.

It requires the constant application of the many techniques of management such as planning, programming, and budgeting plus the use of economic theory, urban planning, politics, art, social sciences, public administration, engineering, law, biology, botony, ecology, political science, investment practice, transportation, philosophy, behavioral science, leadership, real estate practice, old-fashioned entrepreneurship, and so on, and so on, and so on.

Instead [in this case], decisions kept being made on gut reactions based on Don's experience as a Dayton home builder. Political manipulation and influence were assumed to be key to the decision-making process. Consultants weren't hired for the expertise, but to complete tasks deemed necessary by the developer.

One example of the way this operated was the first land appraisal conducted in December 1971 and January 1972. The report did not follow federal guidelines and was rejected by HUD, because it was suspected of contributing to a windfall profit. Other examples were the development of a project master plan without an adequate base map and assumptions that were made in the economic model that had little relationship to facts such as national trends, real estate economics, or public sector commitments and cost. Rohrbach continued.

> I tried many times to establish priorities and to develop strategies for carrying out these goals. They were the basis for the project plan-summary network which was really updated from the McKinsey report. We discussed this every other week at our staff conferences, which Don decided not to attend. He and I were supposed to meet alone on Saturday mornings, but that didn't work out either.
>
> He [Huber] focused completely on tasks. Everything that came up was a crisis, and I started to spend more and more time putting out brush fires.
>
> The scariest area was the fiscal planning. As the summer passed, it became increasingly obvious that there was little or no relationship between what was being done on the economic model in Kettering and what we were doing in Trotwood.

Rohrbach was partially responsible for this dichotomy. His frank opinions sometimes alienated others. His style was one of a strict taskmaster. The long hours and heavy work load that he required often caused people to resent him. But, Huber was also responsible. He approached the project as a series of tasks. He felt no accountability to the general public, even though he was seeking public financial support.

Rohrbach believed that the New Town required a systems approach where the organization was viewed as an integrated complex of many interdependent parts that would be capable of sensitive and accurate interaction among themselves and with their environment. "To take a systems point of view is not only to see the interconnections of things but also to look for process or flow," he said.

> Managers who use a systems approach tend to be adaptive planners. They seek to understand the essential difference between subsystem and total system optimization and the degree to which conventional attempts at control may aggravate the very conditions they are trying to prevent.
>
> The systems approach seeks to place the output of a subsystem in a total system context which is based on what can be found out about the true nature of the performance of the total system.
>
> That was the whole point of the large wall chart in my office, the project plan-summary network. I've called it the musical score to the New

Town symphony. As I saw it, the object was to plan and develop an economically, socially, physically, and politically viable New Town, not housing, shopping centers, or parks.

Talleyrand once said, "War is much too serious to be left to military men." The same thing could be said about new towns. They are much too serious to be left to builders, and planners, in the traditional sense.

In the systems approach, before a solution can be found, it is necessary to discover why a particular phenomenon behaves the way it does. To determine underlying causation, the questioning process has to include both the measurement of characteristics and their systematic analysis. Causation in turn implies flow from cause to effect.

"With the New Town," Rohrbach continued, "we had to consider the interconnections, the compatibility, the effect of each action upon the other, the objectives of the whole, the relationship of the system to the uses and the economic feasibility, more than parts standing in isolation or the functional components. The problem solving process then begins with a statement of the problem. Don never understood process. He couldn't relate to it. I think that's why he got frustrated and stopped attending staff conferences."

Nor could Hyser or Berardinis understand the process. This added to the hostility after they were transferred from Kettering to Trotwood. As the feuding between the two offices and the developer and general manager grew from late summer to early fall, Huber took more action to regain control of the project. His actions would be contrary to publicly stated New Town policy. Rohrbach perceived this as Huber trying to disrupt the process and as illogical activity. Confusion would arise from this, responsible officials would turn to Rohrbach, and he would try to take corrective action that would usually alienate Huber further.

One example of such action were several statements that the developer made to Trotwood councilmen. First he stated that low- and moderate-income housing commitments could be circumvented. This he hoped would convince these officials to approve the community authority. Instead several councilmen questioned the developer's motives and turned to Rohrbach and Rausch. This angered Huber, who threatened that if the officials did not approve the community authority, he would build another Huber Heights. These actions caused Rohrbach to doubt if the developer were really interested in positive social change or building a new community at all. He also began to question the whole premise that the federal government should subsidize private developers' front-end costs and new towns in general.

"While extensive sums were used for political contributions, adequate funds were never made available to be allocated to the community authority," lamented the general manager. "As it started to become obvious in October when we were closely analyzing the economic model for the community authority, there would be little or no funds available for any real social services in the first few years of development. The only conclusion that I could come to was that the New Town was just an illusion. Unless there are massive injections of federal funds in the form of grants and low interest loans, the New Town is potentially nothing more than a series of subdivisions. Implementation of important social goals such as education, health, and other community services was remote, especially for the first few years, because of the priorities of the private developer."

Rohrbach believed in the community authority concept. He also disagreed with how he had seen it implemented. He felt that if part of the rationale for the community authority was to provide a vehicle for public participation and control in the decision-making process, it was essential that adequate time be given for this to happen. As the community authority had developed to November 1972, he had not seen this happen.

Beginning in March, the six members of the New Community Interim Non-Profit Corporation began to meet. A seventh member was added at the request of the ad hoc citizens group that had lobbied for the enabling legislation. Edward Rausch was assigned by Huber as liaison officer to trustees and an effort was made to allocate New Town staff to the Non-Profit Corporation.

Rohrbach concluded that "by summer it became obvious that additional personnel would be necessary to assist the Non-Profit Corporation and to establish an arm's-length relationship between the private and public developers."

During the summer budget discussions, a salary allocation was made for an interim executive director. At one meeting, where Washington attorney Reuben Clark was present, several candidates were suggested. Rohrbach had grown skeptical of Clark's influence and was troubled when he discovered that one of the candidates had assisted Clark and others in writing sections of the Housing Act of

1970, in particular Title VII. Rohrbach also felt it was no accident that Clark was involved with several other Title VII new towns and that in each case similar consultant teams were hired. One of the candidates whom Clark had suggested for the community authority position was employed by a firm of which a principal had assigned Clark and others to write the original Title VII legislation. A similar roster of consultants would arise with each new community application to HUD.

At the time that the Brookwood application was being considered, HUD was concerned because of scandals in the 235 and 236 housing programs about corruption in the building industry. Several questions were raised in the HUD application process about land appraisals that could potentially be manipulated not to reflect potential "windfall profits" to the developer. Rohrbach noted that he "was very much concerned that Don insisted Clark deal directly with the HUD staff on this matter, because he had been a party to the first appraisal which had been rejected by HUD. I guess what concerned me most was that once a project was approved by HUD and loans guaranteed, the developer was relatively safe."

This concern was investigated by Michael Haggans in his special report for the American Institute of Architects Research Corporation dealing with corruption in the built-environment. Haggans cited many examples of corruption in the building industry on all levels. He used one example of a former new-community executive who questioned what he felt to be a planned bankruptcy. When this indivudual approached his mortgage banker employer with the situation, the response that he received was, "As long as HUD guarantees the loans we don't give a damn."[2]

The two issues of the land appraisals and the community authority came to a head in October. Partly because of pressure from HUD, Huber agreed that the Real Estate Research Corporation be engaged to produce an acceptable appraisal report. The timing was crucial. Rohrbach had been pushing for an appraisal following HUD guidelines for several months as part of a workable project economic model. Huber did not agree until it was evident that it was necessary for the application's approval because of the intensified review that accompanied HUD's preparation of the environmental impact statement in October and the Community Development Corporation Board's review, projected for December.

Rohrbach recounted this situation to his colleagues.

> The hiring of RERC was a direct result of my visit to HUD in Washington
> the first of October. The meeting had been requested by HUD for a final
> review of the environmental impact statement. At the September 27 In-
> terim Trustees meeting I recommended that since I was going to HUD it
> would be an excellent time for the new executive director and possibly a
> trustee to fly also to meet with various HUD officials. I hoped that through
> this contact the distance between the private developer and the com-
> munity authority would be further defined.
>   At first Don was reluctant to go along with this situation, I think be-
> cause he was dubious of my relationship with Carl [Laird]. But he then
> suggested that Carl contact Reuben Clark to arrange for appointments,
> which Clark did. Clark was reluctant and told Carl that efforts for the
> community authority representatives to see HUD people was a waste of
> time and possibly damaging. Anyway, Carl and Cecil Swank [an interim
> trustee] met with HUD officials, with Don and Reuben Clark present.

During this period, Carlton Laird, who had many years' experience
dealing with corrupt government officials and developers, grew more
dubious of Huber's motives. Realizing that he was not Huber's first
choice for the position he was filling, Laird was upset at the developer's attempts to prevent him from visiting with HUD officials and
subsequent attempts by Huber to withhold his paycheck and that of
his secretary. Laird accepted that Huber was the private developer of
the New Town, but he was the interim director of a public body that
Huber had agreed to fund until that time when it could become self-
sufficient. In return, Huber would receive a built-in package of
amenities, would be relieved from a significant portion of land costs,
and was put in an advantageous position in the competition for HUD
funds. Laird decided to investigate the situation further.

It was at this point that Rohrbach learned that Huber had assigned
Hyser the task of recalculating the land and unit absorption rates as
well as the housing mix. Hyser proceeded, using Battelle data (which
Rohrbach and HUD had not been able to verify) and Huber's Dayton
home-building experience. Hyser's calculations were meant to substantiate Huber's feeling that the project should be developed with a
60 percent single-family and 40 percent multifamily mix. This was
contrary to the results of all the planning that had been done during
the previous nine months and, Rohrbach felt, would mean that the

New Town would never be able to be economically viable.

On the evening of 2 November Rohrbach called together in his Trotwood apartment several of the senior New Town staff to discuss openly the increasingly divergent directions being taken by the Trotwood
and Kettering offices. "We generally decided that at a scheduled meeting with Huber the following day, we should attempt to stand firm on
RERC's recommendations and that we should also attempt to make
decisions line item by line item for the economic model and get some
commitment to those decisions so that we could proceed in an orderly
process."

At the meeting with Huber, Laird raised several serious questions
about the community authority's economic model. There were $40
million worth of capital improvements that had been projected and
only $17 million of bonds being requested to be guaranteed by HUD.
Laird calculated that by 1994 there would be two dollars of interest
due with only one dollar of income available.

The 3 November conference ended with no decisions. Subsequent
meetings and actions during the next few weeks caused Huber and
Rohrbach to drift even further apart. Rohrbach then suggested a final
compromise. RERC was called in to review housing mix calculations
with Hyser and the sales consultant. The general manager hoped that
a formula could be arrived at that would be agreeable to all parties.
But the recalculated figures came extremely close to those that Rohrbach had used. "The figures came out as you had predicted," Huber
yelled at Rohrbach.

Huber had decided in any case to proceed with his own calculations
in which the dwelling unit and population count appeared to be close
to Huber Heights after fifteen years of development. Rohrbach ob-
jected violently. Subsequently, an accountant, Dee Belante, was hired
to assist Berardinis. When Berardinis resigned, she assumed responsibility for the economic model. Her projections soon showed that the
community authority would either be bankrupt in twenty-two years
or would be so heavily in debt that it would have to buy burdensome
assessments on New Town residents.[3]

On Friday, 17 November, Rohrbach informed Cecil Swank,
Carlton Laird, and his administrative assistant that he was resigning.
"You know I've been contemplating this for some time. I can no
longer give my support to the chaotic decision-making practices of
Mr. Huber," he said. Many things had influenced his decision, one of

which had been an article entitled "When To Resign" by Warren Bennis that had appeared in *Esquire* magazine. "I think it is important for everyone in decision-making positions in our institutions to speak out." Bennis concluded. "And if we find it impossible to continue on as administrators because we are at total and continuous odds with institutional policy, then I think we must quit and go out shooting. The alternative is petit-Eichmannism, and that is too high a price."[4] Over the weekend, Rohrbach arranged a meeting with reporter Pat Fritz.

On Monday, 20 November, Carlton Laird submitted his resignation to the New Community Interim Non-Profit Board of Trustees. On Tuesday morning the *Journal Herald* featured a banner headline story on the resignations by Pat Fritz. "Apparent deep disagreements over policy and financing have led to the resignations of two top executives of the Dayton area's New Town," Fritz's article began.

> With the resignations have come questions of political payoffs and suggestions that future new town residents would be saddled with debts due to over-borrowing and under-financing of the New Town's proposed Community Authority. The two men who have resigned are Gerwin K. Rohrbach, project general manager and Carlton W. Laird, executive director of the Interim Community Authority.
>
> The major thrust of the complaints is that only the appearance of public participation is being made. The developer is attempting to control the public sector of the community to maximize marketability of homes he would build and his profits. The charge is that the Community Authority is being financed in such a way as to leave it in uncontrollable debt after the developer completes his twenty-year program.[5]

Donald Huber was quoted as saying the planning efforts would be "seriously endangered by the resignations and the concurrent accusations."[6]

The claims of possible conflict of interest that were made to Pat Fritz by Laird involved State Representative C. J. McLin, State Representative Frederick Young, and Interim Trustee Cecil Swank. McLin, who introduced an early bill to authorize the community authority and voted for the eventual successful bill, had received $6,500 in New Town funds. Young, who introduced the final Community Authority Bill, had performed paid legal services for the New Town. Swank, a "public" representative on the interim board, had sold a $2.5 million life insurance policy to Huber. All of these charges were substantiated in the article. In submitting his resignation to the community authority, Laird presented a report that was strongly critical of the financing of the public developer and of the business practices of the Donald L. Huber Development Group. Laird charged that there existed strong possibilities the future residents of the New Town could be "saddled with debt" through the community authority, and he mentioned the possibility of default on government-guaranteed bonds.[7]

Pat Fritz identified Rohrbach's dissatisfactions with several issues that centered on his conflict with Huber. According to the article, Rohrbach believed that Huber increasingly attempted to use political clout, showed a lack of concern for the viability of the community authority, had little patience with true citizen participation, and had become extremely difficult to deal with within an organizational framework.

On Tuesday evening, the Joint Citizens New Town Planning Council met. During the meeting, the Reverend David Schneider, the council chairman, suggested that Huber had packed the New Community Interim Non-Profit Board with his own choices, although the majority of its members were supposed to represent the public. Schneider's statement was confirmed by Montgomery County Commissioner Charles Lewis. "Somebody had to pick 'em and as I recall Huber made some recommendations which we were willing to go along with," Lewis said. "As I recall, the nominations were his and the commissioners didn't consider other nominations."[8]

The following day, after the story had been covered by practically all of the local news media, Huber made a statement claiming that Rohrbach had not resigned, rather, he had been fired. In the meantime, the Interim Non-Profit Trustees met and refused to accept Laird's resignation. Rohrbach predicted to one reporter that the New Town would collapse within six months unless drastic measures were taken.

19 Newfields

After the resignations, the Donald Huber Development Group and the New Town office made a quick transition from an open to a closed system. Over the next few weeks, and then months, the staff that had been assembled left one by one. After a period of two years it was reduced to what it had been before Rohrbach arrived.

Others were also affected. Pat Fritz had gotten too close to his story. He had become more than an objective reporter and had taken an active stance on an issue that he had strong feelings about. As a result of this he lost his job.

Coverage of the New Town story continued. Both the major newspapers in the Dayton area are owned by the Cox Publishing Company. Though given a great deal of autonomy, each is subject to certain corporate dictates. For instance, during the 1972 presidential election, the "Cox Memorandum" directed that all Cox newspapers editorially support the Nixon reelection campaign. Donald Huber, also, had contacts with that campaign and had used them in his relationship with the HUD Office of New Communities.

In both Dayton newspapers, Huber continued to aim jabs at the absent Rohrbach. In subsequent interviews Huber made charges that Rohrbach had entered into contracts and had fixed certain things without his knowledge.[1] Yet all consultant contracts had been signed by Donald Huber. Contracts legally required the signature of the chief corporate officer, or consultants would not begin work. All the items that had been fixed, like zoning and community authority legislation, had been a matter of public record. Rohrbach had made a concentrated effort to keep Huber informed through the whole process. After Huber showed no interest in attending weekly manager's meetings, Rohrbach forwarded copies of every piece of information and correspondence generated by the New Town staff not only to Huber, but also to other corporate officers such as Edward Berger, president of Universal, and William Leigh, vice-president of Madden. If there were contracts made or items fixed without his knowledge, then Donald Huber must not have read what he signed, what was forwarded to his office, or what appeared in the newspaper.

The charges that Huber made were designed to make Rohrbach a scapegoat for any failures and to allow himself flexibility in changing items that had been fixed in the public arena.

Early in 1973, the project had a new office and a new name. The Trotwood office, which was accessible to area residents, was closed. The remaining staff was consolidated with the other Donald Huber Development Group employees in a new office in downtown Dayton. In the spring, the project received its new name and graphics system from Ivan Chermayeff. The new name was Newfields.

Also in early 1973, the programs that had been established began to deteriorate. The first program to fall apart was citizen participation.

The citizens had developed a love-hate relationship with Rohrbach. They were skeptical because he was an employee of Huber. Sometimes they were irritated when, during a discussion, he welded a plastic fly-swatter at his secretaries, slamming it down on the desk whenever they failed to respond quickly enough. And they were aware that he was manipulating them.

Planner Kreines, who assumed the position of acting general manager after Rohrbach's departure, recalled his methods in an interview. "He was using those people. He once told me, 'Ted, the citizens are like children. They have to be manipulated. They want to be manipulated. The first thing you have to do when you start a citizens' group is get yourself a Reverend. Then you give people the feeling that they have some power."[2] From that point Rohrbach felt that people could "move mountains."

Although the citizens were aware of this manipulation by Rohrbach, they did not mind. "We got mad and yelled at him about a lot of things," recalled Betty Devers, one of the citizens' group organizers. "But that's what he wanted us to do—that's how he got us going."[3] There was real respect for Rohrbach from the citizens, because even when he was being manipulative, he informed them where it would lead them. "The only reason we got into the New Town was that we saw integrity and real purpose in Gerwin Rohrbach. He wasn't just a developer out to make money," Griscom Morgan of Community Services said. "We had hope in Gerwin. Mr. Huber is a developer, out to make money," Morgan continued. "But the public has a lot of stake in this project; not all of the risk is in the hands of Huber. The people who will be buying the product, who will live there, should have a say. I have a private feeling Mr. Huber, like many, is a relatively 'nice guy' in a business that's been ripping off the public. He needs a watchdog."[4]

With the departure of Rohrbach, effective citizen participation ended. In August, hundreds of private citizens were attending large open meetings. By October, these citizens had formed task forces on specific areas related to the project and were working with experts to make their dreams a reality. On 15 February 1973 only eight people showed up for a meeting to reorganize the group's board of trustees. They waited in the lobby of a local seminary for about an hour hoping in vain that a leader would arise, then they left.

The citizens had tried first through the body designated to represent the public interest, the Interim Non-Profit Corporation. The citizens' group requested answers to a list of thirty questions that they raised about housing, commerce, industry, transportation, utilities, health, education, the environment, cultural activities, and financing. Then the group requested some funds for organization from the interim community authority. The citizens sought answers and some recognition and pledged to offer help in return.[5] Instead, they got what the Reverend Schneider termed a "snow job."

There were some basic ideological differences between the low-income citizens, the working people, the housewives, the social workers and intellectuals involved with JCNTPC, and the upper-middle-income citizens who had been appointed to the interim board of the community authority. These basic differences resulted in an inability to work together. Perhaps these differences could have been worked out by a mediator, but no such individual materialized. Instead, Dillman referred to the citizens as using "confrontation politics" while the citizens demanded the resignation of insurance agent Cecil Swank from the board because of conflict of interests. Next, the group tried to approach Huber directly. They asked for recognition; instead they were ignored. Finally, the citizens went directly to HUD, again asking for recognition. The HUD offices, at the time, were in a state of turmoil. Secretary Romney had resigned several months before, forcing massive reorganizations, and in the

early months of 1973 there was another issue beginning to cause un-
easiness in the Nixon administration. So the citizen group found no
support.

As the JCNTPC fought for survival, other citizens' groups were
forming to oppose specific issues, like annexation, that were related to
Newfields. The first group, composed primarily of people from the
Townview subdivision near the project, called itself the Concerned
Citizens of Madison and Perry Townships. This group was soon joined
by the Madison Township Civic Association.

As the JCNTPC died, so did the hope for real citizen input into Newfields' early planning. The New Town Environmental Planning
Group's activities were terminated and a new urban design consultant
hired. This one designed Newfields in a vacuum in a Los Angeles office far away from Trotwood and Dayton. The new consultant was a
famous architect who had won lots of awards and would perhaps win
a few more at Newfields. Rohrbach's grand scheme for providing a
whole new vocabulary of urban design had been changed for the conventional approach of a designer working on maps and drawings in
isolation on a project receiving input from only other designers and
the sponsor.

During the time that Rohrbach was general manager of the project
there had been no significant opposition from any citizens' group. It
had been his philosophy that potential opposition would be compromised by information and by making potential adversaries a part of
the project. This resulted in the extensive communications program
during the spring of 1972 and the continuing dissemination of information through the summer and autumn. From February to
November 1972 such possible volatile issues as the rezoning of almost
five thousand acres and the community authority had created no
grass-roots opposition. Rather they had mustered some support. Less
than a month after Rohrbach had left, with the JCNTPC's influence
fading, a group organized to oppose Newfields. It opposed annexation
of any of the Madison Township to the City of Dayton. Annexation
was crucial to the success of Newfields. Without the annexation of the
agreed segment of the project to Dayton, the city would not sign the
petition for the formation of the community authority. Without the
support of the City of Dayton or without a community authority, the
future of the HUD application was in doubt. The City of Trotwood
was in a similar position.

Partly in reaction to the growing opposition and controversy caused by the resignations, Huber, eager to get the project moving, made a deal with the City of Dayton. If the city would sign the community authority petition and agree to provide water and sewer services, he would assure the city a seat on the initial Newfields Community Authority Board, deliver the annexation petition he had promised, cooperate with highway studies affecting the area, and post a $25,000 performance bond with the city to assure that he would meet the agreement.[6] On 14 February Dayton signed the community authority petition. The following day the *Journal Herald* responded to the tactics that Huber was using in an editorial.

> The agreement reached between developer Donald L. Huber and the Dayton City Commission gives a needed boost to the project. We wish, however, that the dealings between the commission and Huber had been conducted out in the open instead of behind closed doors.
>
> Even the commission's approval of the accord took place under circumstances that left those in attendance at yesterday's commission meeting puzzled. All that the audience could hear from the front of the room was mumbling as the commission agreed to support the project.
>
> This fuzziness has been characteristic of the project in recent months. Legitimate and important questions have been raised about the details of the plan. What will be the housing mix be? What will be the economic structure of the Community Authority, which is responsible for providing and maintaining public facilities? The answers of these and other questions have not been forthcoming.[7]

Simultaneously, Huber had begun to work out a deal with Trotwood. Trotwood's power had increased over the past year as it became more aware of the control that it held over the New Town. The city was given an added advantage with the broad citizen support for annexation to Trotwood, rather than Dayton. So Huber had little bargaining power with annexation. In fact, his position was weakened by his commitment to Dayton. Though Trotwood officials wanted to honor their agreement in principle with the central city, they also wanted to maximize the opportunities for their own city.

On 20 February the Trotwood city council held an open hearing on the issue and over five hundred people crowded into the high school cafeteria. After nearly four hours of heated debate, the council gave a four to three vote in favor of a resolution agreeing to honor the commitment made to the City of Dayton. One of the dissenters was Mayor Van Schaik, who had worked closely with Newfields for nearly a year and a half and had many unanswered questions and doubts concerning the project. The council then unanimously adopted a resolution to support the community authority. The dissenters joined the rest of the council, realizing that if Newfields were to become a reality, then it would be advantageous to have a community authority, because Huber had promised that the city would be represented on its board.

During the debate two other promises that Huber had made were disclosed. Using his contacts in Columbus, he had been able to convince the Ohio Department of Transportation to use its "best efforts" to have the proposed Trotwood extension, also referred to as the Wolf Creek Expressway (map 2), placed higher on its list of priorities. Huber also agreed to scale down the original plans for low- and moderate-income housing.[8]

What was not mentioned at the hearing was that the highway still faced stiff opposition from various community groups in Dayton, including the powerful Model Cities organization, and that Huber had agreed to cooperate with Dayton officials on the same issue. Also the position on low- and moderate-income housing was a reversal from what Huber had agreed to during the state A-95 review process and had to agree to with City of Dayton, regional planning personnel, and federal officials. If Huber could reverse his position to satisfy one group what prevented him from doing the same thing for other issues? A strong citizens group, acting as a watchdog, could have prevented such inconsistencies.

At this time, Perry Township officials, who had before been inactive in relation to Newfields, began to take action to prevent the project from entering their township. Because of grass-roots pressure from residents who had primarily been opposed to Dayton but in growing numbers were becoming opposed to Newfields, the Perry Township trustees established a zoning commission. Thus the township, by removing itself from the Rural Zoning Commission of Montgomery County, took the first step in blocking the development of the 1,000 acres in that township. Subsequently, the commission moved to rezone 80 percent of the township as agricultural, which would prevent new community development.

The Interim New Community Non-Profit Board had liked and trusted Carl Laird. They had been pleased with his job. The trustees were upset over his resignation and for a time refused to accept it. In their December meeting they finally voted to accept his resignation. Two seemingly positive actions occurred as a result of requests made by the trustees: the board was given a $125,000 loan from Huber and was "authorized" to seek separate offices. Both were agreed to at the December meeting, as well as the hiring of a consultant to fill Laird's vacancy until a replacement could be found. The consultant was from the firm Linton, Mields, and Coston.[9] A principal of that firm was Hugh Mields, who had assisted Reuben Clark and others in writing the initial Title VII legislation. It was from the same firm that Clark had originally suggested as one candidate for the job. Soon afterwards, a $2.5 million loan approval was obtained from the Winters National Bank of Dayton by Huber for the community authority until the time that it was approved by HUD. Over the period of the next few months several more candidates who had been suggested by Clark before were hired by the interim board.

When Carlton Laird resigned as interim director, he raised several major questions about the economic viability of the community authority and its ability to represent the public independently. Laird charged that economic projections showed that the community authority would be bankrupt by 1992, after Donald Huber had sold all his land, made his profits, and left Newfields on its own. Laird based his charges on his own investigation and on separate memorandums that had been prepared by Dee Belante and John Wackler of the accounting firm of Ernst and Ernst.

The Belante memorandum, dated 15 November 1972, held that, based on the latest plans for the New Town's community facilities, the community authority would have to borrow forty million, not the seventeen million that it was requesting to be guaranteed by HUD. It said that after the twenty-year development period the community authority would not have enough income to "meet financial expenses or pay back bonds in the ensuring period."[10]

Wackler prepared a shorter memorandum concluding that the economic model for the community authority failed, because it envisioned borrowing too much too soon for the community authority ever to repay it with the interest.[11]

Attempts to verify these projections by independent parties were thwarted by Huber who refused to release anything but the sketchiest of financial information to the public.

Through the winter the interim community authority board feuded with the remnants of JCNTPC. By spring, because of the action taken by Dayton and Trotwood, the interim board was ready to be phased out and the actual community authority was to begin. In the first week of April 1973, the Montgomery County commissioners voted to create the Newfields Community Authority. A week later, the Montgomery County Commission appointed the five members who would represent the public, and Donald Huber appointed four members to represent the private developer. The county commission appointed Herbert Lewis, a Trotwood councilman; Minnie Johnson of the Miami Valley Regional Planning Commission; Paul Stockett, a county administrator; Paul Roderer, a Dayton City commissioner; and Patrick Foley, a Madison Township trustee. Lewis and Roderer had been appointed to fulfill Huber's promises to Dayton and Trotwood. Huber appointed himself; Joseph Madonna, who had been hired to replace Rohrbach as general manager (Kreines had been appointed acting general manager after the resignation and remained in that position until Madonna arrived); James Gould, Huber's attorney; and Thomas Dillman, who had been a public representative on the interim board.

Immediately, the makeup of the board was attacked. Criticism came from the two sides that had been feuding previously, which was what was left of the citizens' group and members of the interim board. "The interim trustees felt that citizen representatives should be citizens and not elected officials. We made the recommendation to the county commissioners that a citizen from Dayton and a citizen from Trotwood be appointed and then have two carry-overs from the interim public trustees," interim trustee chairman Dillman said. Dillman commented further that his own appointment by Huber as a trustee for the private developer "put him in an awkward position."[12] Francis Brown, who had replaced the disenchanted David Schneider as a JCNTPC chairperson, also criticized the commission for not appointing any private citizens. The *Journal Herald* joined the dispute and criticized the appointments in an editorial on 14 April. "The Montgomery County Commissioners, in our opinion," the editorial stated, "have ignored the intent of the General Assembly by appointing government officials as citizen representatives on the Newfields Community Authority board." The editorial maintained that the elected officials would be acting in the interest of their own governments, not in the interest of Newfields residents. The legality of the appointment was questioned and the county commission urged to reconsider its action.[13]

Donald Huber has stated, "From the very beginning, we have been subject to a great deal of criticism because of the private developer's right to appoint members to a minority position on the Board of Trustees. There are two basic reasons for this. First and most important is the necessary coordination of the two developers working on a single site. Unless there is a great deal of cooperation, the two developers could have two separate plans. This, obviously, would be an impossible situation and would involve much conflict" (1975, p. 109). But did the private developer have the right to appoint the "public" representatives also? If so, the cooperation Huber referred to was with himself. Furthermore there was the question of why the county commissioners were fulfilling promises made by a private developer.

Three weeks after the commission appointed a community authority board, three appointees declined to serve. All three were the elected officials. So the commission appointed three new "public" representatives, Thomas Dillman, who had previously been appointed a "private" representative; Marvin Kuns, owner of a printing company; and Darrell Landis, an insurance executive. Two private representatives were also changed, Anthony Char, the Dayton administrator responsible for annexation; and Fred Izenson, Trotwood's city attorney, replaced Dillman and Gould.[14] So Huber's commitment to Dayton and Trotwood for representation on the board was fulfilled. Though personalities on the board changed, it remained a blue-ribbon type of committee composed of upper-middle-income individuals and representatives of local governments who possessed similar values. There was one black woman on the board (Minnie Johnson of MVRPC); the rest were white males over thirty-five.

On 11 May the interim board was dissolved, and Marvin Kuns was elected chairman of the community authority. In addition to his printing company, Kuns was also a founder and president of the Larch Tree Country Club, a new private golf course bounded on three sides by Newfields. So he stood to benefit from the development of the new community. Two other "public" representatives also had curious relationships to Newfields. Dillman had been previously appointed a private trustee. Landis, the insurance executive, was a relative of Paul Landis, a longtime Huber employee.

On 24 April, a week after the makeup of the community authority board was decided, Dayton filed its first petition to annex land in Newfields. The petition, filed with the Montgomery County clerk, described 768 acres of Madison township property owned by twenty-five individuals and businesses. Eighteen landowners signed the petition, one of which, who owned one-fourth of the land, was Donald Huber. Three other landowners were developers who also owned substantial portions of the rest of the land. Dayton's administrator of development and community authority trustee Anthony Char commented to the press that the petition represented the first phase in a move to have 2,600 acres of Newfields land eventually annexed to Dayton.[15] The remaining acres in Madison and Perry Townships would be annexed to Trotwood, according to the agreement first reached in May 1972 and subsequently firmed up by actions of officials representing both municipalities.

The petition excluded the Townview subdivision. Townview had been one of the main organizing areas of the antiannexation forces that grew in number after Dayton submitted its annexation petition and after Trotwood's council had voted to honor the agreement with the central city (map 5). On 10 July a public hearing was held on the matter and drew pointed opposition from various citizens' groups. "It's a manufactured, gerrymandered, twisted, tortuous, ludicrous effort to take township land," a township trustee remarked. Carrie White, a former member of JCNTPC who was representing the Madison Township Civic Association, presented a petition containing 1,227 names opposed to the annexation. After a Huber attorney remarked that without annexation there would be no Newfields, many of the assembled 100 citizens applauded.[16]

But the Donald L. Huber Development Group had been working for over a year on the annexation petition and it was legally tight. In November the county commission approved the annexation. This caused considerable frustration to many Madison Township residents, especially those of the Townview subdivision who sought to be annexed to Trotwood but were left in near isolation by the annexation to Dayton. "When we met with Huber, he kept telling us the annexation wouldn't stop us from annexing to Trotwood if we wanted to," commented Homer Whited, a spokesman for the Madison Township Civic Association. But the annexation to Dayton left the subdivision of predominantly low- and moderate-income people in a position that

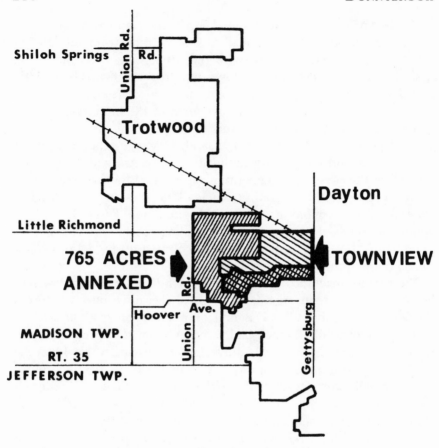

Map 5. City of Dayton Annexation

made it almost impossible for them to be annexed to Trotwood (see map 5).[17]

The Donald L. Huber Development Group's relationship with the Department of Housing and Urban Development during 1973 was like a roller-coaster ride because of the instability within the development corporation and that within the federal government.

Three weeks after Rohrbach resigned, Huber announced that the project would have to be delayed and began an effort to make Rohrbach the scapegoat. Huber contended that the HUD project review would have to be delayed because work on the economic model had not been completed, for which he blamed Rohrbach. This is the reason he cited for "firing" the general manager.[18]

Besides the problems within the development corporation, there were events in Washington that influenced the delay. Secretary Romney had resigned, which caused first a scramble for power and then a reorganization of the HUD staff. Then, in early January, HUD officials announced that funds for subsidizing low- and moderate-income housing construction had been frozen for eighteen months. Though the freeze did not directly affect the new communities' program, it was speculated that it could affect Newfields because the freeze could affect the ability to include the low- and moderate-income housing to which Huber had committed the corporation.

Huber's financial situation grew increasingly precarious. By February 1973 he had spent more than $2 million on the project. He had obtained a three-million-dollar loan from the Kissell Company, a mortgage finance company, and had much of it left. However, the money was necessary to make the ongoing option and mortgage payments on the land, and he had to repay the Kissell loan by October 1973 or renegotiate it.

During the next several months, Huber's negotiations with HUD and the financing arrangements were kept silent. The news coverage of the project concentrated on information concerning the community authority and annexation.

In the spring of 1973, the Watergate story exploded in Washington, throwing the federal government, including HUD, into disarray. In many ways, this situation seemed to work in favor of Huber, who was able to put some distance between himself and the questions raised by Rohrbach and Laird. Meanwhile, he was able to use his political clout in Washington on fresh, new administrators.

In April, with Watergate receiving prime news coverage, Huber filed his final zoning plan for the first section (530 acres) of Newfields with the Madison Township Zoning Board. It included a "village" center, residential areas, and an office-industrial park. The plan was developed by Edward Kreines and a planning firm from Columbia, Maryland.[19]

On Wednesday, 27 September 1973, Newfields groundbreaking ceremonies were held without the project's receiving official HUD approval. Ohio senator William Saxbe was the featured guest, and he told the crowd that he and Senator Taft were "doing everything they could to see that Newfields got the HUD commitment for both developers [Huber and the community authority] to go ahead." About twenty demonstrators picketed the ceremonies with signs proclaiming "Newfields Heartbreaking" and "Welcome to Newfields—Garden of Eden—but Watch out for Snakes." The demonstrators said they were against the project because they were "the ones who'd have to pay for it."[20]

About a month later HUD made a commitment to Donald Huber that it would guarantee to repay up to $32 million in loans to be obtained for the private developer through the sale of bonds. This guarantee had increased by almost $20 million since the original HUD application. The community authority's request for $19 million (a $1 million increase) was not granted at the same time. The community authority continued to operate on the two-and-a-half million dollar loan obtained by Huber from the Winters Bank.

Soon afterwards, the first $18 million was sold in the bond market. An underwriting syndicate, which was the low bidder for the bonds, resold them to some eighty investors, at which time the syndicate paid Huber a half-million dollar deposit. On 15 November the final financial and legal documents were signed by Donald Huber, the federal government, the bonding underwriters, and the investors in the Wall Street office of the underwriters for the remainder of the loan.

While Huber was receiving the $17.5 million in New York, the deeds to 3,600 acres for the new community were being recorded in the Montgomery County Court House. Options on about 2,600 acres were picked up and another 1,000 acres of Huber-owned land were transferred to the Newfields Development Corporation.[21] The transition took place almost a year after Laird and Rohrbach resigned.

The next year, 1974, went more smoothly for Newfields, at least on the surface. In May, though, it was announced that the state of Ohio had delayed plans to begin construction on the proposed extension to U.S. Route 35 and the Wolf Creek Expressway. This was the highway that Huber had promised Trotwood he would convince state officials to place high on their list of priorities. It was also the basis for much of the physical planning after Rohrbach's departure. Rohrbach had contended that the chances for the highway's completion were slim, because of the opposition in the City of Dayton. He had based his planning more on the Interstate 675 beltway, the existing Interstate 70, and a modified version of the Wolf Creek Expressway, which would have connected Trotwood and the New Town to U.S. Route 35 with a minimal disruption of West Dayton.

Also in May a one-million-dollar issue of county industrial revenue bonds for an office building in Newfields complex was approved by the county. Huber's Universal Manufacturing Company was to erect the building and lease it back from the county on a twenty-year basis to pay the bonds back. Universal and other Huber corporations would use the building, which would serve as the first of the buildings in the planned "village center" of the first phase.

As construction on the first phase proceeded through the summer, Trotwood annexed a 641-acre section of Newfields in August. After landscaping the road construction, a lake was constructed, several houses, a row of townhouses, and the first building in the village center.

But by the autumn the project was again beset with delays. HUD still had not approved the community authority, bad weather had delayed spring construction starts, and then the deteriorating economic situation that depressed the housing market affected investment in the project by home builders and developers.

Then in November 1974, a year after its approval of Newfields, HUD announced that it was suspending the approval of future new communities under Title VII. The program had come under serious criticism from many sources, including journalists and city planners. The federally sponsored new towns, being assisted by some $250 million in government-assisted bonds, were moving closer to the brink of financial disaster. The ultimate threat was foreclosures that would force the treasury to pay first the interest to the bond owners, then the principal.

One application affected by HUD's decision would be the community authority. Part of the reason why the community authority's application was not approved by HUD was a pending lawsuit that questioned the legality of the legislation. The suit was settled in favor of the community authority, whose director Brendan Geraghty was optimistic that the application would be approved. "We won't be asking HUD to guarantee our bonds, though," Geraghty, who came to Newfields from the New York Urban Development Corporation, explained. "That's too expensive a procedure, you know. We just want approval so we can be in line for any goodies, if that ever happens. We're still operating on the bank loan from Winters and that'll last for another year or so, then we can float our own bonds, of course we'll have to prove that we're creditable, for any investors to get involved."

Without the community authority, Newfields would be no more

than a well-planned subdivision, perhaps less. As Donald's brother, Charles, stated in an interview when questioned about the new town, "Why should I be impressed? I've built a new community already; I built Huber Heights."[22]

In February 1973 Huber had argued in reference to the charges made by Rohrbach and Laird that HUD would not approve the bankrupt plan. By November 1974, it was apparent, even to Huber, that with several of the HUD-approved plans in bankruptcy or near bankruptcy, the community authority plan would never be approved. In November 1974 Huber dismissed sixteen employees, including General Manager Joseph Madonna. The following June he cut his staff further, laying off ten individuals, including the staff ecologist Ralph Scott. A staff that had once numbered as many as fifty-five after HUD approval now consisted of only fourteen full-time employees. In September 1975, Huber decided to "literally close up" his residential building firm, the Springmont Company, which had been intended to do most of the initial construction. By November, 1975, things were going so badly that Huber was forced to deliberately withhold a scheduled semiannual interest payment on Newfields bonds of $711,000 and a $160,000 annual fee to HUD.[23] HUD delayed foreclosure because it would mean "at least an eight million dollar loss" to the federal agency. Instead, HUD moved to tighten its control over the new-town developer, hoping to avert total "disaster."

An article on 23 November 1975 in the *Dayton Daily News*, three years after the resignations of Rohrbach and Laird, announced that Newfields was "tottering." "The prognosis is not good. We could go under," warned Brendan Geraghty, executive director of the community authority. Huber's executive assistant, Warren Hyser, was more blunt. "We're struggling to survive," he said. Both Geraghty and Huber blamed the federal government for not living up to its original promises. The original goal was for Newfields to have 472 units of housing, a mix of townhouses, garden apartments, and single-family homes built the first year. By 1975 there were to be 919 units, housing 2,849 people. As of November 1975, there were 65 units up, with only 25 of them occupied.[24]

The streets that had been hurriedly constructed for the project's opening already had potholes, some of which had been patched, others not. A lone receptionist occupied the Visitor's Center at the first Village Center. There was a savings and loan with one teller, three parked cars, and several ducks on the village lake, but otherwise the new center was deserted, resembling a ghost town more than a new town.

Newfields Development Corporation was absorbing losses because of the slow sales, Hyser said. They were not enough yet to force default on the almost $18 million in loans backed by the U.S. Department of Housing and Urban Development. "We have funds sufficient to operate for one or two years," he said. The community authority was facing more serious cash-flow problems. Geraghty said that authority's operations were financed by notes. The notes, which would fall due in 1977, were to be paid off with money collected from Newfields residents who would pay 1.25 percent of their adjusted gross income for the special services and facilities. The problem was that there were not enough residents moving in to provide an adequate amount of cash and no federal grants had materialized to help out. Geraghty said that it would be a "disaster" if the community authority went out of business. Hyser said if this happened, the people owning homes or condominiums in Newfields would be forced to form a homeowners' association to take its place. The residents would then have to finance its operations.[25]

In February 1976 Director Brendan Geraghty and two other employees resigned from the Newfields Community Authority, charging that a "substantial segment" of the authority's board of trustees had been trying to reduce his duties without consulting him.

In March, 1976, the *Journal Herald* ran a four-part series proclaiming that Huber's dream of building a new town had been "shattered." Ads were run in the local papers announcing that Newfields was "alive"; there were offers of a free month's rent to prospective New Town tenants; the Newfields Community Authority could no longer afford to pay for the regional transit authority's service to the only existing Newfields neighborhood, and so the bus route was discontinued; and further annexation of New Town land to Dayton was delayed indefinitely.

When Gerwin Rohrbach resigned his post as general manager, he had predicted that the New Town would collapse in six months. He had miscalculated by three years.

20 The Future of New Community Planning

There are several reasons for the interest in new-community planning that occurred in the late 1960s and the early 1970s. The basic notion was that there existed the knowledge of the natural and social sciences, there were the design and engineering skills available, and there were the financial resources to make the urban living environment a more healthy, human, pleasing, and functional place. Funds seemed especially available with men walking on the moon, a needless war being waged in Southeast Asia, and American cities and campuses cleaning up the remnants of rebellion.

As more developers and the federal government became involved in the building of new communities, related professionals, like architects and city planners, were hired for design and planning. The premise that architects used as a rationale for their involvement was that new towns were superior aesthetically to either the blighted cities or the depersonalized suburbs. This premise had evolved through the urban design theory of their profession.

The nineteenth century had been an age of exploration and industrialization. During this period of exploration into the past, the art historians kept an eager eye on the discoveries, for they were engaged in classifying and dispensing the world's architectural knowledge. Artists of the nineteenth century, including architects, reacted against industrialization by withdrawing to the techniques of the past or by creating new approaches. Movements like the arts and crafts in Great Britain and impressionism and art nouveau in France not only affected the pigments on canvas but also the image of cities. Naturalists in both Europe and North America openly reacted against the Industrial Revolution. In Britain, Ebenezer Howard proposed the use of garden cities as an alternative to congested cities like London, where he lived. While in the United States, Olmsted adopted the philosophy of British naturalists, applying it to large urban parks, like New York's Central Park. These early efforts influenced what was called the city beautiful movement. This movement resulted in reshaping cities like Chicago, which had been destroyed by its great fire and afterwards was laced with park and open-space systems (Sprieregan 1965).

By the 1920s architects, including LeCorbusier, Wright, and Gropius, were proposing the wide-scale use of new towns as a means for urban growth based on the experience of garden cities and the city beautiful movement. This philosophy has grown with the architecture, landscape architecture, and urban design professions and remains a part of many practitioners' vision for the future of civilization. Architect Moshe Safdie, envisioning the future image of urban areas, wrote, "The low-density sprawl of little houses consuming every bit of agricultural and open space around the cities continued into the 1980's but late in the decade a number of new large-scale developments, new towns in towns, and new towns out of town were started by private developers." Safdie continued, as if he were looking back from the year 2001,

Mostly these developers were supported by massive public grants. This happened in reaction to the piecemeal development that had become totally bankrupt by the late 1970's. As the city centers proved impossible to manage, except for the rare occasion when a large piece of vacant land was available, new developments were started outside the city centers in the seventies. And so, after twenty-five years of suburban sprawl, came another twenty-five years of dispersal of highly concentrated and planned new communities at the periphery of the existing cities. Businesses, too, moved to these new centers, but the interdependence among the new communities continued to demand highly available and rapid means of transportation among them. As a result, in the late 1980's the government decided to create an all-inclusive rational Transportation Authority. Its role was to plan, design and construct group transportation at the regional and sub-regional scale and to integrate it totally with all other forms of smaller-scale transportation serving individual communities [Safdie 1974, p. 126].

The city planning profession, which was strongly linked in its beginning to architecture and landscape architecture (as well as to law), adopted this philosophical premise for new towns. But during the urban strife of the 1960s, as it became apparent that strictly physical solutions could not solve the serious problems of cities, planners began to turn to other approaches. Social scientists became more involved in planning and, while doing so, criticized most of the previous techniques used in the profession, thus splintering planning into several schools of thought.

The revival of new towns in the late 1960s created a subtle, uneasy merging of these schools. While new communities opened new opportunities for physical land-use masterplan practitioners, it also involved, to a lesser degree, younger social and systems planners. But the planners and architects who did become involved in new towns had very limited power over the crucial decisions that were made. Those with this power were the federal government (in the case of federally assisted new communities) and the developers. It is those two groups who must share the responsibility of failures.

The federal government's involvement in new communities had begun during the depression. As part of the New Deal, greenbelt communities were built similar in some ways to Howard's British models. They had, however, a more dominant American base. Tugwell sought to respond to the economic necessities of the time. While Howard's garden cities were independent and free standing, Tugwell's were satellite towns depending largely on the massive acceptance and availability of the automobile. Though three greenbelt towns were successfully built and several more designed, the program was abandoned before World War II (Myhra 1974).

The federal government's post–World War II involvement in new communities began in the 1960s with a series of legislative acts that made mortgage money more available to developers. These acts culminated in 1969 with the passage of the New Community Development Act, HUD Title VII. There were seventeen new towns approved by HUD's Office of New Communities through 1974. By the end of 1974, these federally sponsored new communities, which were being assisted by some $250 million in government-guaranteed bonds, were moving closer to the brink of financial disaster. The ultimate threat was a federal takeover if HUD were forced to foreclose, causing the treasury to pay interest to the bondholders. For instance, Saint Charles Communities in Maryland was seeking a $4 million loan from HUD's new communities revolving fund to pay the $1 million interest due on the $24 million in long-term bonds that were issued to finance the development.[1] Saint Charles Communities is not an isolated example. Computer analysis by Decision Sciences Corporation of Jenkintown, Pennsylvania, projected that every one of the new communities in the HUD program would go broke without infusions of new money. In November 1974 HUD, faced with scrapping the whole effort, froze all new loan guarantees until the entire program could be studied.

The developers who became involved were a curious collection of eccentrics who adopted bits and pieces of the professional premises that I have mentioned plus some of their own. Some tried to capitalize on the involvement of the federal government, others went on their own. Some, like Robert Simon, the one-time owner of Carnegie Hall and developer of Reston, were idealistic elitists. Others, like James Rouse, shopping-mall developer and Columbia builder, were a combination of hard-nosed entrepreneur and social innovator. While others, like Donald Huber, wealthy suburban home builder and Newfields developer, had motives ranging from guilt to profit. Old American communities had been formed through a combination of economic, idealistic, and romantic notions, the same ones that affected the planning and development of new communities.

Title VII new communities have not been the only projects experiencing financial difficulty. In March 1975, it was reported that the New York Urban Development Corporation, which had sponsored three new towns and used consultants similar to those at Newfields and other federally assisted new communities, had found itself unable to pay off $104.5 million in one-year bond-anticipation notes. It was one of the biggest defaults by a public agency since the 1930s.[2]

The optimism in which the new towns of the late 1960s began turned to disappointment by the mid-1970s. First, the funding that many developers had counted on from the government fell short of their initial expectations. This stemmed from the reality that during the Nixon administration there was no real commitment to the urban environment. Second, new towns failed to live up to their promises for social innovation. This stemmed from the fact that few developers were really committed to social programs.

Criticism about new towns came from two primary sources: journalists and city planners. Journalists attacked the projects from many points. In her series of articles in the *Journal Herald* in 1972, Denise

Goodman made numerous criticisms about the lack of democracy and the social problems of Columbia and Reston. She concluded that planned communities could not in themselves solve the larger problems of racism and self-identity plaguing the larger culture; yet she remained cautiously optimistic, partly because she believed that there were environmental benefits in comprehensive advance planning and cluster design,[3] and partly because she felt that there was evidence in the planning process of Newfields that it had learned from the mistakes of earlier efforts and had begun to solve some of the problems of democracy and social interaction. Efforts, she learned, that the project's development never made a commitment to.

In a 1975 syndicated series of articles, Thomas Lippman and Bill Richards criticized both the manner in which federal government was involved and the financial planning done by developers.

> Everyone agrees on the basic problem confronting the HUD new communities. They borrowed heavily to acquire, grade and improve land, pay their planners, start construction and sell their product. Because of inflation, it all costs much more than they expected, and because of the nationwide housing slump and the general economic recession of 1974 and 1975, both resident and industrial sales lagged behind their projections. As a result, they couldn't pay their bills and many of them can't continue with their development.[4]

City planners have been criticizing the approach of developers to new towns for a much longer time. Herbert Gans, a student of post–World War II suburban developments, was hired as a consultant for Columbia. He specifically criticized the notion of planning heterogeneous communities that was being advocated for new towns. Based on his study, he contended that people prefer to live in more homogeneous neighborhoods. As a result, he predicted various problems for Columbia including social isolation, community conflicts, and persisting individual and family problems (Gans 1968). His changes were not implemented, and subsequently most of the problems that he predicted for Columbia have occurred.

In 1972, when he resigned as the New Town's general manager, Gerwin Rohrbach predicted an economic collapse of the project. He based his prediction on the belief that the federal government was not wholly committed to the new communities program and that the New

Town's developer had not made competent financial forecasts.

Yet there are new towns that are working, both in Europe and the United States. For instance, both Howard's garden cities and Tugwell's greenbelt towns have survived. But though there are many successful new towns, I find it difficult to accept architect Moshe Safdie's image of how future new towns will develop. That is, new communities started by private developers supported by massive public grants. This is the same program that has been tried by HUD Title VII and failed. Perhaps a similar program could be successful, but it would take a different type of "private developer" and another form of public grants coming from a different governmental structure.

New towns can offer a viable alternative to suburbia; planned communities can be better environmentally, aesthetically and, to a limited extent, socially. This is important because there is much evidence that, even with the declining birthrate, there will be a continued increase in the demand for housing to the year 2000. An increase is expected both because of continued family formation and of the decrease in the supply of housing because of increased construction costs. Another factor that will probably have a continued effect on the urban environment is the energy crisis that began in the mid-1970s.

In its market research of the metropolitan Dayton area for Newfields, the Real Estate Research Corporation of Chicago projected this increase in demand and decrease in supply. RERC projected that the Dayton SMSA would increase in population from 850,266 in 1970 to 1,213,209 in 1992. Their projection factored in a significant decrease in the birthrate for the area. RERC projected that most of this increased population would live in multifamily dwellings, because landdevelopment and construction costs would continue to push singlefamily housing out of the reach of a significant portion of American families.[5]

A research team at the University of North Carolina has extensively studied new towns for several years. Their research seems to verify that, though there are problems, there are many positive aspects about new towns. The North Carolina team sampled residents in thirty-six communities, fifteen new towns (including two that had received federally guaranteed loan assistance) and fifteen closely matched control communities, plus six special control communities. Using elaborately prepared questionnaires and in-depth interviews, the team quizzed residents on various aspects of their communities, including schools, health care, recreation, shopping, and working (Weiss, Kaiser and Burby 1971; National Science Foundation 1974; Burby and Weiss 1976). The results were interesting. In the overall rating of their communities, the new-town residents gave higher marks than their counterparts. Of all the residents, only the new-town elderly were less enthusiastic than their counterparts. The greatest improvement in community satisfaction came in the ratings of blacks and moderate-income residents. It should be noted that retirement communities, black suburbs, and subsidized neighborhoods were used as the special control communities.[6]

Based on the overall and the highly favorable environmental ratings, the University of North Carolina study's preliminary results would seem to justify the premise that new towns can offer a viable alternative to suburbs. The North Carolina team went further and made suggestions for federal government policy changes that they felt would begin to rectify some of the shortcomings of new towns.

1. Since residents seemed to rate community satisfaction on the basis of attributes of their immediate neighborhood, rather than on community-wide services and facilities, the team felt it might be wise for federal government to encourage more planned unit developments than large-scale new communities.
2. Since the greatest beneficiaries of new community life seemed to be black and subsidized housing groups, the team felt the federal government could make a meaningful contribution to the quality of life by increasing its efforts to assure facilities for both groups in federally assisted new communities.
3. Since the team found a great acceptance of retirement communities among elderly, it suggested the inclusion of neighborhoods for the elderly in new towns.
4. Since there was a low performance rating by residents in the area of educational, health and shopping facilities, the team suggested developers should be encouraged to provide more social services earlier.
5. Since the two federally assisted new communities received generally low performance ratings, the team suggested that the whole Title VII program be re-evaluated.[7]

The critics of new towns have pointed out that they require a much greater front-end cost than typical suburban development. One such cost is that of "planning." But there was little real planning done.

Physical planners were hired primarily as technicians. Social and other types of planners played only a subordinate role, if any at all. The few planners who reached management roles were removed from the vital basic financial decisions.

The bulk of the front-end costs came not for planning but for the jurisdictional maneuvering that was required and the cost of the land. New communities were in most cases developed in areas that required multilevel approvals for zoning, annexation, extension of utilities, provision of municipal services, school districting, and many other various local, regional, state, and federal requirements. In the case of HUD Title VII new communities, a substantial investment was required just to request assistance and there was no guarantee of approval.

Newfields' developer Donald Huber summed up the frustration involved in the federal negotiations in a statement that he made in November, 1974. "HUD officials say you can't do this without their specific approval, or they order you to change this or that. I can't sell a particular piece of land to an industrial prospect, for example, without their say-so. It takes six months to get that."[8]

If there does indeed exist a knowledge base in the natural and social sciences, there are the design and engineering skills available and there are sufficient financial resources available to make urban environments more healthy, pleasing, and functional places to live and grow. If there is a need for housing, and if new communities have at least begun to provide a working laboratory for satisfying some of the needs of urban residents, then what prevents new towns from providing both a better physical and social environment and from making a profit at the same time?

First, there are the initial problems of *location* and *size*. One reason that Columbia has been the most successful of the recent new communities is that it was strategically located midway in the Washington-Baltimore corridor. The Woodlands, one of the more successful Title VII projects, was located in the sun belt growth region of Texas. The greenbelt new towns were located in metropolitan areas in close commuting distance for automobiles. So far as size is concerned, many of the HUD Title VII new communities were just too large for realistic fiscal planning. They required too much of an initial investment to make them an attractive financial venture.

One solution to the problem of size is planned unit developments

(PUDs) that minimize risks and the length and extent of financial exposure. PUDs are smaller versions of new towns. There is no set rule on size, though they usually run from several hundred dwelling units to as many as 5,000 units on a thousand or so acres, which is approximately 10 to 20 percent of new-town size. Though they differ in some aspects from new towns, they usually employ similar land-planning techniques. PUDs offer a more realistic scale of experimentation than new towns.

The second major problem with new communities is *financing*. Sound financial investment is needed. The next America should not be created by the same type of developers who were responsible for the last. Suburban home builders and shopping-center developers often run highly speculative organizations, are involved in political manipulation, construct shoddy products, and are motivated solely by profit. These builders could flourish in the post–World War II era when there was an overwhelming demand for housing and ready low-interest mortgage funds were available. This same type of developer became involved with new towns. To these individuals the concept appeared to be a trendy product that could be easily marketed while being subsidized by the federal government.

A notable exception to this type of new-town developer is James Rouse in Columbia, Maryland. Rouse sought to involve a broad-based financial backing for Columbia from its beginnings to the early 1960s. The Woodlands was also built with more solid backing than most of the other Title VII new communities. The three greenbelt new towns were built with the full backing of the federal government.

The third problem is the *environmental analysis* of the site. This problem can be addressed by ecological planning. This land-planning method utilizes an interdisciplinary ecosystem analysis to provide alternatives for development. The ecological planning method was successfully used in the environmental planning of The Woodlands in Texas (McHarg 1969; Juneja 1974; Wallace, McHarg, Roberts and Todd 1974; McHarg and Sutton 1975), and the innovative grass-roots new community of Cerro Gordo in Oregon (The Town Forum 1974).

The fourth problem is the *social-systems analysis* of the area where the new community is to be located. One approach to social planning for new communities has been offered by Gans (1968). Another method, which has been suggested by McHarg, Eugene Odum, and others, is an extension of ecological planning, and that is an applied human ecological approach. There are also interdisciplinary human ecology attempts to analyze the relationship between people and the land. Though it has not yet been used for new-community planning, applied human ecology might offer a method for their social planning (McHarg 1969; Odum 1971; Young 1975; Berger 1976, 1977; Richerson 1977; Rose, Steiner and Jackson 1978/1979).

The fifth problem is *urban design.* An effective urban-design program should be able to use economic, environmental, and social information to provide for maximum design alternatives. As with the environment and social-systems analyses, this should be an interdisciplinary approach. Rohrbach and Porterfield with the New Town Environmental Design Team attempted to solve this problem. In addition to using economic, environmental, and social information, people were brought into the design process.

A sixth problem is that *citizen participation,* especially that of low- and moderate-income citizens and minorities like blacks, and other nonwhites, women, young people, and the elderly, who have been excluded from the decision-making process. During the planning period of new towns, when the land was largely uninhabited, citizens were ignored. As development began, residents who moved in during the early stages were again ignored by the developer. The rationale used by developers was that before development began the project owner had to answer to no one except various officials, who were, in some cases, corruptible or had values similar to those of the developer. After development began, developers felt that it was still necessary to control the project for aesthetic or zoning purposes. So in many cases new communities were being developed undemocratically.

Again, some solutions were attempted with Newfields. Organizing various community groups with an interest in the New Town, a broad based citizens group had been formed. Rohrbach hoped that this group would both participate in decisions and act as a watchdog for the project. In addition, the community authority offered a democratic model for citizen *ownership* in new communities. The community authority law as created by the Ohio legislature for Newfields, while recognizing existing jurisdictional controls, gave communities the power to own and control facilities and to provide certain public services.

The seventh problem is *project management.* A solution to this problem lies in systems management. Human communities are com-

plex systems. The planning and management of the development of
these communities should be undertaken through the understanding
of systems. The groundwork for this approach to management has
been laid by von Bertalanffy (1968), Churchman (1968), Ackoff
(1970) and others. Again, this approach was attempted by Rohrbach
in the management of Newfields.

The final problem with new-community planning is that it should
be part of a *coordinated regional planning effort*. Gideon Golany
observed, "Because of its self-contained economic base, the effect of a
new town upon its region is far higher than that of a satellite town
developed exclusively as a bedroom community" (1976, p. 144). This
problem is both regional and national. In most metropolitan areas
there are hundreds, often thousands, of separate governing bodies for
services, sewers, schools, and zoning. Each separate entity clings
tenaciously to its power, often handicapping any possible innovation.
What is needed is a system whereby developmental decisions can be
intelligently coordinated while some local control is maintained.

There are also constraints related to the federal government.
Though there has been a long series of legislative acts directed at stim-
ulating new-town development, the programs for implementing those
acts have been ineffective. In many respects the federal government's
involvement with new communities has been similar to involvement
in other urban programs, like urban renewal and model cities. The
commitment has been at best half-hearted and almost totally depen-
dent on the whims of the particular administration in power. Besides,
in the case of the HUD Title VII New Communities Program, the expenses required in just the application process eliminated participation from everyone except for the affluent. In Huber's own words,

> The most significant problem in current new community development is
> the federal process. Obtaining a federal guarantee is a very slow proce-
> dure and increases the exposure of a developer beyond any reasonable
> risk. Newfields started working with the Title VII federal process in early
> 1971. It has taken almost two and one half years and we still do not have a
> federal commitment. [This statement was published in 1975.] As a result,
> the developer must cope with problems of tied-up funds, expiring options,
> public relations stemming from an association of federal programs with
> minority and low-income groups, varying political atmospheres, chang-
> ing local governments, and a constantly changing HUD office.
> One might ask why a developer deals with HUD in spite of the delays

and difficulties. There is no other source of funds . . . consequently, any developer interested in building a new community is forced to go to the government [1975, p. 111].

In relation to the federal government, the political atmosphere at the time that the Title VII new communities were developed should be noted. In 1972, when the Dayton New Town project was strangled in red tape, the matter was taken to the White House. Huber was a political contributor, and this was 1972, the election year. Political contributions for political favors was the cornerstone of the Nixon era. Domestic affairs advisor to the president, John D. Ehrlichman, a most capable administrator, was able to get the New Town moving. The environmental impact statement was released shortly before the election, and despite the controversy that surrounded Rohrbach's resignation, the New Town progressed for a while. But then came Watergate. And with the exit of Ehrlichman, there was no centralized administrator with the same capability or power to cut red tape and move projects like the New Town. Huber was left to deal with a complicated federal agency that was no longer committed to the program on which he was depending for support.

In published articles and interviews with the press, Huber and his aides blamed the federal government "for not living up to its promises" and the poor economic condition of the 1970s for the failure of his new town. These factors did play a part in the collapse of Newfields. As Clarence Stein (1957) observed concerning the economic failure of Radburn, "Good timing is essential to successful new town planning." But Huber's failure to muster a broad base of support for this project in the local region, his inability to tap other major financial sources besides the federal government, and his continued mishandling and miscalculation of his affairs with HUD also contributed to Newfields' demise.

What is needed from the federal government is a full-fledged comprehensive ongoing commitment to urban areas from the redevelopment of central cities to the preservation and enrichment of existing neighborhoods on to the planned development of new areas. This commitment should come in the form of funding (not limited to the wealthy or determined by campaign contributions), and the creation of guidelines that would force intelligent use of land that demonstrates cognizance of future societal needs.

Appendix: Explanation of Project Plan-Summary Network

A. *Planning and Urban Design*
    1.1   Inventory of existing biophysical features (topography, geology, landform and soils, surface water system, flood plains, vegetation, wildlife, air, noise, climate, microclimate and historic sites)
    1.2   First draft of concept plan
    1.3   Review concept plan
    1.4   Complete preliminary master plan
    1.5   Complete master plan
    1.6–1.15 Continuing master plan analyses
    2.1   Start phase one final development plan
    2.2   Complete preliminary phase one final development plan
    2.3   Complete phase one final development plan
    2.4   Phase two area selected
    2.5   Start phase two final development plan
    3.1–3.2 Planning think tank meetings
    3.3–3.4 Public meetings/workshops including community authority trustees and representatives from the citizens' organizations
    4.1   Hire director of planning and urban design
    4.2   Select urban design consultant
    4.3   Select landscape architectural, architectural and design consultants

B. *Zoning*
    1.1   Brief local officials
    2.1   Submit new community zoning resolution

2.2   County approval of new community zoning resolution

3.1   File for master plan zoning in township

3.2   Madison Township Zoning Commission meeting

3.3   Madison Township Zoning Commission recommendation to township trustees

3.4   Madison Township Trustee hearing

3.5   Master plan zoning approved by Madison Township

4.1   File for master plan zoning in Montgomery County

4.2   Rural Zoning Commission hearing

4.3   Rural Zoning Commission recommendation to Montgomery County Commission

4.4   Montgomery County Commission hearing

4.5   Master plan zoning approved by Montgomery County

5.1   Start Montgomery County Planning Commission review

5.2   Montgomery County Planning Commission recommendation to Madison Township Zoning Commission and Rural Zoning Commission for master plan

6.0   Master plan zoning effective

7.1   File phase one final development plan in Madison Township

7.2   Madison Township Zoning Commission hearing

7.3   Madison Township Zoning Commission recommendation to Madison Township Trustees for phase one final development plan

7.4   Phase one final development plan effective

C. *Construction and Development*

1.1   Hire construction and development manager

1.2   Hire grading superintendent

1.3   Hire construction superintendent

1.4   Complete staffing

2.1   Contract for dam and lake design

2.2   File preliminary application with state for dam

2.3   File formal application with state for dam

2.4   Start construction of dam and lake

2.5   Complete dam and lake and start to fill

3.1   Draft building and construction standards

3.2   Complete building and construction standards

4.1   Start innovative housing design competition

4.2   Select innovative concept

4.3   Engage innovative design architect

4.4   Start innovative design

4.5   Finish innovative design

4.6   Start construction of innovative house

4.7   Finish construction of innovative house
5.1   Start first year engineering
5.2   Begin review of plat plan by local authorities
5.3   File preliminary plat plan for first year
5.4   Preliminary first year plats approved
5.5   File final plans for first year
5.6   First year plat plans recorded
6.1   Design model single family homes
6.2   Start construction of model homes
7.1   Begin FHA approval
7.2   Receive FHA approval
8.1   Develop guidelines and specifications for commercial and industrial facilities
8.2   Design commercial and industrial facilities
8.3   Complete design of commercial and industrial facilities
8.4   Start construction of first year commercial and industrial facilities
8.5   Complete construction of first year commercial and industrial facilities
9.1   Begin design of sales pavilion
9.2   Complete design of sales pavilion
9.3   Start construction of sales pavilion
9.4   Complete construction of sales pavilion
10.1 Start construction of first year trunk lines
10.2 Complete construction of first year trunk lines
11.1 Start project control system
11.2 Complete project control system
12.1 Begin coordination with community authority for design of amenities and schools
12.2 Complete design with community authority of amenities and schools
12.3 Start construction of school facilities
12.4 Start construction of first year amenities
12.5 Complete construction of school facilities
12.6 Complete construction of first year amenities
13.1 Select joint venture partners
13.2 Coordination with joint venture partners
14.1 Select first year development contractor
14.2 Start first year development
14.3 Complete first year development
15.0 Obtain building permits
X   Project opening

D. *Marketing and Sales*
    1.1   Select marketing and advertising firm
    1.2   Select graphic design firm
    1.3   Develop New Town name and logo design
    1.4   Develop New Town development promotion program
    1.5   Begin to prepare sales and promotion brochures
    1.6   Begin advertising
    1.7   Decorate model single-family houses and sales pavilion
    2.1   Select decision research consultant
    2.2   Develop marketing staff plan
    2.3   Hire marketing manager
    2.4   Hire sales staff
    3.1   Begin residential market research
    3.2   Develop residential market profile
    3.3   Select model housing units
    3.4   Develop sales strategies
    3.5   Coordinate with builder's sales staffs
    3.6   Begin residential land sales
    4.1   Begin commercial and industrial market research
    4.2   Develop commercial and industrial market profile
    4.3   Identify commercial and industrial prospects
    4.4   Develop commercial and industrial leases
    4.5   Begin sale of commercial and industrial leases
    5.0   Draft covenants and restrictions
    6.1   Select sales pavilion design
    6.2   Develop sales pavilion design
    7.0   Issue first year annual marketing report
    X   Project opening

E. *Financial Analysis*
    1.1   Begin economic planning
    1.2   Concept plan financial analysis
    1.3   Begin master plan financial analysis
    1.4   Amenity package financial analysis
    1.5   Complete master plan financial analysis
    1.6-1.16   Continuing financial analysis of master plan and phase plans
    2.1   Develop accounting system
    2.2   Develop budgets for both public and private developers
    2.3-2.16   Issue monthly financial reports
    3.1   Determine financial organization
    3.2   Determine cash availability

3.3   Begin action to obtain interim financing
3.4   Obtain interim financing
4.1   Begin negotiating indentures and project agreements with HUD
4.2   Complete negotiating indentures and project agreements with HUD
4.3   HUD closing
4.4   Private placement of bonds
4.5   Complete private sale of bonds
5.1   Begin public audit
5.2   Complete public audit
6.1   Determine private or public placement of bonds
6.2   Form underwriters group
6.3   Issue prospectus
6.4   Make public offering of bonds
6.5   Complete bond sale

F.   *Public Utilities*
1.1   Inventory existing sewer and water trunk lines
1.2   Develop plans for North Branch Sewer and Water District
1.3   Obtain signatures and file petition for North Branch Sewer and Water District
1.4   Hold public information meetings concerning North Branch Sewer and Water District
1.5   Negotiate engineering cost for North Branch Sewer and Water District
1.6   Complete engineering negotiations for North Branch Sewer and Water District
1.7   Advertise public hearings concerning North Branch Sewer and Water District
1.8   Hold public hearings
1.9   Construction approval of North Branch Sewer and Water District
1.10   Obtain easements for North Branch Sewer and Water District
1.11   Contract for construction of North Branch Sewer and Water District
2.1   Develop plans for Wolf Creek Sewer and Water District
2.2   Obtain signatures and file petition for Wolf Creek Sewer and Water District
2.3   Hold public information meetings concerning Wolf Creek Sewer and Water District
2.4   Negotiate engineering cost for Wolf Creek Sewer and Water District

2.5 Complete engineering negotiations for Wolf Creek Sewer and Water District

2.6 Advertise public hearings concerning Wolf Creek Sewer and Water District

2.7 Hold public hearings

2.8 Construction approval of Wolf Creek Sewer and Water District

2.9 Obtain easements for Wolf Creek Sewer and Water District

2.10 Contract for construction of Wolf Creek Sewer and Water District

3.1 Decide on private or public trunk financing

3.2 Estimate cost

3.3 Apply for grant

3.4 Receive grant

G. *United States Department of Housing and Urban Development (HUD) Relations*

1.1 Submit preapplication for federal assistance

1.2 Submit formal application for federal assistance

2.1 Receive HUD environmental impact statement comments

2.2 Respond to environmental impact statement comments

2.3 Environmental impact statement distributed to agencies

2.4 Environmental impact statement issued to HUD New Communities Board

3.1 Complete A-95 Review process

4.1 Revise economic model and land statements

5.1 Update land appraisals

6.1 Submit updated master plan

7.1 Begin intensive review by HUD

7.2 Complete intensive review by HUD

7.3 Formal presentation and commitment

7.4 Begin negotiating indentures and project agreements

7.5 Complete negotiating indentures and project agreements

7.6 HUD closing

7.7 Continuing HUD relations

H. *Jurisdictional Relations*

1.1 Inform local officials of new community plan

1.2 State regional and local officials receive HUD application for A-95 Review

1.3 Draft preliminary resolution of agreement between local jurisdictions

1.4 Approve preliminary resolution

1.5 Develop final resolution

1.6   Statement of final agreement
1.7   Implement agreement
1.8   Assist City of Dayton annexation activity
1.9   Assist City of Trotwood annexation activity
2.1   Develop program for subdivision building and construction standards
2.2   Start coordination of revising building and construction standards
2.3   Complete coordination of revising building and construction standards

I. *Land Acquisition and Management*
1.1   Site selection
1.2   Begin to acquire 4500 acres ±
1.3   Complete initial acquisition of 4500 acres ±
1.4   Continue to acquire property as per master plan
1.5   Submit revised land control statement to HUD
1.6   Coordinate reappraisal
1.7   Continued acquisition
2.1   Hire director of land management
3.1   Develop land control system
3.2-3.15   Monthly analysis of individual parcels for closing, coordination with master plan and final development plans, inspection, coordinate interim uses, disposition, recording of parcels and report
4.1   Establish records
4.2-4.15   Update records monthly
5.1   Start to acquire necessary parcels for City of Dayton annexation
5.2   Complete acquisition of parcels for City of Dayton annexation
6.1   Start to close lake site parcels
6.2   Complete acquisition of lake site parcels
6.3   Start to close first phase parcels
6.4   Complete acquisition of first phase parcels

J. *Community Authority Legislation*
1.1   Lobby for community authority concept
1.2   Finalize draft of Community Authority Bill
1.3   Organize lobbying
1.4   Submit bill to House of Representatives
1.5   Identify witnesses
1.6   Ohio House of Representatives committee hearings
1.7   Ohio House of Representatives action for bill approval
1.8   Organize lobbying

1.9 Submit bill to Ohio Senate

1.10 Identify witnesses

1.11 Ohio Senate committee hearings

1.12 Ohio Senate action for bill approval

1.13 Ohio State Legislature adjourns

1.14 Community Authority Bill becomes law

K. *Community Authority Operation*

1.1 Develop interim bylaws

1.2 Develop interim charter

1.3 Recommend interim trustee appointments

1.4 Monthly interim trustee meeting

1.5 File interim charter

1.6 Issue news release

1.7 Monthly interim trustee meeting

1.8 Engage legal counsel

1.9 Monthly interim trustee meeting

1.10 Appoint HUD negotiator

1.11–1.12 Monthly interim trustee meeting

1.13 Disband interim trustees, form New Town Community Authority

1.14–1.21 New Town Community Authority trustee monthly meetings

2.1 Develop preliminary plans for community authority organization

2.2 Revise plans

2.3 Hire community authority director

2.4 Start coordination with director of planning and urban design, and citizens organization

2.5 Start coordination with local jurisdictions

2.6–2.16 Continued revision of plans, coordination with director of planning and urban design, coordination with local jurisdictions, and coordination with the citizens organization

3.1 Recommend master plan amenities

3.2 Recommend phase one final development plan amenities

3.3 Engage architect for phase one final development plan amenities

4.1 Recommend master plan school facilities

4.2 Recommend phase one final development plan school facilities

4.3 Engage architect for phase one final development plan amenities

5.1   Community authority district petition filed
5.2   Community authority district approved
5.3   Montgomery County Commissioners appoint community authority trustees

L.   *Citizen Participation*
1.1   Organize citizens group, hold membership meeting
1.2   Citizens group's board elected
1.3–1.14   Hold monthly citizens group board meetings
2.1   Individual task forces organized
2.2   Task forces review master plan and make recommendations
2.3   Task forces review phase one final development plan and make recommendations
2.4–2.6   Public meetings and workshops

M.   *Public Relations*
1.1   Prepare special presentation for Community Authority legislation
2.1   Establish format for monthly newsletter
2.2–2.15   Publish and distribute monthly newsletter
3.1   Prepare special news release
4.1   Prepare special presentation for visit of HUD officials
5.1   Prepare special presentation for water and sewer districts
6.1   Prepare special presentation for master plan zoning
7.1   Start preparation of interim brochure
7.2   Complete interim brochure
8.1   New town trip for interim community authority trustees
9.1   Prepare special presentation for formal HUD presentation
10.1   Prepare special presentation for phase one final development plan zoning

Notes and References

Two general types of source material were used for *The Politics of New Town Planning*. The first was information that pertained directly to the New Town story, including newspaper accounts, memoranda, letters, printed documents, interviews and observations. Much of this type of information is quoted directly and cited in notes. The second group of sources contained background information that dealt with new towns and planning generally. This material included books, articles, newspaper accounts more holistic in content, and government documents. These sources are cited as references by chapter and by topic in the selected references.

PREFACE

References

Bridenbaugh, C. 1938. *Cities in the Wilderness, The First Century of Urban Life in America, 1625–1742*. London: Oxford University Press.

Garvan, A. 1963. "Proprietary Philadelphia as Artifact," in *The Historian and the City*. Cambridge: The MIT Press. pp. 177–201.

Mumford, L. 1961. *The City in History, its Origins, its Transformation and its Prospects*. New York: Harcourt, Brace and World.

Tolles, F. B. 1948. *Meeting House and Counting House*. Chapel Hill: The University of North Carolina Press.

Warner, S. B., Jr. 1968. *The Private City: Philadelphia in Three Periods of Growth*. Philadelphia: University of Pennsylvania Press.

INTRODUCTION

Notes

1. *Community Service News*, II: 17. (May–June 1944).
2. *Journal Herald*, 29 August 1972.

3. *Wall Street Journal*, 14 July 1971.
4. Richard M. Nixon. "State of the Union Message from the President of the United States," in U.S. Congress House Document 91–226, 22 January 1970.
5. Hugh Mields covers the development of the HUD Title VII New Communities program in his book *Federally Assisted New Communities*. pp. 24 and 26 especially.

References

Brooks, R. 1971. "Social Planning in Columbia," *Journal of the American Institute of Planners*, 37: 373–390.
Gans, H. J. 1967. *The Levittowners*. New York: Random House.
———1968. "Planning for the Suburbs and New Towns," in *People and Plans: Essays on Urban Problems and Solutions*. New York: Basic Books.
Howard, E. 1902. *Garden Cities of To-morrow*. London: S. Sonnenschein. (1963. Cambridge: MIT Press).
LeCorbusier. 1971. *The City of To-morrow and Its Planning*. Translated from the 8th French Edition of *Urbanisme* by Frederick Etchells. Cambridge: MIT Press.
Mields, H. 1973. *Federally Assisted New Communities: New Dimensions in Development*. Washington: The Urban Land Institute.
Mumford, L. 1961. *The City in History*. New York: Harcourt, Brace, and World.
Myhra, D. 1974. "Rexford Guy Tugwell: Initiator of America's Greenbelt New Towns: 1935 to 1936," *Journal of the American Institute of Planners*, 40: 176–88.
Schaffer, F. 1972. "The New Town Movement," in Hazel Evans, ed. *New Towns: The British Experience*. New York: John Wiley and Sons.
Speer, A. 1976. *Spandau: The Secret Diaries*. Translated from German by Richard and Clara Winston. New York: Macmillan.
Wright, F. L. 1957. *A Testament*. New York: Horizon Press.
———1943. *An Autobiography*. New York: Duell, Sloan and Pearce.

PART 1, BROOKWOOD, CHAPTER 1, THE DEVELOPER

Notes

1. *Dayton Daily News*, 1 April 1973.
2. Department of Housing and Urban Development, Office of New Communities, *Environmental Impact Statement on the Proposed*

Brookwood New Community, Montgomery County, Ohio, 1972 p. 4 (hereafter cited as the Environmental Impact Statement).

3. Dayton, Miami Valley Regional Planning Commission, "State of the Region, A Report on Conditions in the Miami Valley Region with Suggested Interim Guidelines," October 1966, p. 13.
4. "Annual Report of Housing Grants," *Professional Builder and Apartment Business*, July 1974.
5. *Dayton Daily News*, 1 April 1973.

References

Hunter, F. 1953. *Community Power Structure.* Chapel Hill, North Carolina: The University of North Carolina Press.

Morgan, A. E. 1951. *The Miami Conservancy District.* New York: McGraw-Hill.

CHAPTER 2, THE PROJECT

Notes

1. The Donald L. Huber Corporation and the New Community Interim Non-Profit Corporation, acting on behalf of the Brookwood Community Authority, "Brookwood New Community, Dayton, Ohio" (an application for guaranteed assistance under Title VII of the Housing and Urban Development Act of 1970—for the Department of Housing and Urban Development), February 1972, p. 12 (hereafter cited as the HUD application).
2. Ibid.
3. *Wall Street Journal*, 11 May 1972.
4. *Dayton Daily News*, 3 January 1973.
5. McKinsey and Company, Inc., "Project Plan for the Development of Brookwood, New Community" (for the Donald L. Huber Development Group), October 1971 (hereafter cited as the McKinsey report).
6. These two articles were written by Pat Fritz of the *Journal Herald* and Jim Bland of the *Dayton Daily News*. Fritz and Bland would provide the principal coverage on the New Town story for several months.

References

Bertsch, D. F., and A. I. Shafer. 1971. "A Regional Housing Plan: the Miami Valley Regional Planning Commission Experience," *Planner's Notebook*, 1: 1–4.

Downs, A. 1973. *Opening Up the Suburbs: An Urban Strategy for America.* New Haven: Yale University Press.

CHAPTER 3, THE GENERAL MANAGER

Notes

1. This chapter is based on my interviews with Gerwin Rohrbach; several newspaper stories written about him, especially one by Pat Fritz of the *Journal Herald* entitled "Who Is Gerwin Rohrbach and What Is He Doing in Dayton?" (6 September 1972); and Rohrbach's resumé.

CHAPTER 4, EARLY PLANNING EFFORTS

Notes

1. The HUD application.
2. Ibid, p. 32.
3. Ibid, p. 53–88.
4. Ibid, p. 298.
5. Columbus, Department of Economic and Community Development, Development Planning Division, "State A-95 Clearinghouse Review of the Brookwood Title VII New Community Application to the United States Department of Housing and Urban Development," 27 July 1972, p. 2 (hereafter cited as the State A-95 Review).
6. Ibid, p. 3.
7. Ibid, p. 3.
8. Ibid, pp. 3–5.
9. Dayton, Miami Valley Regional Planning Commission, New Town Review Committee, "Review of Application for Federal Assistance by Donald L. Huber for Guaranteed Assistance under provisions of Title VII" (GA72–33), 24 May 1972 (hereafter cited as the local A-95 review).
10. Ibid.
11. Ibid.
12. McGee to Bertsch, 24 May 1972.
13. Robert Deddens, "Community Authority Explanation and Benefits, Basic Statement of Purpose" (Gould, Bailey, and Farquhar memorandum for the Donald L. Huber Development Group, 10 October 1972.)
14. Robert Deddens, "Drafting of Community Authority Act" (Gould, Bailey, and Farquhar memorandum for the Donald L. Huber Development Group, 10 October 1972), pp. 5–7.
15. Ibid, pp. 2 and 3.
16. *Journal Herald*, 11 May 1972.
17. The HUD application.
18. Robert Deddens, "Community Authority Explanation and Benefits,

summary of House Bill 1063, New Town Community Authority"
(Gould, Bailey, and Farquhar memorandum for the Donald L. Huber
Devlopment Group, 4 May and 10 October 1972), pp. 2 and 3. Also
Ohio House Bill No. 1063.
19. Ibid.
20. As reported by Jim Bland, *Dayton Daily News*, 18 February 1973.
21. The McKinsey report.
22. *Dayton Daily News*, 11 April 1972. See also the Environmental Impact
Statement and Montgomery County New Community Zoning Amendment.
23. *Journal Herald*, 6 September 1972.
24. *Journal Herald*, 6 September 1972.
25. The Donald L. Huber Development Group, publicity release, 14 May
1972.
26. Ibid.
27. The HUD application, p. 12.

References

Kahn, S. 1970. *How People Get Power, Organizing Oppressed Communities
for Action.* New York: McGraw Hill.
Mields, H. 1973. *Federally Assisted New Communities: New Dimensions in
Development.* Washington: The Urban Land Institute.
Morgan, A. E. 1951. *The Miami Conservancy District.* New York: McGraw
Hill.

PART 2, REWRITING THE ROSETTA STONE
CHAPTER 5, THE PROCESS

Notes

1. Ian McHarg has said approximately the same thing in numerous public
and classroom lectures. This specific quote was taken from the University of Pennsylvania Graduate School of Fine Arts *Bulletin*,
1973–1974.
2. The most influential figure is von Bertalanffy (1968). Also see Wiener
(1950), Boulding (1966), Churchman (1968), Ackoff (1970), and Laszlo
(1972).
3. The major source for organization development is Lewin (1951). The
best summary of organization development is provided by Schein, Bennis, and Beckhard (1973) in the Addison-Wesley series. For an explanation of action research see Clark (1972).
4. The McKinsey report.

5. Gerwin K. Rohrbach, memorandum to Turner, 10 April 1972. The Donald L. Huber Development Group, Dayton, Ohio (hereafter cited as the Turner Memorandum).
6. Ibid.

References

Alinsky, S. D. 1946. *Reveille for Radicals.* Chicago: The University of Chicago Press.

von Bertalanffy, L. 1968. *General Systems Theory.* New York: George Braziller.

Clark, P. A. 1972. *Action Research and Organizational Change.* London: Harper and Row.

Kahn, S. 1970. *How People Get Power, Organizing Oppressed Communities for Action.* New York: McGraw-Hill.

Lewin, K. 1951. *Field Theory in Social Sciences: Selected Theoretical Papers.* Edited by Dorwin Cartwright. New York: Harper and Row.

McHarg, I. L. 1969. *Design with Nature.* Garden City, New York: Doubleday/Natural History Press.

Schein, E.; W. Bennis; and R. Beckhard, eds. 1973. *Organization Development.* Reading, Massachusetts: Addison-Wesley.

Wiener, N. 1950. *The Human Use of Human Beings; Cybernetics and Society.* Boston: Houghton Mifflin Company.

CHAPTER 6, LAND ACQUISITION AND MANAGEMENT

Notes

1. *Journal Herald,* 10 February 1972.
2. *Journal Herald,* 10 February 1972. See also the Environmental Impact Statement.
3. Ibid.
4. Ibid.
5. *Journal Herald,* 10 February 1972.
6. Huber, memorandum to Turner, 14 July 1974.
7. Donald L. Huber Development Group, "Land Ownership Statement, A New Community, Dayton, Ohio." 31 October 1972 (hereafter referred to as the Land Ownership Statement).
8. The HUD application, p. 33.
9. The Environmental Impact Statement, p. 21.
10. *Journal Herald,* 4 July 1972.
11. Ibid.
12. Ibid.

13. Ibid.
14. *Journal Herald,* 27 June 1972.

References

Leopold, A. 1949. *A Sand County Almanac,* New York: Oxford University Press.

McHarg, I. L. 1969. *Design with Nature.* Garden City, New York: Doubleday/Natural History Press.

CHAPTER 7, ZONING

Notes

1. The Environmental Impact Statement, p. 10.
2. *Journal Herald,* 18 July 1972.
3. *Journal Herald,* 18 August 1972.

References

Mumford, L. 1961. *The City in History.* New York: Harcourt, Brace and World.

Reps, J. W. 1964. "Pomeroy Memorial Lecture: Requiem for Zoning," *Planning 1964.* Chicago: The American Society of Planning Officials.

CHAPTER 8, THE COMMUNITY AUTHORITY

Notes

1. Duffy to Romney, 6 January 1972, Northwest Advisory Council of Montgomery County, Community Action Agency, Dayton, Ohio.
2. James Gould, "Articles of Incorporation of New Community Interim Non-Profit Corporation" (Gould, Bailey, and Farquhar for the Donald L. Huber Development Group, 24 February 1972).
3. Robert Deddens, "Community Authority Explanation and Benefits, Basic Statement of Purpose" (Gould, Bailey, and Farquhar memorandum for the Donald L. Huber Development Group, 10 October 1972).

CHAPTER 9, HUD RELATIONS

Notes

1. *Dayton Daily News,* 18 February 1973. Also, according to the records

of the Ohio secretary of state, Huber himself donated $500 to Governor Gilligan's 1970 campaign. Huber's bookkeeper, Martha Earl, contributed $1,570. C. J. McLin, state representative and Huber's business partner, contributed $1,000 to the governor's primary campaign and another $2,000 to the November election effort. Finally, Edward Berger, the president of Huber subsidiary, The Universal Company, contributed $5,000. All told, Donald Huber and his associates contributed over $10,000 to Gilligan's campaign.

2. Huber, memorandum to Rohrbach, 28 June 1972, The Donald L. Huber Development Group, Dayton, Ohio.
3. Ibid.
4. Gilligan to Romney, 9 June 1972, Office of the Governor, State of Ohio.
5. Rohrbach, memorandum, 21 November 1972.
6. The Turner memorandum.
7. Romney to Gilligan, 10 July 1972, Office of the Governor, State of Ohio.
8. Huber, memorandum to Rohrbach, 5 September 1972, The Donald L. Huber Development Group, Dayton, Ohio.

CHAPTER 10, PUBLIC RELATIONS

Notes

1. Rohrbach, memorandum to Huber, 10 April 1972, The Donald L. Huber Development Group, Dayton, Ohio.
2. *Journal Herald*, 29 August to 5 September 1972.
3. Ibid.
4. Ibid.
5. Ibid.
6. Ibid.

References

Gans, H. J. 1968. *People and Plans: Essays on Urban Problems and Solutions*. New York: Basic Books.

Goodman, D. 1972. "New Towns: Half-way to Utopia" (series of articles), *Journal Herald* (29 August–5 September).

Myrdal, G. 1944. *An American Dilemma, The Negro Problem and Modern Democracy*. New York: Harper.

CHAPTER 11, JURISDICTIONAL RELATIONS

Notes

1. Rausch, memorandum to Rohrbach, 6 April 1972, The Donald L. Huber Development Group, Dayton, Ohio.
2. *Trotwood Argus-Sentinel*, 20 April 1972.
3. *Dayton Daily News*, 28 April 1972.
4. *Trotwood Argus-Sentinel*, 2 March 1972.
5. Rohrbach to Pope, 22 May 1972, The Donald L. Huber Development Group, Dayton, Ohio.
6. Gould, memorandum to Huber and Rohrbach, 23 May 1972, The Donald L. Huber Development Group, Dayton, Ohio.
7. Rohrbach, memorandum to Huber, 26 June 1972, The Donald L. Huber Development Group, Dayton, Ohio.
8. Ibid.
9. Steiner, memorandum to Rohrbach, 14 June 1972, The Donald L. Huber Development Group, Dayton, Ohio.
10. Rohrbach, memorandum to Huber, 15 June 1974, The Donald L. Huber Development Group, Dayton, Ohio.
11. The Donald L. Huber Development Group, "Fiscal Impact Statement, a New Community, Dayton, Ohio," 19 September 1972, p. 2 (hereafter referred to as the Fiscal Impact Statement).
12. Steiner, memorandum to Rohrbach, 4 October 1972, The Donald L. Huber Development Group, Dayton, Ohio.
13. Ibid.
14. *Journal Herald*, 26 October 1972.
15. Ibid.

CHAPTER 12, PLANNING AND URBAN DESIGN

Notes

1. The Donald L. Huber Development Group, "New Town Innovative Features" (The Innovative Features Report).
2. Ibid, pp. 10–14.
3. Ibid, pp. 50 and 51.
4. Steiner, memorandum to Rohrbach, 29 June 1972, The Donald L. Huber Development Group, Dayton, Ohio.
5. Ibid.
6. Steiner, memorandum to Rohrbach, 30 August 1972, The Donald L. Huber Development Group, Dayton, Ohio.

7. Ibid.
8. *Dayton Daily News*, 7 September 1972.

References

Caro, R. A. 1974. *The Power Broker, Robert Moses and the Fall of New York*. New York: Alfred A. Knopf.
Gans, H. J. 1968. *People and Plans: Essays on Urban Problems and Solutions*. New York: Basic Books.
Goodman, R. 1971. *After the Planners*. New York: Simon and Schuster.
Jacobs, J. 1961. *The Death and Life of Great American Cities*. New York: Random House.
Ripley, S. D. 1968. "Premise," in *The Fitness of Man's Environment* (The Smithsonian Institution Annual Symposium, 16–28 February 1967). New York: Harper and Row.

CHAPTER 13, CITIZEN PARTICIPATION

Notes

1. Duffy to Romney, 6 January 1972, Northwest Advisory Council of Montgomery County, Community Action Agency, Dayton, Ohio.
2. McGee to Bertsch, 24 May 1972.
3. The HUD application, p. 32.
4. Robert Deddens, "Community Authority Explanation and Benefits, Basic Statement of Purpose" (Gould, Bailey, and Farquhar memorandum for the Donald L. Huber Development Group, 10 October 1972).
5. The Environmental Impact Statement, p. 62.
6. The Innovative Features Report.
7. Ibid, p. 19.
8. Rohrbach, memorandum to Huber, 7 July 1972, Donald L. Huber Development Group, Dayton, Ohio.
9. Ibid.
10. Ibid.
11. Rausch, memorandum to Rohrbach, 7 August 1972, Donald L. Huber Development Group, Dayton, Ohio.
12. *Dayton Daily News*, 10 August 1972.
13. Ibid.
14. Schneider to Romney, 23 October 1972, Joint Citizens New Town Planning Council, Trotwood, Ohio.
15. David Schneider, "Agreement Between Joint Citizens New Town Planning Council, Inc. and Huber Development Group, Inc.," Joint Citizens New Town Planning Council, Trotwood, Ohio (no date).

16. I was directly involved in the events that I have described in the text as an organizer, participant, and observer.
17. Neil Porterfield, "Planning for New Town First Year Development—Progress Report/October 16, 1972," The Joint Citizens New Town Planning Council, The Huber Development Group, and HOK Associates/New Town Environmental Planning Group, St. Louis, Missouri, p. 2 and 2a.

References

Burke, E. M. 1968. "Citizen Participation," *Journal of the American Institute of Planners*, 34: 287–94.
Mields, H. 1973. *Federally Assisted New Communities: New Dimensions in Development*. Washington: The Urban Land Institute.

CHAPTER 14, FINANCIAL ANALYSIS

Notes

1. The Donald L. Huber Development Group, "A New Community—Dayton, Ohio" (A Proposal for equity participation in the New Town Development), Dayton, Ohio (no date), Exhibit D (hereafter referred to as Equity Proposal).
2. The Turner memorandum.
3. Gerwin K. Rohrbach, "Project Plan—Summary Network," The Donald L. Huber Development Group, Dayton, Ohio, June 1972.
4. Equity Proposal, p. 7.
5. Ibid.
6. Ibid.
7. Rohrbach, memorandum to Huber, 16 October 1972. The Donald L. Huber Development Group, Dayton, Ohio.
8. Ibid.

CHAPTER 15, MARKETING AND SALES

Notes

1. The Real Estate Research Corporation, "Housing Marketing Analysis, The Brookwood New Community, Dayton, Ohio" (report for The Donald L. Huber Development Group). Dayton, Ohio, April 1972.
2. Ibid.
3. Ibid.
4. Ibid.

5. Ibid.
6. Chermayeff and Geismar Associates, "Criteria for the Selection of a Name for a New Community Located between the City of Trotwood, Ohio and the Village of Brookville, Ohio" (report for The Donald L. Huber Development Group), Dayton, Ohio, 27 October 1972.

CHAPTER 16, UTILITIES AND CONSTRUCTION

Notes

1. The Turner memorandum.

References

McHarg, I. L. 1969. *Design with Nature*. Garden City, New York: Double-day/Natural History Press.

CHAPTER 17, SUMMARY

Notes

1. Huber, memorandum to Rohrbach, 24 July 1972, The Donald L. Huber Development Group, Dayton, Ohio.

References

Carter, G. 1952. Action Research in Community Planning. *Social Work Journal*, 33: 23–28.

PART 3, DONNYBROOK, CHAPTER 18, THE RESIGNATIONS

Notes

1. Much of this section is based on interviews with Gerwin Rohrbach and my observations of the events described in the text. I tried to reach Donald Huber for his comments, but I received no reply.
2. Michael Haggans, "Corruption: An Element in the Process of Producing the Built Environment," A report for the American Institute of Architects Research Corporation, January 1972, p. 22.
3. *Journal Herald*, 8 February 1973.
4. Warren Bennis, "When to Resign," *Esquire*, June 1972.

5. *Journal Herald*, 21 November 1972.
6. Ibid.
7. Ibid.
8. *Journal Herald*, 22 November 1972.

CHAPTER 19, NEWFIELDS

Notes

1. *Journal Herald*, 10 February 1973.
2. *Dayton Daily News*, 21 February 1973.
3. Ibid.
4. Ibid.
5. *Journal Herald*, 4 January 1973.
6. *Journal Herald*, 15 January 1973.
7. *Journal Herald*, 15 February 1973.
8. *Journal Herald*, 7 December 1972.
9. *Journal Herald*, 7 December 1972.
10. *Journal Herald*, 9 February 1973.
11. Ibid.
12. *Journal Herald*, 13 April 1973.
13. *Journal Herald*, 14 April 1973.
14. *Journal Herald*, 3 May 1973.
15. *Dayton Daily News*, 25 April 1973.
16. *Journal Herald*, 11 July 1973.
17. *Dayton Daily News*, 22 November 1973.
18. *Dayton Daily News*, 16 December 1972.
19. *Dayton Daily News*, 14 April 1973.
20. *Dayton Daily News*, 27 September 1973.
21. *Journal Herald*, 16 November 1973.
22. *Dayton Daily News*, 21 March 1976.
23. *Journal Herald*, 15 March 1976.
24. *Dayton Daily News*, 23 November 1975.
25. Ibid.

References

Huber, D. L. 1975. "Newfields, Ohio: The New Community Planning Process," in *Strategy for New Community Development in the United States.* Stroudsburg, Pa.: Dowden, Hutchinson and Ross, pp. 103–12.

CHAPTER 20, THE FUTURE
OF NEW COMMUNITY PLANNING

Notes

1. "The High Cost of Money Threatens the New Town Program," *Engineering News Record*, 31 November 1974, p. 7.
2. "Securities, A Moral Issue," *Time*, 10 March 1975.
3. *Journal Herald*, 2 September 1972.
4. *Cincinnati Enquirer*, 2 February 1975 (Thomas Lippman, *Washington Post*).
5. Real Estate Research Corporation, "Housing Market Analysis, The Brookwood New Community, Dayton, Ohio." (Report for the Donald L. Huber Development Group.) April 1972.
6. See Burby and Weiss, *New Communities U.S.A.* and also an article entitled "New Towns: How Are They Doing?" which appeared in MOSAIC, a National Science Foundation publication, in the summer, 1974, issue.
7. These suggestions first appeard in the MOSAIC article.
8. *Dayton Daily News*, 18 November 1974.

References

Ackoff, R. L. 1970. *A Concept of Corporate Planning*. New York: Wiley Interscience.

Berger, J. 1976. "The Hazelton Ecological Land Planning Study," *Landscape Planning*, 3: 303–335.

——1978. "Toward an Applied Human Ecology for Landscape Architecture and Regional Planning," *Human Ecology*, 6: 179–199.

von Bertalanffy, L. 1968. *General Systems Theory*. New York: George Braziller.

Burby, R. J. and S. F. Weiss. 1976. *New Communities U.S.A.* Lexington, Massachusetts: Lexington Books.

Churchman, C. W. 1968. *The Systems Approach*. New York: Dell.

Huber, D. L. 1975. "Newfields, Ohio: The New Community Planning Process," in *Strategy for New Community Development in the United States*. Stroudsburg, Pennsylvania: Dowden, Hutchinson and Ross. pp. 103–112.

Gans, H. J. 1968. *People and Plans: Essays on Urban Problems and Solutions*. New York: Basic Books.

Golany, G. 1976. *New Town Planning: Principles and Practice*. New York: John Wiley and Sons.

Juneja, N. 1974. *Medford*. Philadelphia: Center for Ecological Research in Planning and Design, University of Pennsylvania.

McHarg, I. L. 1969. *Design with Nature.* Garden City, New York: Double-day/Natural History Press.

McHarg, I. L. and J. Sutton. 1975. "Ecological Plumbing for the Texas Coastal Plain, the Woodlands New Town Experiment," *Landscape Architecture,* 65: 78–89.

Myhra, D. 1974. "Rexford Guy Tugwell: Initiator of America's Greenbelt New Towns: 1935 to 1936," *Journal of the American Institute of Planners,* 40: 176–188.

National Science Foundation. 1974. "New Towns: How Are They Doing?" *MOSAIC,* 5 (summer).

Odum, E. P. 1971. *Fundamentals of Ecology.* Philadelphia: W. B. Saunders.

Richerson, P. J. 1977. "Ecology and Human Ecology: A Comparison of Theories in the Biological and Social Sciences," *American Ethnologist,* 4: 1–26.

Rose, D.; F. Steiner; and J. Jackson. 1978/1979. "An Applied Human Ecological Approach to Regional Planning," *Landscape Planning,* 5: 241–261.

Safdie, M. 1974."Beyond the City Limits," *Saturday Review/World* (August).

Spreiregen, P. D. 1969. *Urban Design: The Architecture of Towns and Cities.* New York: McGraw-Hill.

Stein, C. S. 1957. *Towards New Towns for America.* Cambridge: The M.I.T. Press.

The Town Forum. 1974. *The Cerro Gordo Experiment.* Cottage Grove, Oregon.

Wallace, McHarg, Roberts, and Todd. 1974. *Woodlands New Community* (four-volume report for the Woodlands Development Corporation, Houston, Texas.) Philadelphia.

Weiss, S. F.; E. J. Kaiser; and R. J. Burby, eds. 1971. *New Community Development: Planning Process, Implementation and Emerging Social Concerns.* Chapel Hill, North Carolina: Center for Urban and Regional Studies, University of North Carolina.

Young, G. L. 1974. "Human Ecology as an Interdisciplinary Concept: A Critical Inquiry," *Advances in Ecological Research,* 8: 1–105.

Selected References

ACTION RESEARCH

Carter, G. W. 1952. "Action Research in Community Planning," *Social Work Journal*, 33: 23–28.

Clark, P. A. 1972. *Action Research and Organizational Change*. London: Harper and Row.

ADVOCACY PLANNING AND PLANNED CHANGE

Alinsky, S. D. 1946. *Reveille for Radicals*. Chicago: The University of Chicago Press.

Arnstein, S. R. 1969. "A Ladder of Citizen Participation," *Journal of the American Institute of Planners*, 35: 216–224.

Bennis, W.; K. D. Benne; R. Chinn; and K. Corey, eds. 1976. *The Planning of Change* (third edition). New York: Holt, Rinehart and Winston.

Burke, E. M. 1968. "Citizen Participation," *Journal of the American Institute of Planners*, 34: 287–294.

Davidoff, P. 1965. "Advocacy and Pluralism in Planning," *Journal of the American Institute of Planners*, 31: 331–337.

Kaplan, M. 1969. "Advocacy and the Urban Poor," *Journal of the American Institute of Planners*, 35: 96–101.

COMMUNITY ORGANIZATION

Aiken, M. and P. E. Mott, eds. 1970. *Structure of Community Power*. New York: Random House.

Hunter, F. 1953. *Community Power Structure*. Chapel Hill: The University of North Carolina Press.

Kahn, S. 1970. *How People Get Power, Organizing Oppressed Communities for Action*. New York: McGraw-Hill.

ECOLOGICAL PLANNING METHOD

Berger, J. 1976. "The Hazelton Ecological Land Planning Study," *Landscape Planning*, 3: 303–335.

——— 1978. "Toward an Applied Human Ecology for Landscape Architecture and Regional Planning," *Human Ecology*, 6: 179–199.

Giliomee, J. H. 1977. "Ecological Planning: Method and Evaluation," *Landscape Planning*, 4: 185–191.

Hills, G. A. 1961. *The Ecological Basis for Land Use Planning*. Toronto: Ontario Department of Land and Forests, Research Report No. 46.

Juneja, N. 1974. *Medford*. Philadelphia: Center of Ecological Research in Planning and Design, University of Pennsylvania.

Leopold, A. 1949. *A Sand County Almanac and Sketches Here and There*. New York: Oxford University Press.

Lewis, P. H., Jr. 1969. "Ecology: The Inland Water Tree," *American Institute of Architects Journal*, 51.

McHarg, I. L. 1962. "Ecology of the City," *American Institute of Architects Journal*, 38: 101–103.

——— 1968. "Values, Process and Form," *in The Fitness of Man's Environment* (Smithsonian Annual II). New York: Harper and Row.

——— 1969. *Design with Nature*. Garden City, New York: Doubleday/Natural History Press.

Odum, E. P. 1971. *Fundamentals of Ecology*. Philadelphia: W. B. Saunders.

Steinitz, C.; T. Murray; D. Sinton; and D. Way. 1970. *A Comparative Study of Resource Analysis Methods*. Cambridge: Department of Landscape Architecture, Research Office, Harvard University.

Richerson, P. J. 1977. "Ecology and Human Ecology: A Comparison of Theories in the Biological and Social Sciences," *American Ethnologist*, 4: 1–26.

Rose, D. and J. Berger. 1974. "Human Ecology in the Regional Plan." Philadelphia: Department of Landscape Architecture and Regional Planning, University of Pennsylvania (mimeo).

Rose, D.; F. Steiner; and J. Jackson. 1978/1979. "An Applied Human Ecological Approach to Regional Planning," *Landscape Planning*, 5: 241–261.

Steiner, F. and K. Brooks. 1978. "Ecological Planning Information for the State of Washington," *Land Use Planning*. Pullman: Washington State University Cooperative Extension Service.

Young, G. L. 1974. "Human Ecology as an Interdisciplinary Concept: A Critical Inquiry," *Advances in Ecological Research*, 8: 1–105.

FAIR-SHARE HOUSING

Bertsch, D. F. and A. I. Shafer. 1971. "A Regional Housing Plan: The Miami

Valley Regional Planning Commission Experience," *Planner's Notebook*, *1* (April).

Downs, A. 1973. *Opening Up the Suburbs: An Urban Strategy for America*. New Haven: Yale University Press.

GENERAL PLANNING

Bridenbaugh, C. 1938. *Cities in the Wilderness, The First Century of Urban Life in America, 1625–1742*. London: Oxford University Press.

Caro, R. A. 1974. *The Power Broker, Robert Moses and the Fall of New York*. New York: Alfred A. Knopf.

Friedmann, J. 1973. *Retracking America: A Theory of Transactive Planning* Garden City, New York: Anchor Press/Doubleday.

Gans, H. J. 1962. *The Urban Villagers*. New York: The Free Press.

Garvan, A. 1963. "Proprietary Philadelphia as an Artifact" in *The Historian and the City*. Cambridge: The MIT Press.

Goodman, R. 1971. *After the Planners*. New York: Simon and Schuster.

Gottman, J. 1961. *Megalopolis*. Cambridge: The MIT Press.

Jacobs, J. 1961. *The Death and Life of Great American Cities*. New York: Random House.

Macaulay, D. 1974. *City, A Story of Roman Planning and Construction*. Boston: Houghton Mifflin Company.

MacKaye, B. 1928. *The New Exploration: A Philosophy of Regional Planning*. New York: Harcourt, Brace and Company.

Meyerson, M. and E. C. Banfield. 1955. *Politics, Planning, and the Public Interest: The Case of Public Housing in Chicago*. Glencoe, Illinois: Free Press.

Morgan, A. E. 1951. *The Miami Conservancy District*. New York: McGraw-Hill.

Mumford, L. 1961. *The City in History*. New York: Harcourt, Brace and World.

Reps, J. W. 1965. *The Making of Urban America: A History of City Planning in the United States*. Princeton: Princeton University Press.

Warner, S. B. 1968. *The Private City: Philadelphia in Three Periods of Growth*. Philadelphia: University of Pennsylvania Press.

Whyte, W. H. 1968. *The Last Landscape*. Garden City, New York: Doubleday and Company.

NEW TOWN PLANNING

Brooks, R. 1971. "Social Planning in Columbia," *Journal of the American Institute of Planners*, 37:373–379.

Department of Housing and Urban Development, Office of New Communities. 1972. *Environmental Impact Statement on the Proposed Brookwood New Community, Montgomery County, Ohio.* Washington, DC: U.S. Government Printing Office.

Burby, R. J. and S. F. Weiss. 1976. *New Communities U.S.A.* Lexington, Massachusetts: Lexington Books.

Evans, H., ed. 1972. *New Towns: The British Experience.* New York: John Wiley and Sons.

Gans, H. J. 1967. *The Levittowners.* New York: Random House.

——— 1968. "Planning for the Suburbs and New Towns" in *People and Plans: Essays on Urban Problems and Solutions.* Pp. 127–202.

Golany, G., ed. 1975. *Strategy for New Community Development in the United States.* Stroudsburg, Pennsylvania: Dowden, Hutchinson and Ross.

——— 1976. *New-Town Planning: Principles and Practice.* New York: John Wiley and Sons.

Goodman, D. 1972. "New Towns: Half-Way to Utopia," (series of articles) *The Journal Herald* (August 29 to September 5).

Howard, E. 1902. *Garden Cities of To-morrow.* London: S. Sonnenschein.

Huber, D. 1975. "Newfields, Ohio: The New Community Planning Process" in *Strategy for New Community Development in the United States.* Stroudsburg, Pennsylvania: Dowden, Hutchinson and Ross. Pp. 103–112.

Karmin, M. W. 1971. "The Next America, Columbia, Planned City Finds It Shares Woes Facing Unplanned Cities," *The Wall Street Journal* (July 14).

McHarg, I. L. and J. Sutton. 1975. "Ecological Plumbing for the Texas Coastal Plain, The Woodlands New Town Experiment," *Landscape Architecture* 65:78–89.

Mields, H. Jr. 1973. *Federally Assisted New Communities: New Dimensions in Development.* Washington, DC: The Urban Land Institute.

Myhra, D. 1974. "Rexford Guy Tugwell: Initiator of America's Greenbelt New Towns: 1935 to 1936," *Journal of the American Institute of Planners,* 40:176–188.

National Science Foundation. 1974. "New Towns: How Are They Doing?" *MOSAIC,* 5 (summer).

Safdie, M. 1974. "Beyond the City Limits," *Saturday Review/World* (August).

Stein, C. 1951. *Toward New Towns for America.* Chicago: Public Administration Service.

The Town Forum. 1974. *The Cerro Gordo Experiment.* Cottage Grove, Oregon.

Wallace, McHarg, Roberts and Todd. 1974. *Woodlands New Community.* (Four-volume report for the Woodlands Development Corporation, Houston, Texas.) Philadelphia.

Weiss, S. F., E. J. Kaiser and R. J. Burby (editors). 1971. *New Community Development: Planning Process, Implementation and Emerging Social Concerns.* Chapel Hill: Center for Urban and Regional Studies, University of North Carolina.

ORGANIZATION DEVELOPMENT

Lewin, K. 1951. *Field Theory in the Social Sciences: Selected Theoretical Papers* New York: Harper and Row.
Schein, E., Warren B. and R. Beckhard 1973. *Organization Development* (series of books). Reading, Massachusetts: Addison-Wesley.

PLANNING LAW

Bosselman, F., D. Callies and J. Banta. 1973. *The Taking Issue.* Washington, DC: U.S. Government Printing Office.
Gray, O. S. 1970. *Cases and Materials on Environmental Law.* Washington, DC: Bureau of National Affairs.
Sax, J. L. 1964. "Taking and the Police Power," *Yale Law Journal,* Vol. 74.
Strong, A. L. and K. T. Pearlman. 1976. *Environmental Law: Cases and Materials* (two volumes). Department of City and Regional Planning, University of Pennsylvania and Department of City and Regional Planning, Ohio State University.
U.S. Congress. 1969. The National Environmental Policy Act of 1969 (P.L. 91-190).
U.S. Congress. 1970. The Environmental Quality Improvement Act of 1970 (P.L. 91-224).

SYSTEMS APPROACHES

Ackoff, R. L. 1970. *A Concept of Corporate Planning.* New York: Wiley-Interscience.
Ackoff, R. L. and P. Rivett. 1973. *A Manager's Guide to Operations Research.* New York: John Wiley and Sons.
von Bertalanffy, L. 1968. *General Systems Theory.* New York: George Braziller.
Boulding, K. E. 1966. *The Impact of the Social Sciences.* New Brunswick: Rutgers University Press.
Churchman, C. W. 1968. *The Systems Approach.* New York: Dell.
Laszlo, E. 1972. *The Systems View of the World.* New York: George Braziller.
Wiener, N. 1950. *The Human Use of Human Beings; Cybernetics and Society.* Boston: Houghton Mifflin Company.

URBAN DESIGN, ARCHITECTURE
AND LANDSCAPE ARCHITECTURE

Alexander, C. 1964. *Notes on the Synthesis of Form.* Cambridge: Harvard University Press.

Bacon, E. N. 1967. *Design of Cities.* New York: Viking.

LeCorbusier. 1971. *The City of To-morrow and Its Planning* Translated from the 8th French edition of *Urbanisme* by Frederick Etchells. Cambridge: The MIT Press.

Lynch, K. 1960. *The Image of the City.* Cambridge: The MIT Press and Harvard University Press.

Malt, H. L. 1970. *Furnishing the City.* New York: McGraw-Hill.

Morris, A. E. J. 1972. *History of Urban Form, Prehistory to the Renaissance.* New York: John Wiley and Sons.

Newton, N. T. 1971. *Design on the Land, the Development of Landscape Architecture.* Cambridge: The Belknap Press of Harvard University.

Simonds, J. O. 1961. *Landscape Architecture; the Shaping of Man's Natural Environment.* New York: F. W. Dodge.

Speer, A. 1976. *Spandau, The Secret Diaries* Translated from German by Richard and Clara Winston. New York: Macmillan.

Spreiregen, P. D. 1969. *Urban Design: The Architecture of Towns and Cities.* New York: McGraw-Hill.

Wright, F. L. 1943. *An Autobiography.* New York: Duell, Sloan and Pearce.

——— 1957. *A Testament.* New York: Horizon Press.

Index